Homeschool Genesis:

A Story-Sourcebook

Cathy Gileadi

CONTENTS

ACKNOWLEDGMENTS

For their help in preparing this manuscript, and for their cheering support and encouragement, I thank Michael and Elizabeth Gauthern of Mamaranui, New Zealand, and Jani Sue Muhlestein of Brigham Young University, Provo, Utah.

I am grateful to Dr. Dennis and Sandy Packard for their insightful editorial assistance.

Special thanks go to Growing Without Schooling, 2269 Mass. Avenue, Cambridge Massachusetts, for permission to reprint John Holt's article on the uses of computers.

Without the babysitting and housekeeping help of my own children, especially David, Sammy, and Yoni, I could not have even attempted this book.

I owe a special thank you to Jim and Elaine Harmston, who materially eased the preparation of the manuscript.

Thanks to Gerald Pulsipher of the Franklin Institute who facilitated the editing of the manuscript and gave useful editorial insight.

I am grateful to Peter and Lori Reynolds for the many hours they devoted to this project in creating the cover and the book design, and their kind encouragement in every way.

Most of all, I must thank my husband Avraham who encouraged, suggested, criticized, and edited this book for me. He also cooked meals, cleaned house, babysat children, and in many other ways facilitated what would otherwise have been an impossible project.

PREFACE: HOW TO USE THIS BOOK

Home school is such a personal thing; like family life itself, each home school distinctively forms (and constantly changes) as the family grows. For this reason, I have never felt comfortable telling people just how, in ten easy steps, they can homeschool their own children themselves. Our experiences can only reflect what we ourselves have learned, yet I feel that our long span of homeschooling with a large family has provided many useful examples of what can be done.

As you read this book, you might underline those ideas or experiences that appeal to you, that you think you could use, that seem to fit into your family's style, or that you wish you could move toward. Make notes in the margin about how you might incorporate things you like. The book teaches inductively, which means that instead of telling you ahead of time everything you need to know about homeschool, it shows lots of examples and lets you draw principles from them--although you will find plenty of recommendations as well.

Because of this inductive nature of this book, families who are not choosing homeschool right now can still find many suggestions they can use with their children during holidays, vacations, or just during family times together. I hope that this book can find a much wider application than serving only homeschool families; the ideals we have been seeking can apply to teaching children anytime, whether in homeschool or not.

I hope, also, that you can visualize and enjoy the book as you read. I have tried to be frank and honest in presenting our voyage into homeschooling. In reality, it is a kind of family portrait as well as a homeschooling manual.

INTRODUCTION: AN AUTOBIOGRAPHY

Over the past several years my husband Avraham would often ask me, "Well, when are you going to start writing your book on homeschool?" I evaded his question, feeling such a project overwhelming and maybe a bit presumptuous. But the idea of a book kept growing, especially after I would lecture at homeschool conferences, when people would tape and ditto off my talks, and some would ask me for written information, "even just a pamphlet?" Experimental and ever-changing though my homeschooling seemed to me, we were doing some things that appealed to people.

So many seemed to be groping for better ways to educate and raise their children. Feeling intuitively that the typical public school experience was cheating their children of their real potential, or developing personalities foreign to the family's philosophy, they nonetheless lacked some direction in which to go. Many would start homeschools, attempting to use school approaches and materials at home; but most felt disappointed and disillusioned by their efforts, often ending up by sending their children back to school. Others tried correspondence courses and outlined studies with some success but still felt that they were missing some vital element in their programs—without knowing just what it was.

We began finding our way into our own homeschool approach by reading Hal Bennett's *No More Public School*, which basically gave us the confidence to try educating our children outside of the system. Raymond and Dorothy Moore's *Better Late than Early* and *School Can Wait* (and, later, *Homegrown Kids*), gave me much moral support during the early years of our homeschooling. *School Can Wait*, a research project funded by the federal government, showed that children consistently performed better academically (and also demonstrated adequate emotional maturity, with ability to make moral decisions) if their formal schooling were delayed at least until the age of 8 or 10. We also liked John Holt's *Teach Your Own*, but generally kept away from the mainstream of the homeschooling movement. In these early years, reading such material as we found in the excellent newsletter *Growing Without Schooling*, merely boggled me: the multitude of approaches and attitudes made me feel confused and unclear about what I was trying to do myself.

1

Instead, I concentrated on adapting the Montessori approach for my young children. Constructing some of the Montessori equipment, buying some, and simply branching out on its philosophy and point of view, I began to hit on the idea of parent (teacher) as *facilitator* rather than instructor or dispenser of knowledge. To be sure, I spent a great deal of time reading aloud to the children, suggesting projects, providing instructions and materials for crafts, but more and more I allowed the children to lead the way, letting myself fade into the background as their interests and growing skills led them to learn for themselves.

This is what listening homeschoolers seemed to be hungry for. Sometimes they found it so difficult to let go of the authoritarian role of parent-teacher, but then sometimes they swung too far the other way, letting the children range freely without guidance or enough parental interest to give form to the children's explorations. So often these searching homeschoolers would ask me for a program, for a list, for a course outline; I would find myself at a loss, because I didn't have one. Thus evolved the idea of writing a book about our experiences, not as a prescription, or even as a recommendation, but just to clearly show some of the things that have worked—and others that have not—in our own homeschool, and to chronicle the ideas and philosophies that have formed it.

After a few years, beginning to read in Growing without Schooling and in other publications about the experiences of homeschoolers, I was amazed to find that families throughout the country, and indeed the world over, had taken much the same path we had. I felt a kinship and brotherhood with all of these families, and felt that perhaps there was a spiritual or conceptual movement taking place at the grassroots in many places; people were seeking a superior way of raising their children that included a closer relationship with the natural world and an emphasis on being skillful. A good estimate of homeschooling families in the U.S. now sets the number at about ten thousand.

Finally Avraham and I agreed that during our year abroad, in the Cook Islands and in New Zealand (where he planned to complete a book he had long been working on), I would write my book on homeschool. Beginning in Rarotonga, and thereafter in New Zealand (where, ironically, my children attended public schools), and again on our return to America, I finished the project with our homeschool in recess. Practicing and prospective homeschoolers have expressed so much interest and support for this book! Though it only presents a picture of where we are right now, I feel it offers some valuable insights into what homeschooling has been like in our family of eight children, and looks at some important questions we need to answer on how we feel about children, about learning, about growing up.

Like many families, our spiritual life encompasses the whole of our intellectual path. As you read this book, you willl notice that I refer often to experiences with church and the Spirit. Instead of trying to impose dogmatic ideas onto the children, we find spiritual viewpoints woven so thoroughly into the fabric of our life and learning that the two could never be separated. Although many in today's world reject religion, I can't offer them an apology for our approach, but I hope that this point of view can add a dimension to what they glean from this book, instead of turning them from it. An early elder of our church described the interplay of spirit and intellect:

> Not only does the religion of Jesus Christ make the people acquainted with the things of God, and develop within them moral excellence and purity, but it holds out every encouragement and inducement possible, for them to increase in knowledge and intelligence, for every branch of mechanism, or in the arts and sciences, for all wisdom, and all the arts and sciences in the world are from God, and are designed for the good of His people. (Brigham Young, *Journal of Discourses* 13:147)

Throughout our homeschooling, and throughout this book, I have tried to find the joyous and positive in home learning rather than carping on the negative aspects of public education. True, many people consider homeschooling because they despair of their children's experiences in the school systems. Yet throughout these systems we find teachers who express our same dissatisfactions, staying in the schools as long as they can, working and hoping to improve the situation there.

We can appreciate the good things the schools have to offer, realizing that by homeschooling we are seeking a superior alternative. This approach leads us to an exciting philosophy of learning, the idea of living together as families, working together, learning together, traveling together, helping each other through difficult times and totally enjoying the happy ones. We can never "hark back to the good old times"—supposing they ever existed—as some fundamentalist homeschoolers wish they could. The times we live in now certainly offer their own challenges, and I supposed that more and more people will be reaching toward homeschool as the social public school present more dangers or simply offer negative experiences.

Some mothers have confided to me that they took their children out of school after their young ones had been forced into the school bathrooms and submitted to exposure to tobacco, drugs, or sexual scenes. Many a young girl restrains herself all day long, rushing to the bathroom as soon as she gets home, to avoid this kind of experience. Although these negatives cannot be widespread yet, many parents worry about them. Even so, these concerns must not form the philosophy behind our choosing to homeschool. Instead, I feel it is how we perceive the wholeness of the world, how it refines us, how it leads us toward the great minds of the present and the past, that sharpens our interest and delight in the world around us and in peoples everywhere.

From School To Homeschool

Because this is a homeschool book, you might be expecting me to be strongly anti-school. In some ways, this is true; but when I began this chapter, four of my children—three for the first time—were attending school in New Zealand. And I do believe that school can have an appropriate place in the homeschooler's life.

Without lamenting the high rate of illiteracy present in the United States, a country long committed to compulsory education, and without dragging you through the shocking facts about the decrease in discipline and increase in violence, alcohol, and drugs in ever-younger children at school, I maintain—for yet other reasons—that schools are not good places for developing superior children. Of course, the times being what they are, most parents are not willing to devote themselves to educating their children at home; many women wish to work out of the home, sometimes legitimately, sometimes to add luxuries rather than necessities. And even when the mother chooses to stay home, she often cannot stand the presence of her children. How often have you heard women say, "How glad I am that summer vaction is nearly over. I can't wait to get these children back to school!"

Granted, the reason for her reaction is not totally her fault, for school life develops in children many of those behaviors that seem intolerable at home.

To illustrate what I consider the bad effects of school, I find myself looking back to my childhood. Most of the memories, bleak, and not very happy, still make me cringe inside so many years later! I remember at kindergarten age, walking what seemed to me miles and miles, to school. I remember sitting on a smooth, cold floor at story-time, the teacher saying very strongly, "Now, nobody is to interrupt the story, and nobody is to get up for any reason." I had to go to the bathroom, but, young as I was, I took her words literally, and so I wet on the floor. When we got up, there was the puddle. "Who peed on the floor?" the teacher demanded. Of course no one spoke up; young as we were, we had already learned the lesson that you don't get yourself into trouble at school if you can help it. Soon my wet pants were discovered, however, and with much shame I changed into some dry school-panties (I can still see them in my mind, grayish-white cotton) and was given my wet ones, wrapped, to take home.

Most of my classroom memories blur into one persistent image, sitting at an uncomfortable desk in a stuffy, poorly ventilated room, illuminated with electric lights, doing endless book-work on subjects that seemed to me to have little relationship to what my life was all about. Such requirements as not wiggling, only speaking when given permission, waiting in lines until all the class was quiet, eating limited portions of cafeteria food (eating is a critical issue in childhood!), and, most of all, being subject to the sarcasm, criticalness, and whims of an all-powerful teacher seemed to me, and still does, to contradict the essence of what being a child is all about; and it made me miserable while growing up. In fourth grade, I remember having been placed in a "lower class" while my special friends were in a "higher" class. I slumped at my desk and scribbled my papers sloppily. Acting on my complaints, my mother requested a shift into the desirable upper class, where I found, to my astonishment, the classroom was exactly the same. However, I applied myself there so as to merit such elevation.

One of the bright lights from my school days still makes me glow inside. After our family moved to another home, I attended a school where I was considered gifted. With other such children, I received lessons in writing poetry—the real kind, working through forms—Spanish, music (how I dearly loved the harmony singing; how I sang enthusiastically so everyone would know I appreciated it), and math. Also, the teachers, and most especially the principal, treated me with a good deal of solicitude, tenderness, and respect, as though I were someone to take care of, listening to my feelings about friends and my home, and encouraging me in every way. Thus, though I spent much of my time in conventional classrooms, these extra attentions—which every child deserves, feeling that he or she is a special, gifted, extraordinary, and darling young person—made that school year precious to me. Unfortunately my parents divorced and we moved to yet another location.

And the school memories grind on much the same, worrying because I received a B instead of an A, knowing that I was just as bright as the other A children, but not willing to expend myself memorizing lists of things so as to do well on exams. The year I was fifteen, however (when I was baptized into the Church of Jesus Christ of Latter-day Saints), a sort of happy glow illuminated my life. During that year I was chosen as a cheerleader and placed in accelerated classes, where we enjoyed a great freedom of expression and much more variety in coursework. Again being considered a worthwhile and special individual, instead of someone who must be kept busy and under control, made all the difference to me.

All during these years, and indeed through the rest of my life, I went on privately with what I consider to be my real education—trekking to the public library and hauling back loads of books to read on my own. I only wish that I had had some good guidance in my reading, though I concentrated mainly on the classics and on crafts books, interests that still dominate. I recall biking in hot, southern-California summer weather, with a double basket behind the bike seat, full of heavy books, toiling some miles to and from the library.

At this time, because of family difficulties (my mother had remarried), I left home to live with friends in New Mexico. Their daughter had become a special friend, and they graciously allowed me, at fifteen, to come to live with them. At this time of my life I received schooling in how to be a good member of my Church (something I critically needed then), because at home circumstances hampered such learning. But my public schooling ground on pretty much the same. Fortunately, however, we were able to arrange for my graduation from high school at age sixteen, so that I missed two years of tedium.

I entered the University of New Mexico soon after my seventeenth birthday. After a year's attendance there (facilitated by my great-aunt's sending of tuition and money for books), I moved on my own to Brigham Young University, where I supported myself through the rest of my bachelor's degree. I worked first as a janitor (from four a.m. to seven a.m.—an impossible schedule for one who needs much sleep), and then as a part-time secretary in the College of Religion and later in the President's Office.

My academic memories, however, comprise roughly the following: much dull reading (I realize now that it was dull because most textbooks are written abominably, in heavy institutional English); much memorizing of masses of facts for tests (again a good deal of it useless, as, for example, being able to relate in sequence each of the places the Apostle Paul visited and how long he remained there for a New Testament class); and, most of all, attending lots of unrelated classes without the opportunity to draw together any conclusions about the relationships of one field to another, one point of view to its contrary, such as the full dose of evolution we received in our geology class and the unequivocal denial of evolution in the scripture classes.

Thinking of the undergraduate days for the most part makes me feel tired and somewhat unhappy, especially because socially I entered into mundane activities that I rarely enjoyed--attending football games, or light-minded parties, where we played silly games; or rock dances.

Some experiences at college, however, fed what I needed at the time. The modern dance program at BYU was superb, and I took as many of these classes as I could. Also, majoring in English, I was able to do what I loved the best, read literature, think, talk, and write about it; though I still detested having to memorize facts to regurgitate on examinations in order to be graded. Most of my education classes, which were necessary to certify as a secondary teacher, were dull and useless. In contrast, I remember Dr. Rex Wadham's class. He strove to develop our ability to teach by the Holy Spirit, to teach worthwhile matter, to create a safe and happy learning environment in our classrooms. Dr. Wadham, now deceased, produced much penetrating research on what good learning is and how to facilitate it at home and in school. As you might imagine, he was very different than most education professors, and not often well accepted by them.

After I graduated, I was to take a job—doing what? Teaching school, of course! After some searching, I landed a job in a Utah school district a couple of hours from Provo. It was located on the edge of the Ute Indian reservation, in a town that was split into two populations, long-time Mormons and newly come oil workers.

At the high school in which I taught, an incredible tension between the three types of culture brewed and festered, mostly beneath the surface. I was faced with six periods per day—Spanish, English, and a hodge-podge of leftover classes that no one else could take: drama, health, world history, and (of my own choosing) modern dance. Students trooped into my classroom for a fifty-minute period, tense, bored, perhaps angry—teenagers. Other teachers, examining my class rolls, said, "Hmm, in this class you have six Indians—too bad for you."

Not wanting to duplicate the negative schooling that I had experienced, I struggled to develop ways of teaching, of dealing with young people that could make them happy and make a difference in their lives. I remember thinking, "If only I could have these students full-time for several years running, what progress we could make!" And then the thought came, "That's what being a parent is." I used many songs and games in my Spanish classes, and brought in a variety of books and writing experiences (and talking experiences) to my English classes.

But I found it took most of the class period to unwind the students, to release them from the student-teacher enmity they experienced in other classes in order to bring them into working condition. And some of them could not tolerate that release and responded with totally anti-learning and anti-social behavior. Fortunately I was able to shift these to other classes. (The principal at the school, though he was heavily criticized by many, supported my feeble efforts wholeheartedly and gave me courage where otherwise I would have faltered.) I began to ask for "slow" classes—mostly the Indian students there. I soon learned that these students were not slow at all. Experienced in the school game, they simply feigned stupidity so as to avoid the grinding boredom of school work.

One day in particular stands out. I had borrowed a set of poetry books from the school bookstore. I spread them out on the desks, which I had arranged in a circle. The students entered and idly picked up the books, browsing through them, continuing as the bell rang and class was to begin. I said nothing. Soon they started calling each other's attention to this or that poem, and I drew out of them what they liked about them. And there ensued such an energized discussion of image, alliteration, onomatopeia, assonance, rhyme, form and feeling! Of course they did not know the terms, but they observed their presence and their effects. I did not press them to memorize those terms, but tears still come to my eyes remembering the high level of discussion that day.

During the second year of teaching I met my husband and terminated my job mid-year. As he worked on his bachelor's degree (which, by cramming, he completed in two years instead of the usual four), I commenced a master's degree. Then, for the first time, I began truly to enjoy college, spending my time reading, writing, talking, and thinking about literature. Of course I still had to sit in uncomfortable desks in stuffy, badly lit classrooms; but I was allowed to write a creative thesis, consisting of a collection of poems, rather than toil on a research thesis.

This culminating of a lifetime of classroom experiences vibrantly illustrates a truth: most of us are born with a disposition, a gift, a talent for certain things, in other words, a mission to perform something in a particular way. True education, while it does not neglect other matters (such as mathematics and science, as in my case), helps a person unfold these gifts and directs him into work that utilizes the gift. That work must make him happy, because he was born to do it! Thus, the old approach to education, "no gain without pain," is all wrong for our little ones. Instead, though the learning process may require intense work, it should be interlaced with joy and excitement. (Notice, I do not say fun, which is a misdirected effort that many classroom teachers try!) The motive for learning should not be to fit oneself out for a posh job and higher pay; it is, as Arthur King's grandfather taught him when he was young, to "learn all you can, but do it for its own sake." Later, Dr. King realized that he should do it for God's sake.

By observing our little ones, and prayerfully understanding them, we can see their mission unfold from a very early age. Mothers confide to me that they somehow know that this child will become such-and-such a man or woman when grown. Each child comes into this world so individual and different from others, even from the beginning. And the disposition and interests of the child strongly manifest themselves in a homeschool environment. Materials and books are available for the child to explore and use in a self-directed manner—always guided by a loving parent, but not forced. (This individuality most often is suppressed in the school environment, and its bad effects are felt for years. In some cases it can be destroyed entirely, with devastating effects on the person and on a society.)

By the time I was finished with my master's I had two children, David and Sammy. I was awed by how intelligent and clever they seemed to be (of course all babies and young children are smart that way); and, as you see in my chapter on Toys, I did everything I could to develop their minds. When the time came for David to go to school, I could not imagine putting my own little one into the same vise that I struggled in for so many years. So we decided to homeschool him, being acquainted with books and families that promoted the same.

Despite the negative comments I have made about my own school experiences, I still feel that the nuclear homeschool is not the ultimate answer. How can it be? Parents and children isolated from other families, duplicating efforts, materials, and equipment, struggling to juggle household, work, and child-rearing responsibilities, mistrustful of practices in the society around them, having to evaluate anew the things that we have for so long taken for granted?

In today's world I feel homeschooling is the only satisfactory solution. Even in good schools, such as the ones in New Zealand—equipped with reading nooks in the classrooms, supplying creative activities and field trips throughout the day, providing lots of outdoor play and snack-times, and generally being very relaxed (mothers and babies are welcome to visit classrooms anytime; much of the work is independent; and the society itself is comparably wholesome and oldfashioned)—the bad effects still manifest themselves.

The children come home exhausted from a long day on someone else's emotional turf. They are exposed to bad language, and though it seems to roll off the older boys' backs, the younger children absorb it, use it, and live it in their minds. As Avraham said, "You know, the level of morality in our family has noticably dropped since the children went to school." They must cope with bullies, teasing, cliques. They endure being chastised by teachers who are exhausted by bad behavior. They must sit in uncomfortable classrooms much of the day, doing work that is imposed and forced on them, rather than originating work on their own. And so on.

It would surprise you how much work a child will do without being assigned—if he is homeschooled in a television-free, video-free, computer-games-free environment loaded with books and interesting learning materials. Even when she went to public school, during the evening Chava would station herself near my work-space and sound out words, copy little books, ask for endless spellings. And each of the children, at his own level, does the same.

Public school can help in one important way: it stretches the older children's capacity to write at length and, indeed, to do other extended tasks that they might not regularly do for me, which is one of the challenges of homeschool—older children (rightly and naturally) growing away from mother as they mature, may rebel in completing assigned tasks. I have observed, in families with one or two children, that much of this can be avoided by allowing the maturing children to accompany the father on business trips, or be answerable to him, or in some other way leave the mother.

In homeschool families other than our own, too, when there are many younger children pulling at the mother's energy and attention, and more household tasks to handle, older children can grow restless in this limiting environment. They may begin to complain, resist, and in irritated ways to resent their homeschooling experience, though they may not know what is wrong themselves. The first time we sent David to school, at eleven, we just had a new baby (Sarah). At that time, David was lounging around, reading the same books over and over, bursting into temper when asked to do the smallest tasks, doing things slip-shod. The thought came strongly into my mind that he should go to school, and my husband, quite separately, had the same impression. When we approached David, he agreed surprisingly that he would like to go, and he attended from February until May.

School did a few important things for him. He was able to measure himself against other children his age, and to see how he and they operated in the system. Thus he was rescued from a somewhat boring home situation, because my baby had not been well and Avraham was working long hours on a demanding project. He played more serious sports for the first time; he was pretty poor at it at first, but soon improved. Overall, he toughened up a little and experienced something of a normalizing. I have noticed that certain children who have always been homeschooled occasionally need that.

But David also suffered the bad effects of school: exhaustion, meanness, a teasing spirit, some bad language, imbalance of his physical body (partly because he missed a mid-day vegetable meal, instead lunching on sandwiches and fruit), and a growing mistrust of adults. Fortunately, when school ended in May, one month at home brought him back to his cheerful, good self.

We considered several alternatives to sending David to school when we woke up to his need. Because of his interest in wood-work and metal-work, we thought of sending him either to a retired neighbor who worked in wood, or to a general handyman neighbor—in both instances to be a sort of free apprentice for a couple of hours each day. We would have liked to have sent him to school only a few hours each day, perhaps for math and art and physical education. We also considered community school classes and evening school classes. Had we been located closer to relatives, such as we were in New Zealand, with a grandfather (a retired electrician), or an uncle (a practicing electrician and a gentle person), we might have followed the first course; but the schedules, personalities, and practicalities of this didn't suit where we were. As for part-time schooling, we lived five miles from the school, and in winter weather we felt that school attendance was the only workable solution.

Quite apart from the benefits that came to David, I was grateful for the experience so as to measure my opinions against the reality in the school. As it turned out, my feelings were not far wrong. David loved the experience and minimized the negative aspects; in fact, he never mentioned them until the middle of summer vacation, because he loved going to school so much! He was afraid that I might stop him from going to Middle School during the following year. I resisted this strongly, knowing that the situation there was much worse than at the elementary school he had attended. We decided to let the decision wait, and that fall our family traveled to the Pacific.

New Zealand school proved to be a super experience for Sammy, whose natural disposition for facts and intellectual work made him shine. (His teacher, a loving, positive woman, told me he was brilliant and often asked him to stand before the class and read his compositions and poems.) Sammy also got into sports in a total, delighted way. I visited David's class casually one afternoon, and his teacher, a young, first-year instructor, confided that after she saw his evaluative exams, in which he tested off the tops of the charts in every subject, she asked him, "Where did you go to school before?" and was shocked at the answer! The only complaint either teacher mentioned was the atrocious handwriting each boy displayed; in New Zealand they teach an attractive script, rather than cursive. But the boys improved rapidly.

Yoni, on the other hand, was assigned to a classroom headed by a teacher well known in the community for his negative approach. In addition, Yoni could barely read, and felt terrible at the bottom of the class. Although we became friends with the teacher, and suggested reward-for-positive-behavior techniques, using craft activities for rewards, the atmosphere only sometimes improved. We then decided to allow Yoni to stay home whenever he chose, which was about half the time. Eventually this developed into his staying home completely. In all, the New Zealand school experience totalled six months. But our return to the United States ended a very interesting experience with New Zealand public school.

At the same time, the children's attendance at school enabled me to write this book, which otherwise might have been impossible. A few months after our return to the U. S., Sammy (ten), Yoni (eight), and Chava (six), trotted off to the same local—very country—elementary school that David had attended. They loved going to this school, just as David had. Although they worked more diligently in some areas, such as writing, than they had at home, I felt dismayed at the busy work, pressure of grades, unrelatedness of subject matter, and just solemn nonsense I felt was going on. And they began to show the same negative symptons—and change of face and expressions—that David had.

Despite all this, I was glad for this five months' experience. They were much happier in school than coasting at home during a transitional period, and they experienced something that was new to them. I personally took the time to recuperate from morning sickness and to regroup—and to finish this book! But how I longed to recommence homeschooling and bring the children back into balance again!

I have noticed that when children attend school they cry more easily when reprimanded at home. They often endure the teacher reprimanding the class for whatever poor group performance. Sometimes they are punished as a class for the misdemeanors of a few. And despite the caring, personal approach that characterizes New Zealand schools (at least in small towns), they too experience group maneuvers—standing in lines, waiting for things to be handed out, being herded here and there. I am not saying that these things are bad in themselves, but I cannot believe that they should be the fabric of a child's everyday experiences. Children, as people in their own right, are not made that way. Nor should any human, large or small, live in a tension-fraught social structure where teasing, fault-finding, or belittling are habitual.

Still, as I have watched my homeschool children develop, I grow in certainty that homeschool, in our present counteractive manner in this society, is not the ultimate answer. Children often need to be out among peers at an early age. I observe Chava, for instance, who at age five delighted to operate in a group of children outside the home. She especially loves the company of other girls, big and small, and of other women besides myself. The older boys like to play sports; but deeper than that, there comes a time when they need to gradually break away from home, to find their place among other people including peers (but not exclusively peers, as school tends to provide; though in New Zealand schools, mixed-age classrooms predominate, so as to give children a broader age-group experience!).

Spending more and more time with Father can be an answer, providing he is available. But our society dictates that men work at a living outside their homes and families, and few there are who forge their living at home. Even when they can, as Avraham has in many instances, the demands of their work separate them from the children for large blocks of time. To be fair, Avraham's pressing dream is to work a family small-farm with his boys. Children also need the extended family experience—aunts, uncles, cousins, grandparents; or the equivalent, loving neighbors. They need good friends from homes enough like their own that they will not suffer from spending their time there. They need to be able to move freely in their neighborhoods, to be safe, to explore. Children, above all, need access to the natural world outside. How paradoxical it is to teach and quiz on the predative nesting habits of the cuckoo, or on the life cycle of the monarch butterfly, or on formations of clay or sandstone, in the dry classroom manner, while the real thing is going on outside the child's own window! Instead, the family can observe these fascinating goings-on, and, ignited to know more, scour available books for the information.

The children need access to the natural world for another reason. Being inside all day denies us the healing, cleansing, rejuvenating effects of sun and air. I think of the two hundred years of peace that ensued after Jesus' visit to the American continent, which is detailled in the Book of Mormon. If you have read that book,   you will remember that the centerpiece of his visit was his remarkable blessing on the children. I feel sure he gave instructions for their proper upbringing; I cannot think that he wished for them to sit inside rooms, many hours per day, forced to complete repetitive paper work, on which they should be graded A, B, C, etc. Wouldn't it be instructive to be able to see what they actually did each day? It must have included a good balance of intellectual and physical work, indoors and outdoors, with appropriate spiritual instruction as well. Most likely they spent time with people outside the nuclear family, secure in an unpolluted culture.

Becoming a Homeschool Family

During the first years of our marriage, Avraham went to Brigham Young University full-time and also worked part-time, doing translation work and teaching Hebrew and, later, teaching scripture classes. Working on my own degree, I also taught as a graduate assistant, later teaching as a part-time faculty member, until the birth of my third child, Yoni. By that time, home responsibilities overcame me! Whenever I was gone teaching, Avraham made sure he was home to take care of the children.

When I finally began to stay home full-time, Avraham was working on his master's degree, with a thesis comprised of a new translation of part of the book of Isaiah. He later finished and polished the entire translation of Isaiah in his own time, teaching part-time to cover our family's expenses. I also worked—at home—as a freelance editor and writer.

We had just bought an acre and a little home, and had settled down to what we thought would be some long-term homesteading. Avraham made a large garden, raised chickens, planted an orchard, built a greenhouse, and we benefited from a block of raspberries. At the time Avraham did his Ph.D. studies, however, members of his committee felt he should acquire some academic experience away from BYU. And so, after two years on our little farm, we had to sell it to pay our way for study in Toronto, Canada. Avraham wanted to work with Dr. R. K. Harrison, a noted conservative biblical scholar, who welcomed Avraham. We enjoyed a year in Toronto, a city that surprised us for its cleanliness, decency, and a variety of ethnic groups (some second- and third- generation Chinese, Portugese, Latin-Americans, etc., so closely knit that they hardly spoke English).

We returned to Utah, living close to the university. Avraham completed his Ph.D. dissertation, a study on literary structure of the book of Isaiah. This later became the foundation for a landmark book on the subject--destined to "change Isaianic scholarship for the next hundred years," as Dr. Harrison kindly commented.

We lived in Provo for several years thereafter, receiving two new children into our family, Chava—our first girl (named after my great-great grandmother—meaning Eve), and Avi, named after Avraham. The summer before Avi's November birth, we had ventured on our first extended camping trip as a family, a three-month forway into the Alaskan wilderness.

The landlady of our Provo home decided that five children were too many, so we moved again, this time living for a winter in the home of our honorary grandparents, Arthur and Patricia King. These dear near-relatives had become our close friends a few years back, providing us with the extended family we lacked. We benefited from their constant counsel and support in forming the ideas to raise our growing family. Equally important, they provided counsel in Avraham's academic career. When they returned from their winter's stay in Arizona, we located a little cottage south of Spanish Fork where we lived for two years.

The summer we moved, however, we also traveled to Mexico. We found a marina in a small fishing town, Kino Bay, and camped in a lean-to and tent near the beach. We had prepared for this stay by employing a tutor in Spanish several months previous, but the children hardly used the language, as it turned out. We enjoyed the culture, the beauty of the sea, the different foods and customs, the friends we made. During that time Avraham continued working on expanding and refining his literary analysis of Isaiah.

Returning to Utah, Avraham worked alternatively on a translation project, his Isaiah analysis and a book of essays honoring Dr. R.K.

Harrison, written by Jewish and Christian scholars around the world.

Soon our sixth child, and second daughter—Sarah—was born, named after another great-grandmother. During this two years in our cottage in the Utah foothills, I continued working at home as a freelance editor and writer. During Sarah's infancy, we developed the idea of a big family adventure—a trip to the southern hemisphere to see Polynesia, and especially New Zealand, there to visit Avraham's parents and family. But how could we finance such a venture, and what would we do there? It seemed almost as though we were merely subsisting as it was; yet we had a feeling that such a trip could be possible, even for a family with six young children.

By writing a book for a local company, I helped earn half of the return-trip fare; Avraham worked at his translation employment extra hours and sold our car as well. The university made available research funds for Avraham to complete his literary work on Isaiah. Frenzied planning and packing ensued, and before we were aware we found ourselves launched on the adventure.

On our return, we stayed with friends for a time, then located a rental home, where I finished this book. Meanwhile, Avraham had published two books. Soon we found we were expecting our seventh child. Just a month before Joseph was born, we decided to move to a more suitable home in the hills above Salem. There Avraham continued his translation employment and work on his Isaiah analysis. In addition, he completed a book of essays on our times in prophecy.

Before Joseph was born, three of our children (Sammy, Yoni, and Chava) attended school for several months, as I have mentioned. I anticipated this experience happily, recalling their good times in New Zealand schools. But I soon found myself disappointed and alarmed. Despite the good things each child experienced, including loving understanding teachers and an expanded social circle, I saw them quickly change. They paralleled David's earlier experience, developing a mistrust of adults, a hyper and painful awareness of peer opinion, a super-sensitivity to the prospect of being teased (as there was an unusual amount of teasing in the school), a concern for making mistakes, and an abnormal awareness of getting less than 100% on any paper or test. In addition, they brought home language and sex concepts I disliked, and they became progressively meaner and unkinder to each other. We still cannot eradicate the "boys can't play with girls" and "I hate girls" attitudes that found their way home with the children.

Another interesting development: in our local school, there was an emphasis on "benchmark skills." Each child was tracked through his learning and then tested on basic academic skills. Each child seemed to be doing fine at passing off these skills. Yet, when I got them back into homeschool, I found that only Sammy really had retained them—and he had entered school with most of these already learned. In particular, I found that Chava, who passed the tests in phonics and math concepts, still needed help in understanding them, especially in math. When we sat down to do some simple regrouping and to evaluate, I found she didn't understand the concepts at all. This reflected a comment that Yoni's teacher once made to me: "If these benchmark skills were all they are cracked up to be, we'd have a school full of brilliant scholars running around the halls. And it just isn't so."

I was grateful for this brief school experience, however. Not only did I get the break that I needed, but I also had confirmed to me again that my frustrations with public schools were well-founded. Despite the good experiences the children had, including different social interaction and the chance to play more sports, I felt the negatives outweighed the positives.

The year following, we recommenced homeschooling, with, however, some differences. The older boys became more active in their scouting programs, going out one or more times weekly. Chava began dance lessons; and Avi, Chava, and Yoni began Suzuki string lessons. David and Sammy commenced a ham radio class that lasted almost three hours on Saturdays. All of the children were spending hours at friends' homes, and friends were visiting our home more often.

Especially exciting, a family began homeschool up the street, and the two of us did things together, including sharing of field trips. Avraham began doing his work three days a week at BYU, taking with him David, Sammy, and occasionally Yoni. Thus the texture of our homeschool dramatically changed, the boys working primarily with their dad, the younger children having more direct access to me. David moved entirely from my jurisdiction when he started on American School's high school coursework, and Sammy followed suit a year after.

During that year, Chava, at seven, seemed to be needing something more than I was able to give her. Because of the new baby, I wasn't available one hundred percent of the time—nor had the inclination—although she was demanding that kind of attention. Finally, she began to clamor to go to public school. For a time I pacified her by letting her play during the day with a homeschool friend or two; but she still was pulling on my energies more than I could give.

A public-schoolteacher friend, noticing the problem, offered a solution. She approached her principal and asked if a homeschool child a year younger than her class age could attend spottily, whenever the parents decided. Surprisingly, the principal agreed: if we registered the child, she could attend whenever she showed up; and she could be in a class higher than her grade level. This schoolteacher ran a pretty unconventional classroom: small groups, children reading to one another and giving each other math problems, lots of different, creative activities going on, everyone working at her or his own level. At first fearing to inconvenience this kind teacher, I found myself convinced to try it. And so Chava began attending Mondays, Tuesdays, and Wednesdays, all day. Thursdays we went to music lessons, and Fridays Chava visited with a homeschool family of girls in Provo and enjoyed dance lessons in the BYU Creative Dance Program. Her life suddenly became more interesting—and my life depressurized considerably.

I learned from this experience that if we think hard, pray hard, and wait patiently, the right answer can come—the miracle we would like will happen. It has been freeing to find more alternatives than just two—either home or school attendance.

That is our picture right now. One thing is certain: it will all change, metamorphosing into something different again--just as our lives change.

Our search for a higher kind of learning and living is the subject of this book. I keenly feel its faults, its omissions, its incompleteness, even as our homeschool itself is yet incomplete. Yet I also feel earnest and sincere in our explorations; our years of homeschooling have yielded some tangible, satisfying results, and I hope that you enjoy reading about them as you move toward your own family's ideas in learning.

HOW TO START A HOMESCHOOL

Almost always, beginning homeschool families beg for an outline, a how-to-do-it manual for homeschool. It's pretty difficult to supply one, because each family differs so much one from another. If our family is to be taken as an example, the homeschool is constantly in flux, always changing and adapting to growth in both parents and children. Nevertheless, we are able to offer some broad guidelines for starting a homeschool. The actual, nitty-gritty details, though, still have to be worked out by families themselves. The following ideas may help.

1. **Make the conceptual leap into homeschool.** This can happen before you have children, before they are school-age, or while the children you already have are still in school. It can be the most difficult step of all, because most of us are so deeply enculturated into thinking that school offers the prime source of education. Even though we lament the shortcomings of the system, we can hardly conceive of working outside of it. If we are going to homeschool our children effectively, we must be able to visualize what that kind of education will bring to our lives, how it will actually change us. Sometimes visiting other homeschool families can help us to do that. A neighbor once visited our homeschool and said to herself, "I could do that!" She took her children out of school and began a successful and continuing homeschool.

To help you make this mental shift, you can read the chapters, **Myths about Children, The Schedule: Child-Initiated Learning,** and **Homeschool Theory.** These help create an alternative image in your mind to what homeschool now means to you. Entering into meditation and prayer about the subject will help you additionally reach into the quiet, deeper part of yourself: What are my real feelings on the matter? Do I have a confirmation that homeschool is right for me? I wouldn't attempt a homeschool without that confirmation.

2. **Reorganize your home to accommodate the homeschool.** If you have children already, you probably have spaces for their toys and paraphernalia. You may want to reorder that space to include school materials. Most parents have already removed items that are breakable or valuable to "child-proof" their homes. Or sometimes they place these items in a formal room that children only enter with permission. You

may have to purchase—or build—bookshelves if you need more than you already have. Do some thinking about how your children can help you around the house. Sometimes they don't work up to our standard, but I try to accept an honest effort, helping with the difficult chores. This may be a big pill for the meticulous housekeeper to swallow; but I believe that a family cannot keep a spotless home and successfully homeschool as well. Children need room to make their messes and the chance to learn to clean them up. And sometimes it is easy enough to fall behind in the laundry or scrubbing when a homeschool project carries you away. The chapter, **Keeping House**, gives some suggestions about how we have handled housekeeping.

3. **Start gathering materials you want to use for homeschooling.** Some families begin homeschooling with rather structured materials, so they can wean their children more easily from the structured school schedules they are used to. You can use textbooks from the schools, if you and the children like their quality. Once in a while you may come across a text that really appeals. Many school districts are willing to help you with texts, as this permits them some financial remuneration from the government. We have always purchased some workbooks, as I note in the chapters on subject matter.

In addition, you may want to form the habit of browsing through bookstores, especially used bookstores, to glean books on all sorts of subjects that appeal to you. Over a period of time, you can amass a formidable collection—the heart of your homeschool. At used bookstores and especially at school sales, we have collected many back issues of *National Geographic* and, I am bemused to say, the *Readers Digest*, both of which the children adore. We have bought some tantalizing craft books at used book sales, and some beautiful volumes about life and science in various locations of the world. I have found some kits at school sales, to help with phonics, math, etc.

Think about which magazines you might like to subscribe to. Our favorites include *Natural History, Smithsonian, Boys Life, Readers Digest, Science Digest, Insight, Time, Ranger Rick, The Friend, New Era,* and *Ensign.* Magazine subscriptions are an inexpensive way to enrich your reading, and they surprise you with new stuff every month. You can also get the appropriate age-level *Weekly Reader* if you children have enjoyed that at school.

Being book addicts ourselves, we have welcomed this opportunity to build an interesting library. If you are like us, you will find much satisfaction in your growing collection of books. We have followed a standard of making sure that what be bring home is in good taste, of lasting value, and still of high interest to the children—and to ourselves. There are so many choices out there that fall within these guidelines.

4. Decided what style of homeschooling you are going to start with. There are actually many more options than we sometimes imagine. After you determine the way you are going to approach the basics—scripture study, core learning skills, chores, outside activities—there still remain so many options. We have taken a handicrafts approach to homeschool, learning through the hands. Some families travel during their first year of more of homeschool, learning history and geography first-hand. Some go for strictly correspondence courses (one family had its ten children receive their B.A. at 14 and their M.A. at 16, simply through correspondence).

Occasionally, some families have their children attend the public schools part-time, reserving the rest of the day for intensive music practice, handwork, home business, or other activities. Others send their children to the office with Mom or Dad, pursuing homeschool where they can participate with family businesses. Some children attend school for a part of the year, homeschooling during the other part. Some employ tutors for basic subjects or for difficult ones. There are as many possibilities as you can imagine, often providing your children with real-world experiences they might not have otherwise.

5. Talk about homeschooling often with the whole family. The idea at first may delight your children, or if they don't understand what it could mean for them they may resist it. Visit other homeschooling families that impress you. Read aloud parts of this book or other homeschooling books that you like. Most important of all, ask each child to pray about the venture until he or she gets a confirmation about his or her part in the undertaking. Be sure that everyone is beginning to feel okay about homeschool. Often the parents' united, good attitude is critical in this step.

6. After ascertaining that homeschooling is indeed legal in your state, find out what the actual requirements are. Must you test at certain intervals? Must you be supervised by an accredited teacher? Must you submit curriculum? Must you notify your local school? Do the spadework to meet the legal requirements. Your local homeschooling association may have the suggestions about the easiest, most direct way to do these things. Holt Associates provides documents and suggestions about legal problems.

7. Arrange—prayerfully—an initial schedule for your opening homeschool. This of course may shift as you develop, but posting a schedule helps focus everyone as you start. Just before the birth of my seventh child, I was in a quandary about how to handle all of the other children, stretching myself to meet the needs of young teenagers through a newborn. One morning a schedule presented itself to my mind, including weekly science and social studies reports and weekly handcraft assignments, in addition to our usual freelancing. I got some good ideas about out-of-home activities for the different children. As it turned out, we altered this original schedule; but just having it in mind gave me the confidence to hurdle our new addition to the family.

8. Finally, set a day—perhaps after a vacation or at the end of a term (though not necessarily)—and come home! You can expect your children to endure a period of unschooling, getting over their acquired resistance to assignments, workbooks, papers, and reading. They may try some of the tricks on you that they have learned in school, that subtle resistance to adult intervention in their lives. You may struggle over your feelings about their language or emotional patterns or certain expressions of the face you hadn't really noticed before.

This cooling-off period may take months, and I can't promise that it will be easy. But the important idea is to be relaxed, positive, and noncoercive, if you can manage that. Remember that the children have their whole lifetimes to learn things, and that this interim should most importantly provide good attitudes and happy experiences. They won't inevitably fall behind their peers at school it they don't keep a rigid schedule every day! We have found, as this book demonstrates, that children learn just fine with or without constant adult supervision. Your prime job in this beginning time is to teach cheerfulness and joy at being home, having to freedom to learn and find one's interests and work in life.

THE SCHEDULE: CHILD-INITIATED LEARNING

Envisioning a six-hour replica of the standard school-day, most prospective homeschool parents doubt they can make that kind of commitment. Well, they certainly can't—and few practicing homeschoolers do, either. I have only met one homeschooling family that observed the regular school hours; and that family wasn't happy in homeschool, soon sending their children back to public school.

In our homeschool we only devote one to two hours a day to the basic subjects. After that, the parent acts as guide through whatever activities she or the children may have in mind. If she's baking bread, she might include interested little ones in measuring, warming, mixing, kneading, and, of course, in making bread sculptures to decorate with seeds and raisins to gobble up for lunch. For older children not otherwise involved, she could have them multiply a recipe to make a large batch, or adapt it, and then casually set on the table an encyclopedia, article or book on the history of breads throughout time, an important and interesting subject.

A walk outdoors always develops some engaging subjects—rocks stimulate a geology study, especially if you carry a sack to bring home samples. We ever pursue the names and uses of plants in our area, carrying home specimens especially of wildflowers—to press in our homemade flower press and mount in a nature notebook. The names of the various cloud formations, the directions of winds, the different kinds of precipitation, fog; the making of roads, the organizing of neighborhoods; the growing and harvesting of various crops and the machinery needed for this; animals and birds and their care, habitats, and uses. The subjects for study, endless and interesting, comprise the real world surrounding the child and are therefore very interesting to all.

This is not to say that the parent needs to design all the different areas of study. In my experience, she usually just makes herself available to answer questions, guide children to the right books, when necessary, make trips to the library, provide needed materials and a helping hand with the difficult parts, and anticipate and forestall quarrels or moments of boredom.

As an example, some years ago the older boys went through the typical dinosaur stage. So we bought and borrowed books about dinosaurs, including one complex and scientific book that detailed the various prehistoric periods. We bought a plastic set of dinosaurs and the children made a scenic panorama, labelling each creature, using a bit of mirror-glass for a lake and twigs for trees. We made dinosaur poems and we drew dinosaurs. We sewed a lovely, velour brontosaurus from a pattern in a children's magazine that became a bedmate, and we constructed, I am bemused to report, a big papier maché bronto as well.

We learned our lessons so well (that is, the children initiating the activities and myself facilitating) that when we visited the Ossuary, the dinosaur-bone laboratory and museum of Brigham Young University, we were happily conversant about many of the things we saw. We went there with another family, and the mother was sure that a certain mounted head belonged to Monoclonius, but because of our immersion in dinosauria, I was equally sure that he was Protoceratops—which he was.

The curator at the museum, "Dinosaur Jim" (now retired), the famed discoverer of the largest dinosaur in the world, Ultrasaurus, explained his views on the conflict between prehistoric finds and the biblical account. He felt that with Adam, the earth's history proper began, but before that time, many other creatures could have roamed the earth during its stages of creating. The scriptural term "day" did not likely mean a day as we know it now, thence the dinosaur bones and man-like creatures that scientists debate about.

A year later we camped near Dinosaur National Monument, exceptional because the bones that have been uncovered there are preserved intact *in situ*.

Before our homeschool encounter with prehistoric study, I had little knowledge (and less interest) in the subject. But I learned to love it with the children, and now I know a little about it myself. The same thing happened with astronomy. At one point in my own education, I began to feel that I could never learn the constellations, developing an emotional block to the subject. Then Sammy, our second child, wanted to learn the constellations and begged me to sit outside with him at night (we lived in an unpolluted, country area) to view the stars with the aid of a comprehensive star map we happened to have. This was too difficult for me, so at the library we found the delightful classic, H. A. Rey's *Know the Constellations*, a book I recommend to every family. After a few fun sessions of reading it together, we took it outside, flashlight in hand, bundled in woolly hats, jackets and boots (it was the middle of winter), to view the stars. For the first time I made friends with Orion, The Big and Little Bear, the Crab, and other formations. Soon we were making outings to the planetarium at BYU, viewing the moon and stars through their telescopes and hearing their lectures.

Although some proponents of this kind of learning mostly leave the children to their own devices throughout the day, waiting for the child to ask to be taught, I believe in a short period of parent-guided study, if only for the discipline of following through a daily study and work schedule. Certain subjects, such as spelling, math, and handwriting, need frequent practice or you lose ground. Furthermore, a short study session gives form to the daily activities.

The Schedule

Wake up, read one or two chapters of scripture individually (depending on age), say prayers.

Wash face or shower, brush teeth, comb hair, a drink of water, dress.

Some chores, such as milking goat, feeding chickens, tidying house.

Breakfast, with Father reading and explaining a passage from the scriptures.

School session, at desk or sitting on sofa:

Math—usually a lesson from a workbook or a course; or later, from books at the appropriate level, such as Algebra or Geometry.

Spelling—a lesson from a purchased workbook or borrowed school-text, from a standardized list of spelling words of graduated difficulty, or a list of words taken from the child's writing, or from his own dictation.

Handwriting—practiced from a purchased book or from exercises the parent devises.

Science—reading one section or chapter from a pre-determined book.

History or Social Science—reading from various books such as *World Book*, the *Landmark Series*, or *National Geographic*, if the parents deem it necessary (usually the children study this without any formal instruction).

Writing—perhaps a daily journal entry and, for the older children, composition.

Music—practicing a preassigned lesson, in our case piano, strings and recorder.

Physical Fitness—weight lifting, basketball, running, calisthenics, sledding in the winter, etc.

For younger children, we do fewer subjects, and I read aloud for an hour during this formal time and sometimes in the afternoon as well. For older children, we include grammar, a typing lesson, and Scout projects.

In one or two hours in this way the child covers more material than most children see in a day at school. And then, from about ten o'clock, the children are free to choose whatever they would like to do, with the parent guiding the activities as needed. Sometimes the children have in mind a definite activity: building a fort; playing with water in the sandbox; working at the workbench with wood, metal, glass, paper products; painting; playing with friends; exploring in the bush; cooking; building with Legos; listening to story tapes; etc. Basically the choices are limited to what resources are available and what the parent is willing to put up with!

By providing art materials, access to the kitchen, a proper workshop environment with tools and materials, appropriate toys, and carefully-interspersed trips to the library, pool, craft shop, neighbors, Scout troop, specialized courses, Church activities, sports functions, the children will fill their days with happy activities. You create what we call a safe learning environment, in which the child feels free to explore without being reprimanded or chided at every turn. Children learn quickly how to work safely with tools and to control materials so they don't make a horrendous mess—especially if you insist that everyone cleans up his own mess (sometimes with help from you, if the mess is big and the child is small).

Every child is well aware of "the big I," himself, and of course doesn't want to be hurt. We should stop ourselves from saying, "You're going to fall, you're going to cut yourself, you're going to burn yourself, you're going to break that, watch out, watch out!" In *The Continuum Concept*, Jean Liedloff points out that these warnings sometimes turn into self-fulfilling prophecies. During her study of the Yequana Indians, none of the children were drowned, though from an early age they all had access to dangerous waters, both swift streams and still pools. They learned to be safe around water. She related the story of a family who installed a swimming pool, and then constantly warned their child of its dangers, locking the gate against his entry. One day, the child somehow found his way in and did drown.

Of course, we are careful around water, but I have tried to be relaxed with saws, files, knives, graters, glass. We do put the limit on electric tools and appliances that can cause irreparable damage instantly; and super-sharp tools such as wood-carving or lino-carving sets, which can injure even craftsmen unless they work very carefully and consciously. Our philosophy is to give the child access to the tools and work of the real world; supervise him only as much as is necessary; let him do whatever he can.

But will children really do all this wonderful intellectual exploring? Most of us have grown up having been forced to do our schoolwork, do our housework, do our yardwork, to do our lifework. Our culture teaches us that work is to be avoided and leisure jealously sought. We only work as much as we are forced, getting away with whatever we can and cutting corners as often as possible. Carrying this heavy cultural baggage, we find it impossible to let our children go, to let them work at what interests them. We assume that human beings will fritter away their time uselessly if they are set free. Perhaps they will only play, we worry, but we forget that play is work to children, and that building a log house, damming and directing a stream, cutting, pasting, coloring, carving—all the wonderful things that children like to do—even playing house—all teach something, all are positive. I measure it this way: if the children are doing something positive, it is school. Nearly every play activity requires thinking, imagining, working out.

If you have spent a half-hour reading fairy tales together, what could be more appropriate than a costumed rendition of "Little Red Riding Hood," complete with musical background, make-up, props? If someone turns on a piece of music, what is more beautiful than a room full of dancing children? When the little children play house, they move furniture, fold and unfold blankets, put on and take off play-clothes, make food, and generally work out the roles they see around them. What I am saying is that play is not negative, to be replaced by some adult-initiated, supposedly superior activity. If you feel the play is becoming light-minded, silly, or destructive, you can usually channel it back into a positive mode. For example, if playing house turns into a bout of arguments, you can ask the children to come fix a snack or to take the play-house baby for a walk in the stroller or backpack.

Sometimes the children may spend a morning arguing, fussing, teasing. By putting some craft material on the table, without comment, you can silently direct them into a happier activity. Sitting on the sofa with a stack of read-aloud books—again without calling out—will draw children to you. If the older ones insist on abrasive behavior, I sometimes say, "Either find something productive to do, or you can do some more chores." Then, insisting that they work if they don't busy themselves, they usually redirect their energy. Popping corn and making caramel (we just cook butter and honey until it candies, flavoring with vanilla and mixing with seeds or nuts, lightly roasted), making homemade lemonade or peanut-butter balls can sweeten behavior.

As for boredom, during all our years of homeschool I have noticed that no one has said, "I'm bored," unless they were overtired or getting sick. If all else fails, the children read—and they do spend many hours per day with books.   Indeed, self-initiated reading creates the basis for their expansive education.   People often comment on how much "general knowledge" our children have.   The mother cannot take credit for this; we buy books, trade for books, and borrow books, which are often strewn all over the house.   By this means, the children educate themselves, and they love books.

Few trips generate so much excitement as a trip to the library, and we dismay some librarians—and delight others—by taking forty or fifty books out each time, hauling them off in boxes.   I must confess that we have at times spent money in overdue fines.   Sometimes I joke that we keep the library stocked in new acquisitions with our overdue fines!   Fortunately, in New Zealand, in the town we lived in, the librarians didn't notice if the books were a week or so overdue.   They started charging fines after about a month!   And truly, we don't usually keep books over very long.

Amidst these reassurances that children will spend their days productively if facilitated, I sound one negative note.   They will really only do it in the right environment—and by now you can guess what will stop child-initiated learning dead: the presence of media in the home.   When a television comes on in most children's homes, everything else goes off.   Eliminate the television, the videos, the computer games, all prefabricated entertainment, and self-initiated education proceeds.   These media gimmicks stultify the mind, plugging into it a narrowed notion of what is interesting and worthwhile.   Additionally, they bind up much valuable time, being linear in nature; you have to wait and wait for the next thing rather than proceeding spontaneously at your own pace.

I realize that the media is a hot issue, and I hope that my explanation of our approach to it (see **Technology**) will interest and not offend.   The homeschool families in my experience that have failed to produce vibrant, motivated, wholesome and happy children have been the ones that permit watching television.   And as strongly as these people argue for the good things available on TV, the children tell their own story. A nonmedia homeschool, on the other hand, produces children who don't know what it is to depend on passive, entertaining kinds of "learning." They grow up with the notion that no one is going to lay it on for them.

As the children grow, the boys ideally spend more time with their father, perhaps working outdoors or sharing in his work. Children may need to break away from the strong mother-presence at about age ten or eleven, it seems to me. Father can challenge them and structure their experiences to suit their needs for an expanding world; he also better channels their growing strength and energy into fitting work. Failing this ideal, you could try some of the options I mention for the time children outgrow the stay-at-home, mother-dominated schedule. Of course, they can pursue some interests on their own: long hikes, sleep-outs, gardens, animal raising, sports, extensive building projects like tree huts, and so on.

Probably the best benefit of child-initiated learning is the resourceful, cheerful, confident person that emerges from it. Most of us as adults don't know how to properly utilize our time; we constantly switch on some program or other to fill in empty hours. How delightful it is, then, to watch a neighborhood child enter our home, survey the premises, decide that there is nothing to do here, and then have one of our children draw him into art, woodwork, Lego construction—whatever. Sometimes neighborhood children come over to work on crafts with me, not necessarily to play with my children!

Adults who have grown up in self-discipline, as opposed to external discipline, feel they can do any sort of work that appeals to them. They understand how to learn necessary skills; and they know they can do it directly, without too much stress and without a lot of help. They have developed a strong concept of their own interests and abilities, not faltering from one employment to another. As a result, they also become happy, balanced, useful individuals—quite refreshing in our modern society!

Albert Einstein said,

It is, in fact, nothing short of a miracle that the modern methods of instruction have not yet entirely strangled the holy curiosity of inquiry; for this delicate little plant, aside from stimulation, stands mainly in need of freedom; without this it goes to wreck and ruin without fail. It is a very grave mistake to think that the enjoyment of seeing and searching can be promoted by means of coercion and a sense of duty. To the contrary, I believe that it would be possible to rob even a healthy beast of prey of its voraciousness, if it were possible, with the aid of a whip, to force the beast to devour continously, even when not hungry, especially if the food, handed out under such coercion, were to be selected accordingly.   (*Contemporary Philosophy* 2:12:1)

KEEPING HOUSE

The most often-asked—and the most heartfelt—question homeschoolers ask me is, "How do you manage it all—teaching the children and keeping up with the housework?" Homeschooling stands or falls by the mother's ability to master her house. And it is so easy for the work to overwhelm us!

How well I remember the time when I was expecting my third child. David was three and Sammy one, and their messes seemed to overflow the entire (quite small) house. I had been donating breastmilk to a neighbor's sick baby, and my body was depleted and worn out. My husband was struggling with an illness along with a demanding piece of scholarship, and our finances were very limited. Every day, almost, I woke up to a sink full of dishes. The bedrooms always seemed like faraway dark corners of dust, behind the toilet made me think of wet must, and then there were the toys never quite in control. When people came to visit, I could only weakly apologize for the mess!

That seems to me to have been our lowest point, but we have had many variations on this theme along the way. To top it off, I am not a natural housekeeper (my husband is, however, and when things get out of hand he can make cleanliness and order much faster and better than ever I can). But I have found some good ways to deal with housekeeping as we have homeschooled.

Whenever someone asks me how to start a homeschool, I advise them first to work through their houses, room by room, eliminating those things they don't use and don't want. I know there is a whole course that teaches people how to strip their homes of clutter; the principle is to dispose of all things not used within the past year, and never to acquire something new unless one throws away something old. I am not so strict as that, but our principle is to weigh things by the Spirit, and to throw away not only unnecessary and unwanted items but also items that violate the spirit of Zion. In other words, we throw away anything that might seem out of place in a Zion society, whether it's in poor taste, too worldly, or excessive or vulgar in some way.

Do this room by room including a close look at books (I threw away some long-kept volumes by following this standard), and records or tapes (most of us could throw away the larger part of a collection in this way!). You may find that your home ends up looking somewhat bare, as ours does.

I recall how we house-tended for a missionary couple for a year or so. Their luxurious home remained quite bare and unadorned during our stay. What a shock it was to visit them some months after they returned to find it stuffed full of gilt and gew-gaws and an overabundance of furniture! Visitors to our home might be shocked to find it as undecorated as it is—few knick-knacks, not many pictures on the walls, quiet paint and rarely wallpaper, just a minimum of furniture. But the fewer extraneous things you have, the fewer things you have to take care of, and the more time and attention you can devote to other matters—your education and the education of your children.

If you find this pruning difficult to do, I suggest a measure that has helped me. We have often moved house, especially during the years of Avraham's education, which required sorting and throwing away. If you don't need to move, take a vacation for a month or more, living someplace where you can only take with you the minimum of belongings. Camping is a good choice but any housekeeping type of stay away from home works. There you will realize how little you actually need to function, and you will see what items are actually vital to you. When you return home, your belongings will appear in a new light. You will be able to sort through them with a fresh perspective, praying as you go over what will be needed in the future and what is extraneous.

The first time we tried this, during our move from Utah to Toronto, Canada, we overdid it. We felt such a release from the weight of many belongings that we got rid of too much. I remember in particular a beautiful indoor slide Avraham had made, complete with crawl-through hole. We gave away many toys. We sold our living-room set, and got rid of much that we had to buy again when we returned from being away.

Camping for three months in Alaska, entirely out in the wilderness, I realized just how little I needed to be entirely happy. For the campfire I used cast-iron cookware; we used dishes and cutlery, knives and wooden spoons, etc. We used a grinder to make flour for our bread, as we couldn't adjust to eating only cooked grains. We used a tent over our heads, mattresses and warm sleeping bags, raingear. We were happy with the most minimal wardrobes, for we only left camp to go to church; one nice outfit was all we needed, plain sturdy clothing sufficing in the camp. We didn't need toys, but we did use books, paper, scissors, paints, pencils, etc. We needed, but didn't have, good music; a nice tape player might have been ruined in the wild anyway, I'm afraid. Your imagination can fill in other essentials—an ice-chest, food, bowls, buckets, soap, tools of various kinds—surprisingly little, when you consider the overload we labor under in our American way of life.

Our experience in the Cook Islands validated this idea. Because we could take only forty pounds of luggage per ticket, including one bicycle per person, we carried very very little with us. When we arrived, we bought a mop, a broom, a few toys, etc., but still operated on the minimal household idea. For the first time since I'd been camping, I felt that I had control over my house again. I knew the status of everyone's clothing (there wasn't much of it there) and could visualize every corner of the place and its state of cleanliness.

Because Rarotonga is so undeveloped and wet, the children tracked in much dirt, but people there do not carpet their floors. Although the local linoleum can sometimes bear outrageous colorings (ours was a bright red covered with active patterns), it is easy to clean and I felt convinced that I didn't want to live with wall-to-wall carpeting again. (I have heard it said that carpeting is the dirtiest of floor coverings, because even when you shampoo and vacuum the carpet can remain soiled.) To me, carpeting never feels truly clean. Rather than red linoleum, however, better would be a nicely-finished wood floor.

After you have pruned away the nonessentials from your living space, giving them away to friends—or Deseret Industries or the Salvation Army—or simply throwing them away (once my husband and I felt impressed to discard a certain record we had because it was unfit for anyone to hear!), you still have to allocate the work around the home. Here is the difficult part for you as mother; you must break away from the mother-martyr syndrome that compels you to do your imaginary duty and do all the work yourself.

Still, you yourself have to make sure that the work gets done, because from my experience you can't run a homeschool in an untidy, disorganized, or dirty house. Order is a law of heaven, and when you live outside it your mind is continually pulled to that crowded corner, those unsorted boxes, the streaked curtains. No one can express this with as much certainty as a mother who is naturally untidy! So I suggest that the first task is to conceptualize exactly what needs to be done in every room, and to organize how often it needs to be done, who will do it, etc. Again, I have seen commercial programs that tell you how to go about it. *A House of Order* by Daryl Hoole gives an excellent system for this. Don Aslett's

Is There Life After Housekeeping? and other books helped me streamline the work as well.

I would add, as a woman who grew up more skilled at reading books and writing papers than scrubbing floors and folding diapers, that one needs to develop a joy in the process of making a home clean and orderly. Passing the buck of unpleasant chores to your children or a housekeeper just because you don't like to do them yourself is not fair. I honestly learned to enjoy doing dishes, finally. My children started doing dishes during our Alaska camp. I would assign one boy to be the pilot (wash) and the other co-pilot (rinse). This trick worked for a while, but they did not really enjoy it. They still may resist me when I want them to do the dishes, but once they begin, they often enjoy it. After months of practice, they can take a dirty kitchen and put it into order without too much complaining.

Aside from that, one should let go and delegate the work. A friend, not a homeschooler but herself a superior mother, had her children put the entire house in order before they left for school, including folding and putting away the laundry. During the day, she could study, write, sew, or work at church jobs. Recently she was able to take a job, soon rising to an executive position, yet keeping child rearing as a priority.

My children now do the housework regularly, picking up, vacuuming, sweeping, dusting, washing windows and mirrors, spot-cleaning the woodwork, putting away laundry, washing dishes, cleaning sinks and toilets. I mop the floors, do the cooking, and wash and fold laundry. I occasionally work with the children or take over some of their chores, but almost never pick up toys or dust.

Once someone asked me what I do when the children won't cooperate with the chores. My answer: "I scream and yell and carry on. . ." Not always, though! Sometimes I tell them they can't go swimming or biking until the work is done. Usually the habit of our routine carries the children through their work.

At eight years, Yoni was the surpassingly superior babysitter in the family and he continues to be so. He could take the baby and amuse her for a morning or more while I did other work. He often will do this without being asked. The other children, not realizing what a help he is, might ask me what Yoni did for chores. His babysitting is as valuable as their contributions; in times of pressure it is a lifesaver. If possible, I tailor the chore to the child's interests and capacities, but don't stretch this idea past its usefulness. Not long ago, Sammy, then ten, raved, "I can't do the dishes, and I won't do the dishes!" But he did do the dishes and, very typically, got to enjoy doing them. And as he grew up, he became an uncommonly good babysitter as well.

When we lived in the Cook Islands, a hurricane uprooted several huge trees around our house and stripped the remaining trees and bushes, littering the large yard and driveway with branches, twigs and leaves. Avraham and the boys worked every day for many hours; after a week the yard was spotless. This may seem minimal to some, but for my book-reading, project-making boys to work most of every day was a triumph. Since then they have helped Avraham with prolonged building, yard, and gardening projects (and someday, I hope, will with farming).

At first, however, this outdoor work upset the boys. After an hour or so, they grew tired of hauling branches and raking leaves. When they complained, my husband added another task to the list of things to do, until the words subsided. This seems to me a useful way to deal with complaining workers. As you may know, Mormon church leaders and other Christian leaders ever implore parents to teach their children to work. We sometimes labor with the idea that our children must receive plenty of learning, so we take on ourselves the physical work while they pursue their interests. It is a mistake I have made. Perhaps we think that children can't sustain their work efforts beyond a half-hour or so. But children can learn to work alongside the adults, and they need to experience the mental and physical state needed for this enduring kind of work, the work people all over the world do every day.

I never understood the real importance of this sustained working effort for children until I saw little ones working in the Cook Islands, each performing patiently according to his abilities, relaxed, slow perhaps, laughing and joking often, the smaller ones stopping and starting, everyone pulling together to finish the job. My husband did his translation work in one of the small chapel rooms there, and the local caretaker's entire family of ten children worked with the father and an older brother to keep the huge grounds and also the chapel spotless. Typically, the mother sat under a frangipani tree, sewing, while the children dusted, washed, swept, mopped, mowed, stopping sometimes to climb a coconut tree and distribute to everyone a drink and a snack all in one! No harsh words, no bickering, no debating whose job was more or less; they enjoyed each other's company. Avraham said you could see and feel the love and affection between them.

After most of a day's work, the mother got up and and went home to prepare dinner, taking with her the younger children. I am emphasizing this point because most of us would not think of requiring sustained physical work from our children. I do not say that we should slave our children; they didn't. But at garden time, harvest time, moving time—hurricane time!—let's not neglect the important task of teaching our children work.

How well I remember canning ten dozen quarts of applesauce from our tree. The boys helped Avraham harvest the apples; he washed them, I cut them and steamed them, he dumped them in the Victorio strainer, all the children took turns turning the handle; the boys rotated filling the jars, wiping the rims, putting on the lids and rings; Avraham put them in the steam canners; I took them out. I must also add here that this is unusual. As a rule, Avraham has done the canning (our job has been to stay out of his way!), though lately this has been changing into a cooperative effort.

When we moved from Orem to a country location in Spanish Fork, all family hands helped us move. Our friend Peter Reynolds was observing our family for his Ph.D. dissertation on homeschool (Reynolds, *How Home School Families Operate on a Day-to-Day Basis: Three Case Studies*, BYU, 1985). He wrote of this move: "Everyone was very busy. However, tempers weren't lost during this time. Everyone willingly pitched in. The children, more often than not, only had to be told once what they were supposed to do before they did it. This was very impressive to me. . . ." (p. 203).

In addition to the children, the husband can be an important help at home. A friend's husband comes home from work and does the cooking, which he has done for more than ten years. He likes cooking, which my husband doesn't; instead, when I am behind in my work, he will take over the laundry or the sweeping, mopping, or vacuuming. When our rented home in the humid climate of Rarotonga grew mold on the walls, he organized the family to clean it off. We all worked at it, but the problem was bigger than our ability to handle it. So he took off a whole day and scrubbed the walls with bleach. Avi, then three, got himself a soapy cloth and went after finger marks all day too.

However, when my husband and I were both in school we tried unsuccessfully to divide the household chores equally between us. I found myself wanting to do things my own way, frustrated at adapting to Avraham's schedule. Margaret Mead points out that the best way for husbands to help with housework is to voluntarily take over jobs they want to do:

I think we should treat homemaking tasks with greater respect and, where it is desirable to do so, divide the responsibility for making our homes pleasant and comfortable in ways that enhance each person's contribution...Pushing the baby carriage, vacuuming the rugs, polishing the floors... stuffing the turkey, putting in new lightbulbs, weeding the garden—any of these activities can be defined as male or female. . . .

Whatever tasks a man takes over as his own, he has a right to regard his contribution with pride. (Margaret Mead, *Some Personal Views*, 39–40)

I once read about a homeschool mother who hired household help a couple of days a week. At the time, I felt, "How improper. A woman should do her own housecleaning!" But since then I have changed my mind! There's no inherent virtue in doing everything yourself. I advise homeschooling mothers that after they have organized their homes so that they are running properly, they hire help as it is needed. Sometimes you just can't get to everything, and it is nice to have the dirty corners of the bathroom scrubbed out and the fingermarks cleaned thoroughly from the walls.

One mother said she only had hired help *in* when she was *out*, because she tended to spend her time working, trying to keep up with the housekeeper. I found that to be true myself. Maybe you can barter for housecleaning. I met a professional housecleaner whose husband was writing a book. It required extensive editing before publication; with a new baby, I could sit, nurse the newborn, and edit, but I could not scrub behind the washing machine so easily. We traded, and some places in my house came clean that badly needed it.

Finally, I can share with you some tips I have learned about housekeeping while homeschooling. I read an article by a young mother who, prior to her marriage, had paid close attention to her personal appearance, spending much time brushing her hair, maintaining her clothes, putting on her makeup. With two small children, however, she would find herself arriving at a meeting with perhaps unbrushed hair, a spot from a spilled bottle on her skirt, a rumpled blouse. An older friend wisely complimented her on her evident spiritual growth in caring for the children before herself. The same applies to a house. You need a clean and tidy home; you don't need a decorator home, not while you're raising small children, or perhaps ever! Once you pare down the work to be done, you can handle it much easier.

One homeschool mother folds all her laundry into colorful plastic dairy baskets you can find at the variety store. They're much easier to store in a central place, a dressing/laundry room, so her work is even more reduced.

Having used both bureaus and baskets, I prefer the basket method for its tidiness and control. Too often grimy clothes (I hate to say) can be stuffed into a bureau drawer to perfume the entire lot. I recall one of my boys claiming that he had no idea whatever how all of his undershirts (and, sigh, socks) had ended up dirty and inside his bureau drawer!

We generally clear the table and do the dishes right after dinner. In New Zealand even guests are expected to help with this chore after a meal. The gleaming counter in the morning, if we don't let dishes wait overnight, repays the extra ten minutes taken from the evening. Sometimes when I wake up in the morning I measure my cheer by whether the kitchen counter is empty or full!

Doing all your chores together as a family before you start schoolwork or projects is a good idea. As I have said, you cannot operate a good homeschool in a mess. The order imposed by chores will build into lifetime habits. One homeschool family puts the whole house in order as well as deep-cleans one room a day before they start their school activities. For us, however, this does not include laundry; I do this throughout the day.

We simplify our cooking and eating. How embarrassed I was when, hoping to entice our young eaters, a dear family friend prepared vegetables in nice sauces, piping out mashed potatoes in beautiful patterns, mixing lovely mixtures. My children told me (not in her hearing, so as not to hurt her) that they like their vegetables plain. A baked potato, a piece of cheese, finger salad, and there is lunch. I must add here that I prepare many of my foods from scratch, incubating the yogurt, grinding the wheat for bread, simmering the soup, squeezing the lemons for lemonade. When I can, I even make butter and cheeses. But making food from scratch, if you keep it simple, doesn't take the time that complicated mixtures and elaborate menus take. Furthermore, children enjoy cooking most of all the household activities, and you can assign progressively more cooking to them as they grow.

Most importantly, you should adjust your housekeeping mentality to allow for some untidiness. You cannot put together a papier-maché dinosaur without a big mess. Nor can you sand a wooden car, poster paint, or stuff a cloth animal in perfect orderliness. Children can and should clean up after themselves (this requirement has deterred some papier maché in my home). But you should be able to relax and permit (enjoy?) the mess in progress. Some women feel they can't, but it is a definite requirement if you are going to homeschool.

A homeschooling friend once said to me, "The dirt in the corner is always going to be there, no matter how often you sweep it out. But the children aren't always going to be there. You won't take the dirt to heaven with you. But you hope to take your children with you." I try to temper my housekeeping with that wise saying.

SOCIALIZATION

Almost without thinking people ask you, "But what about socialization?" when you tell them you teach your children at home. It's a fair question. But first we must ask, What is socialization? What do we mean by socialization? It might be better to think in terms of positive socialization when we use the word, because all human interaction socializes a child, whether it is good or bad.

Are we socialized if we can fit into a group of peers our own age, able to speak their language, excel at their games? Or are we socialized if we can fit into groups of all ages, conversing freely and confidently, participating in a variety of non-age-related activities?

Perhaps we are socialized if we can compete in a competitive world, carving out for ourselves a success by rising above our foes. Or is socialization the ability to cooperate with others, to consider their needs as we consider our own?

Is socialization the assimilation of one's own culture, feeling competent and confident in the superiority of one's own way of life? (You can observe this everywhere, not only among Americans, but in people of many countries.) Or is socialization the ability to accept and to love many different cultures, other ways of looking at life, other ways of doing things?
Is socialization learning the rules of correct appearance and practice, the etiquette of society? Or is it the ability to seek for true, proper relationships and behavior among people, despite appearances?

Is socialization moving upward, from job to job, ever searching for a bigger paycheck and more material comforts? Or is it finding your life's work, doing what you love to do and what you do well?

We can ask more pairs of questions—and we must not deceive ourselves into thinking that all the answers could be right. Unless we are raised in a dark closet, we are going to be socialized; homeschooling simply offers a different kind of socialization than schooling does. Further, parents, becoming aware of different aspects of socialization, can refine the way they run their homes so that their children can become socialized in a better way, the way of Zion.

Once, on visiting the home of a friend who ran the most efficient and organized homeschool I have ever seen, I asked, "What do you hope for your two girls? What are you trying to raise them to be?" She answered immediately, "I want them to be successful, contributing members of our society." I replied, "That's a good thing to want; but I want something different for my children." She was quite surprised. I said, "By the time my children are grown up, I feel the world will be quite a different place than it is now. Our society cannot continue as it is at present; the prophets in ancient times and in modern times have told us that. We know what kinds of things are coming, the hardships, the trials, the difficulties. We see some of them already. And we know what kind of people will survive those things—only Zion, the pure in heart. I see it as my job to find out what kind of person a Zion person needs to be, what kind of social being he would be, and to help my children grow into that kind of person. I also want to teach them to be resilient, self-reliant, adaptable, to handle anything that is thrown their way, if our society breaks apart, if calamities come, whatever comes."

Of course, I don't know all the ways to achieve this, and even when I know thé right way we don't always live up to it. But I feel very sure that school socialization doesn't achieve this ideal. Once when we were visiting a school, I observed that schools are superior socializers aimed toward modern, industrialized society. That seemed to me to be their primary function, the academic "basics" taking a far back seat to this social reality. The children learn to compete in order to establish themselves above all others. They value outward forms of excellence, such as achievement in athletics. They tend to homogenize, minimizing any differences among themselves so they won't get teased and belittled.

When our oldest boy David was 11 years old, we felt impressed that he should go to school for a while. It was near the middle of the school year, February. This was the boy who had said, "If you ever send me to school, I will hide in the fields till the end of the day and come home then." But when we mentioned that we felt he should go to school now, he answered, "There are some things I don't feel confident in; I don't know my multiplication tables well." We worked on flash cards, and he happily prepared for going to school. We drove to visit the principal, a man well-known for his opposition to homeschool. At first he couldn't bring himself to look me in the eyes as we discussed David's enrolling in school. Finally I told him I had been a classroom teacher, so he relaxed a bit.

David had to ride his bicycle a couple of miles to catch the bus, which took about an hour to reach the school. He would bundle up, with gloves and stocking cap, sliding through a couple of inches of snow. David loved going to school, and I felt he needed it for several reasons. He lost some of his awkwardness and shyness, both of which can be problems in homeschooled children. He enjoyed the stimulation of having many children around, though he never made a truly close friend that year. He loved being in a classroom, as he put it, doing all the same thing. He participated in team sports for the first time, and although he was not very good, he got better, once hitting a home run in baseball to the amazement of his classmates and himself! He was able to measure himself against others his own age, to see who he was among them.

Later David told me that in school you are measured mainly by your prowess in sports, so that he couldn't become popular at all in that way. But he began taking to school some of his crafts, particularly his self-made wooden "transformers," his version of a popular toy that you can change from, say, a car or a camera to a robot and back again. This gave him a measure of popularity. His teacher thought he was a cooperative and considerate boy; David thought his teacher was just this side of perfection! If Mr. Thorpe said a thing, it surely must be so!

Not all results from school were positive, however. After the long day and long bus ride, David was exhausted when he returned home each day. He had no energy or interest in much that was happening at home; he would throw himself on the couch and read a book. He got irritated easily, not wishing to tend the little ones or help around the house, which he normally did with good humor. He began to tease the others in the family more than usual, and more meanly than usual. He began to use some vulgar language. But the worst development, to me, was a certain look that I have always noticed in school children when an adult enters the room: the child looks up, quickly glances at the adult to size up his mood and reaction generally, and then slides his glance away. I have always despaired of this quick look, up and then away; for me it symbolized the basic distrust of children for adults.

I love the relationships of homeschooled children with adults. When one or the other would enter the room, the child or adult might look up from his work and smile or comment, but never unduly tense up or worry. Most of all, David's normal expression changed; he just didn't look like himself, but more like a hardened, stereotyped, school-kid version of himself. Could this be what happens to all school children, turning from their real selves into another, altered version of themselves?

For me, the last weeks of school dragged on interminably as we endured these negatives along with the positives. With school out, after about a month at home, David bounced back to his normal self, the warm, tender expression in his face returning again. But only after a couple of months would he discuss his negative experiences in school (he was afraid that we would not let him go back!). Evidently he had been excluded in some activities because he was so awkward in sports. We might have alleviated this beforehand by enrolling him in community sports programs, as we have done with the other children. But David never was much interested in these things, as the others have been.

At that time, we had not firmly decided what we were going to do in the coming year. David was pressing strongly to be enrolled in middle school, the sixth grade, which would add another half hour to his bus ride and subject him to the junior high school influence, enlarging the primary school problems. At the time I felt very much against the middle school, having heard of drinking, drugs, and various other social aberrations. We discussed the matter back and forth, finally hitting on the answer that I recommend to every homeschooling family: when the time comes, we will both pray about it and we will know what to do. We can have perfect confidence that God will help us decide what to do, and that both of us can know for sure the correct answer. This not only eases the decision-making process, but it also takes the weight of deciding from either party's shoulders. It allows for the right decision to be made every time.

Sometimes homeschooling parents call me, saying their son or daughter really does (or really doesn't) want to go to school, and that they can't convince them otherwise. I just say, "Both of you should discuss all aspects of the situation. Then you should both pray about it, and you will know what to do." (Quite apart from helping in making a decision, this process is central in the education of our children. More important than any academics, they will acquire the ability to humble themselves, to repent of obstructing sins, and to obtain the mind and will of God for themselves in their daily needs.)

In a family, large or small, there are endless lessons in socialization being learned. Children learn that a household operates by the joint efforts of everyone in it. We help get the meals ready, clear the table, clean the house, tend the babies, work in the garden, do the bottling, etc. Everyone is needed and therefore everyone helps. This is so different from the consumer society, where things are provided for us; in a cafeteria or restaurant, foods are served to us, special workers clean up the dishes; classroom activities are provided for us so we can learn, movies and television programs are offered to us so we can be entertained; and so on. In former times, people took it for granted that everyone had to produce so that everyone could consume, but it is not so now.

In his penetrating dissertation, *Anthropology as a Resource in the Analysis of Educational Process*, Dr. Bill Hoyer compares education in industrialized and nonindustrialized societies and notes that this new viewpoint is much more critical to our interrelationships than we might think. When we go to a restaurant, we receive a single helping of food, produced as if magically from an unseen kitchen. We all begin to eat, and when our portion is finished, we stop. If we cannot finish our portion, we leave it on the plate, but only infrequently does someone eat something from someone else's plate. On the other hand, in nonindustrialized (or we might say old-fashioned, or traditional, or producing as opposed to consumer) societies, everyone works to help produce, gather, and process food.

Many of these societies acknowledge and seek for an Unseen Power's help in the acquisition of food; frequently the family, eating together, prays to give thanks, seeking a blessing on the food. Members of such a family, which often include extended family members such as uncles, aunts, grandparents, cousins, serve themselves out of a common pot or common dishes; they are sensitive that everyone gets plenty to eat. In some societies, members eat out of large common dishes, scooping out their portions on bread or in spoons. As commonplace as this example may seem, it teaches vital lessons about the way we approach food, and from this elemental aspect of life, how we approach life itself and one another.

Quite unconsciously, our family has in some ways replicated this way of looking at food. Gardening and raising animals, we have all worked at producing some of our food. We all help with the table-setting and clearing, and with doing the dishes. We pray at each meal. My husband's work has allowed him to sit with us at most meals, so are together more than many families who often gather only at dinnertime. We share our food much more than is conventional. Everyone also tastes and shares a treat. Visitors have noticed how the children seem to share around everything; and it always quietly delights me when one of the children relinquishes a part—or all!—of some special treat to a sibling who didn't get any. "You can have mine," Yoni will frequently say, handing over the remainder of an ice-cream cone or a piece of honey-and-bread. Maybe this sharing also spreads germs, but I feel it engenders a generosity you can't get otherwise.

One of the important reasons to sit together at meals perhaps supercedes food; it is the opportunity to converse together, to enjoy "the discursive dinner table." Here the family can freely talk about anything. The adults might discuss something we have read, some point about their work, a matter of translation or a new view of scripture. The rest of of the time we bring up things we are reading, jokes or riddles we have heard or read, problems we are having, ideas, and often we hash over plans for travel or family activities. These discussions, alongside our evening devotional times, are rich and much more fruitful than formal interviews. Everyone is allowed to speak without restraint (though not allowed to shout, slurp, whine, kick, or bring up certain matters scatological!)

Although mealtimes can turn tense, feeding the baby and toddlers, we discuss so many subjects that I can hardly think of any particular examples. At breakfast, Avraham reads a scripture exegetically, which is to say he pauses to explain things or ask questions. Everybody can comment and explain, though sometimes he may question a particular child. At other meals the talk is open.

I remember a couple of years ago when we were all reading what I call Russia books. I had started with Solzhenitzyn, the children with John Barron's *Mig Pilot*, and my husband with Arkady Shevchenko's *Breaking with Moscow* and several *Reader's Digest* articles. Discussing these Russia books, the children formulated their feelings about Russia: the people there were not wicked, they thought, but the leaders were, and the people's lives became miserable and hopeless because of the way they were forced to live.

Preparing much of our food from scratch has encouraged an accepting attitude toward producing/consuming. My husband, a sincere proponent of food storage, is always on the lookout to buy needed items in bulk. We grind our wheat for our homemade bread; we soak our beans for our homemade frijoles. We always fall back on quantities of home-bottled tomatoes, peaches, apple sauce, grape juice, and so on, that my husband puts up. (If the canning were left to me, we would never have the quantities he produces: twelve dozen quarts of tomatoes in a day, similar quantities of peaches, over a hundred gallons of juices in season; we all help with apple sauce.)

When we lived in the Cook Islands, after a severe hurricane hit Rarotonga, fresh foods became very scarce. You couldn't get much fruit, almost no vegetables, and the only bread available was white loaves made from stale, imported flour. People lived on tinned food and meager quantities of sweet potatoes and taro. We developed something of a food-scarcity mentality, which my husband, born in Europe during the Second World War, already knew. We learned first-hand that a variety of food is extremely important for people to be happy and content.

Not only do you need good food, you need plenty of it—fresh fruits and vegetables, good grains, and lots of everything. Otherwise you focus on food too much. We met a dear family in Rarotonga who shared many of our views on life; he a New Zealander and she a Maori, they had been on the island two years. Due to a lack of variety and quantity, they had suffered from this food-scarcity mentality, now accentuated by the hurricane. Local scarcity, which can occur quickly, can truly "eat you up," so we believe you need a feeling of control over the sources and preparation of your food.

Imagine this scene: Mother sitting at the typewriter, father washing the dishes and hanging out the laundry, each child taking a turn walking the baby, pushing her in the stroller, reading to the little ones. When I am writing or editing a manuscript, everyone gets to help out. In addition, each child has responsibilities to serve throughout the day. While I regret that we have done too little service outside the family, having only prepared meals for families who needed it or tended children when parents were away, we have done well in teaching service within the family.

For example, during school time Yoni or Chava might have a question about how to spell or decipher a word, or how to solve some problem. Quite naturally David or Sammy would stop his work to answer the question. When Chava and Avi still used to nap after lunch, the two older boys would give them a drink, take them to the bathroom, read them a couple of books, and lie down with them (reading their own books) until they were asleep. During this time I would lie down with the baby and rest or sleep myself. The odd man out, Yoni, would look at books; when he finally began to read, he would read too. More often he would find his way outside, and if it were school vacation, would play with neighbor children.

So frequently we ask the children to perform a service—give a younger child a drink, fetch something for one of us, especially for my husband while he is working in the yard or repairing something, take organic wastes to the compost heap, and so forth. These requests often interrupt the children in their projects or reading, so that their individual work sometimes seems to be continually subordinate to the family's needs. Unfortunately, an important project might be stopped at a point where it is hard to pick it up again, but most of the time the children have adapted to these demands and can drop and pick up their work quite easily. The little ones are learning by example, and frequently you will see Avi and Sarah "reading" to each other and to neighbor children. They virtually demand to help with the cooking or the dishes—often more so when I, being pressured, try to put them off!

Visiting my relatives in California and Avraham's in New Zealand gave us a chance to test another principle we have tried to instill, tolerance. Occasionally you hear of some child saying to a smoking relative or friend, "If you smoke, you'll go the Devil," or something like that. We have tried to teach our children that we don't smoke or drink, but that other people do; and if others have not been taught that it's wrong, we must not think badly of them. When we arrived in New Zealand, Avraham's parents and five brothers and sisters, with their families, joined us for a grand family reunion. They drank champagne and beer, and I was secretly delighted to see our children nonchalantly accept that, although they have been taught not to use those substances in conformance to our Church's teaching, the Word of Wisdom.

When we lived in Rarotonga, we lived with the people, not as tourists. So it was proper and natural for the children to learn to dance like islanders, not to enjoy just looking at the dances as visitors do. Tolerance, I hope to teach them, is accepting people as they are. Being well socialized also means feeling confident in varying circumstances.

My children can feel as shy as anyone. (I'll never forget Sammy, at age eight, bicycling down to his first Cub Scout meeting, lingering several hundred yards away from the house because he didn't see the other boys going in and he was too shy to approach by himself.) Yet most people find my children easy to talk with. Avraham's mother said, "These children are wonderful! You can discuss anything with them!" Once they get their bearings, the children adapt quickly to many situations: flying in an airplane for twelve hours, riding for hours in a car with newly-met relatives, sitting with a new church class, working on a friend's or relative's farm, even attending school in a new culture, as they did for a few weeks in Rarotonga, with all the Maori kids crowding around to ask questions and offer candy.

I hope I am not overstating my children's goodness; they can be as rude and thoughtless as humanly possible, I sometimes think, yet I feel that by being in the home with parents who converse in adult language from the time they are babies, children develop a mature adaptability and ability to communicate properly with others. Sarah, then just a year old, stood in the home of a neighbor in Rarotonga. We had been chatting when a hen sauntered in; the neighbor told the baby, "Go chase the hen out." Sarah toddled to the door and began waving her hands and growling at the chicken (who took no notice).

By using correct, mature English with the children, by avoiding cutesy babytalk, we can develop mature language abilities in our children at quite a young age. By reading to them frequently as well, and by providing a broad variety of reading material when they themselves have begun to read, you continue the process. Once a well-educated visitor happened by the sandbox when the boys were playing there with the garden hose. Sammy, then seven, was just saying, "This is the disintegrating mechanism..." The visitor said, "I approve of any game that develops such language!" Of course it wasn't the sandbox but the other techniques that do it. Children who speak with maturity and skill seem to me to possess an important tool for proper socialization.

I must add here as well that long hours in front of the television or video weaken, and in some measure destroy, this kind of skill. Not only do the children sit without speaking, but they miss the correct role model of the parent, and hear inferior speech into the bargain. We then have no control over what kind of speech they internalize; TV certainly does not provide the articulate, eloquent model that they could have from a sensitive parent or from good literature.

Probably the most important issue in socialization is the hardest to explain. In Rarotonga we met the director of seminaries for northern New Zealand and its related areas, including the Pacific islands. He was also a church leader, a stake president, not a tall man, at first not particularly impressive. But as you spoke to him, you felt a strong influence radiating from him, a vibrant positiveness, an uplifting feeling. From speaking with this man, we were able to put into words an important truth we had long been learning: each person radiates a certain reality composed of the things he believes in as well as the way he lives them (which may be two different things, causing darkness or weakness to radiate from him when he fails to live up to what he believes).

LDS Church President David O. McKay, who himself exuded such great goodness, said much the same thing:

There is one responsibility which no man can evade and that responsibility is personal influence. Man's unconscious influence, the silent, subtle radiation of his personality. The effects of his words and acts. These are tremendous. Every moment of life he is changing to a degree the life of the whole world.

Every man has an atmosphere which is affecting every other. Man cannot escape for one moment from this radiation of his character. This constantly weakening or strengthening of others. He cannot evade the responsibility by saying it is an unconscious influence. He can select the qualities he would permit to be radiated. He can cultivate sweetness, trust, generosity, truth, justice, loyalty, nobility, and make them vitally active in his character. By these qualities he will constantly affect the world. This radiation to which I refer comes from what a person really is, and not from what he pretends to be.

Every man, by his mere living, is radiating sympathy, sorrow, or morbidness, cynicism, or happiness or hope, or any other of a hundred qualities. Life is a state of radiation and absorption. To exist is to radiate. To exist is to be the recipient of radiation. (David O. McKay, "Mission of The Brigham Young University," an address given at Brigham Young University, 27 April 1948)

If you follow your instincts for good, your reality emanates with a beautiful, spiritual power, influencing others around you. If you compromise what you know is right, your guilt or self-defenses in covering your guilt radiates from you. Whatever you are radiates from you and cannot be hidden.

Over the years, we all formulate the standards of what we feel to be a proper reality; and we try to measure all that we encounter by these standards, integrating into ourselves what is positive and rejecting the negative. The final and true measure of everything we meet is the Holy Spirit, by which I feel it is possible to judge everything, a sure and unfailing guide. We have tried, by living this way, to help our children do the same, and it is so interesting that children have a built-in ability to feel the promptings of the Spirit even in the small, everyday matters of life. When we attended a folk festival of dances, they all reacted similarly to a troupe from one of the South American countries: "They have such a wild, dark spirit." David said, "They are organized chaos," quite a comment from a boy then eleven years old.

So we try to help the children learn to let the Holy Spirit be the ultimate guide by which to measure all things, and to live up to the truths they learn. If they do this, then the reality they project, the feeling that radiates from them, will become a powerful influence for good. Maybe it's because they are child-like, as the scriptures enjoin us to be, but they are very good at feeling the influence of the Holy Spirit. They seem to know right away when they have gone wrong.

One day a neighbor boy in Rarotonga, some years older than Yoni, invited him to swim in the sea. Yoni had a feeling that he shouldn't go but the older boy's persuasion overpowered him. At the beach the boy was somewhat rough in playing with Yoni, putting him in some danger as a nonswimmer. Yoni knew right away that he had been wrong, that he should have followed his feelings. (Not long after, he taught himself to swim!) More recently, as the eldest in his church class, Yoni was invited to choose someone to say the opening prayer. When he hesitated, the teacher asked him what was the matter. He replied that he was feeling in the Spirit who to ask, which he soon did.

This all sounds simple and straightforward, and would be, except for the impinging of other realities on the ones we are trying to teach our children. In nonindustrialized societies, everyone basically shares the same beliefs and practices, so there is little conflict. When a child misbehaves, everyone—grandmother, aunties, neighbors—understand which is the correct reality and can therefore help the child back into balance. But in our society, it is quite different and more complex. Even in extended families, we can sometimes believe and practice very different things. Certainly in neighborhoods we differ widely, even in homogeneous neighborhoods. And when one reality confronts another, we influence each other.

As with the stake president I mentioned above, some of us exercise a powerfully good influence over others, but sometimes the powerful attraction may be dark. Take the influences on Laman and Lemuel, for example, two characters in the Book of Mormon. They lived in a quite different reality than their brother, Nephi, did; you might say that while they lived in exactly the same circumstances, they experienced completely different realities. They chose to. And when our children are exposed to varying belief systems, and varying behaviors (I keep differentiating these two because we might share the same stated beliefs, but the manner in which we live them may conflict in some basic ways), they are influenced by them. Of course they always have the choice, but sometimes the influences are very strong.

We knew a neighbor who had chosen to live in a reality of darkness, continually suspecting others of malice, contriving ways for revenge, criticizing political and church leaders, and so on. He possessed a gift for language and thus convinced many people that he was correct. When you were with him, you had to make a moral choice, even if you didn't speak, to accept his reality or to reject it. In this case, rejecting it meant disassociating oneself from the person, because his reality was very demanding; he seemed to insist on pulling people in with him.

These powerful personalities appear in all ages and represent a multitude of points of view. Reading Tom Brown Jr.'s description, in his book *The Search,* of marijuana-smoking young people trying to force him into drug-taking reminded me that people who do wrong generally know in their hearts that they are wrong, yet they try to draw others into their wrongdoing. Perhaps they do this in order to justify their point of view or to placate the way they feel. If our young ones do not firmly understand what is right, possessing within themselves the moral stamina to do right, a persistent purveyor of a dark reality can draw them in. The more they are exposed to the incorrect reality, the more they are pulled into it.

And yet, even as we guide our children in choosing a better reality, we must always be careful that they don't learn to criticize or feel negative about others. Foremost comes our love for others—despite what they are—and our willingness to accept them and to help them if we can. The problem becomes more complex when we add to it the popular media, because the reality portrayed there is a perverse and enticing one. Illicit sex, murder, violence of all types, fierce competition, self-indulgence, argumentativeness, light-mindedness and just plain silliness all comprise some of this reality. On top of all this, a sick sort of self-consciousness is engendered by the ever-present camera. I wonder if our generation's self-consciousness might begin with the expressions we imbibe as we watch TV.

When you watch television or a video, you are drawn into a fast-moving, all-encompassing, and consciously thought out reality. Some people say that they will discuss improper items on television with their children, but I say this is nonsense. It all moves too quickly—a glance, a response, a blow, a word, a bit of music, a conversation, a sequence—you cannot possibly discuss all those things you might disagree with. It all goes past, into our brains, sometimes the very vilest kinds of things right in front of the family and no one says a word, so as not to interrupt what follows. As bad as any of it are the commercials, which hawk a foolish, materialistic world that none of us should aspire to.

The things we absorb from TV are generally the coarsest of human feelings, a most objectionable way of becoming socialized. The more television and videos we watch, the more we come to accept the realities portrayed thereon, until we become more and more like the television world. I know one retired man who watches television almost constantly, and he thinks and feels as one does in a television world. He refused to wait in the car one afternoon while a friend shopped, for he feared he would be mugged. His mind is filled with the senseless and dangerous nonsense he views constantly. His reality is part fiction and part real.

When you consider that the TV is on for an average of seven hours per day in homes in the United States, you realize the dangerous socializer that television can become. To my mind, the only way to manage the problem is to eliminate it—no television!

Through the gift of the spirit of discernment, we can examine the realities of any person—or group—that we meet. We can learn a lot just by perceiving, for example, "This person measures my success by money—what clothes I wear, what car I drive, how I furnish my home. His reality revolves around the material world; even though he says he is interested in spiritual things, he never talks about them." This is a rather superficial example, but you can develop a sense of what the actual realities are as distinct from the apparent ones.

Sometimes we may feel uncomfortable about a person or an experience without knowing why. If we try, in a spirit of prayer, to examine what underlies the thing, we can understand a great deal as well as know how best to deal with it. And if our children, through us, can learn to do the same thing, then they can grow in the spirit of discernment, which will give them a very refined approach to socialization.

With the unswerving example of Jesus Christ before us, I think we can formulate a course toward socialization that transcends the question of whether or not a child should attend a schoolroom. If we find ourselves wavering when someone challenges us about socialization, we can discuss the weightier issues, not the polarization between school and home environments.

For us, homeschool has nonetheless developed a few problems in socialization. The worst is a certain awkwardness, what you might call an uncustomariness that comes from being "out of it." Yet, "out of it," for our children, very often means being unaccustomed to the artificial reality I have been talking about. We have found that the easiest way to solve this is a short stint at school. For the eight months we lived in New Zealand, our children attended the public school system. In the primary grades, the classrooms were fairly noncompetitive, the only tests given being in math. The second day of going to school, Sammy took a math test, scoring 45 out of 50. His "mate" (New Zealand lingo for friend) only scored 10 out of 50, and began to cry. Sammy put his arm around the boy and said, "Ah, well, don't worry about it. You'll probably do better the next time." This was the triumph of the homeschooled child, not the good grade on the test!

Usually, however, the children spent their school days writing stories, drawing natural objects from observation, singing, playing music, and doing much physical exercise. While of course the schools aren't perfect in New Zealand, they seemed to me much more relaxed, open, and wholesome than their U.S. counterparts. If you cannot feel comfortable about a child spending his entire day at school, sometimes just a few classes or a half-day's attendance will smooth the behavior of an awkward child. Sometimes school attendance is the only way to help a shy child into the mainstream, being in constant contact with neighborhood friends, feeling accepted—for homeschool children may often be branded as being "different," unpleasantly so.

And maybe this fault is not so serious after all, certainly not in the long-term. While we were in Rarotonga, the most outstanding missionary on the island, who was from Alaska, said to David, "While I was growing up, I was really a nerd. The other boys played football and basketball, while I read books and practiced the piano. Everyone made fun of me. But I avoided many of the temptations that they fell into. And when I was 17, I began to blossom. Suddenly everyone began to take notice of me. My reading and music have really paid off for me, too. I don't feel that I missed anything that important."

When some of my children attended school in Utah for a few months, I felt very happy about some of their experiences, particularly their quick sympathy for kids in the "out" group. Sammy staunchly stood up for one fellow everybody persecuted: "I don't see why you tease him so much; he has a personality just like you do." Yoni, impetuous, would sometimes use his fists to defend a sufferer. I have always taught the children not to fight back, but to use words to handle marauders. Yet I felt a humorous tickle at this anecdote from Yoni: "I was sitting at my desk when the teacher went out of the room, and a big bully came and slugged me in the head and knocked me out of my seat. I sat on the floor, deciding not to get revenge. But then he started to call me a girl, so I got mad and got up and punched him really hard right in the belly. He backed away and never bothered me again—but I felt kind of bad to see it hurt him so much."

I have enjoyed seeing the children expand into multiple friendships at school to encircle a much wider group of friends, to make judgments about what they liked: "Adam is rough and a bully," confided Yoni, "but there's something about him I just like, and I want to be his friend."

Despite some good things, many times I have felt negative about the children's school experiences—quite apart from disagreeing with the worksheet, deskwork, testing approach ("I missed 11 on this one," sighed Chava; I said, "If you miss some answers, it just meant that you haven't learned that thing yet. Don't feel bad about it. I'll help you learn anything you want!"). More than that, I have sometimes observed the children's faces grow fatigued and hard, suspicious in their expression and weary in their approach to things. At one point, worried about Yoni and feeling a great deal of love for him, his teacher asked me to come in and discuss his hurt reaction to the brutal teasing that went on at school. Her basic assumption was that children in school simply behave that way; that you need to let it roll off your back without hurting. I said that I didn't think that people had to act that way. In the larger world, we don't pick on each other, bully and tease. She agreed, but asserted that in school we have to put up with it. As much as I looked forward to getting the children home, rested, fed, relaxed, and learning on their own, I kept them in school for the time because I felt spiritually impressed that, at this point in time, school was the right thing for them and for me—a hard direction to follow when I so opposed the basic supposition itself. This experience taught me, however, not to let myself get polarized, but to be ready to accept lots of different experiences, provided they are within God's plan for us—a heavy lesson for an avid homeschooler!

We have always pursued Boy Scouts to the fullest, and wish we had access to Brownies and Girl Scouts. I like many things about Boy Scouts, primarily the opportunity for the boys to go out every week and have a good time with friends. I like the camping and activities, especially as the boys get older. I have always felt a little uneasy about emphasizing external awards, with all the fanfare and attention for completing a list of activities in a certain area, but the children seem to take it casually so I don't let the theoretical conflict bother me much. When one of the boys becomes very serious about completing merit badges and requirements, my husband and I support him as much as we can, trying to be as serious as he is. Recently, at a Boy Scout planning meeting, the leaders pointed out that usually the mother is the moving force behind a boy getting his Eagle Scout Award. My boys smiled at me, because I am very casual about getting awards, any awards. As long as the children keep receiving the intrinsic rewards of work for its own sake, of learning for its own joy, I don't see too much harm in the outward form.

Trying to remain positive about conditions in schools, I nevertheless have found myself exasperated by one pervasive social practice that my children experienced repeatedly when they attended, and which, to some degree, they brought home and had to overcome: the disposition to tease, pick at, hurt, and cut down others. For any reason—and for no reason—school children here in the U.S. can't seem to leave one another alone. At a band concert during a Scout activity, we observed one youngster who kept poking at a reclining young listener with a short pole, for no other reason than that he wanted to tease.

Any variation in appearance or behavior, clothes, accent, gesture, or even just general demeanor, evokes relentless teasing, often pushing, bullying, and fighting. Any mistake or blunder receives hoots and derision. Yoni, nine, went through a couple of bad weeks with two of his classmates, but he decided that he would persist in trying to be friends, walking with the teasers, talking with them, making himself present and friendly all the time, and thus wore them down and made friends. Sammy, eleven, on the other hand, a little more aloof and in the presence of older, more practiced and sophisticated tormenters, just set his teeth and endured it; sometimes in his morning prayers, he would say, "And please bless us that we won't get teased too much today."

What causes teasing? I can only suggest that the climate of U. S. school life, competitive, tense, herded, might itself breed teasing. To be fair, the teachers of my particular children were very sensitive and human; when Yoni's teacher finally heard about this teasing, quite by accident, she said she would do anything, even confer with the parents and expel the offenders if they teased Yoni any more, because she loved him! Fortunately, without the teacher's going that far, Yoni worked out the problem for himself.

And I have found no answers to dealing constructively with this problem. One day, four young teenage neighbors found Sammy and Yoni playing with a tube in the river. They proceeded to pelt them mercilessly with mud until they started to cry. "That's life! That's life!" one kept taunting. "Is that your idea of life," shot back Sammy, "to hurt and fight those smaller and weaker than you?" Anytime such an incident occurs, I try to keep myself out of it—not wanting to be one of those meddling mothers that enters the fray with the children—but I fervently wish I lived somewhere children knew how to live cooperatively and peacefully, instead of with this frightful picking and teasing.

I specify American children, because in New Zealand the children behaved differently. True, you observed the usual give-and-take between children, and I think that young people there possess a particular drive to excel at sports (our nephew, at thirteen, was one of the outstanding athletes in the community, and he took it seriously, too). But we saw little of this frantic drive to put others down. The emotional climate in each of the schools I visited—even the high school, but most dramatically in the lower levels—was pleasant, congenial, loving. I felt none of the tension and uncomfortableness that beset me when I visit an American school—and I was on the lookout for those feelings.

Kids ran around the schoolyard and classrooms in shorts and bare feet during the warm weather; indeed, the teachers would often wear bermudas (so did doctors and other professional people of all levels). We never heard about any dress codes; but the culture there created a natural limit on dress as well as other behavior, and we never saw any children immodestly or outrageously attired or coiffured. In addition, from age eleven through graduation (at age fifteen, though academically motivated kids would attend longer), students were required to wear uniforms, simple and not particularly stylish. This was meant to ensure an equality among all economic levels; and I think it also relieved a lot of headaches among parents!

What makes the difference between the children I observed here and there? They seemed to watch as much television in both cultures. Perhaps the easy-going Polynesian culture softened the competitive spirit, but I am not sure about that. I don't have any real answers, but I am convinced that this teasing and meanness is purely a cultural behavior, not a prerequisite of growing up. We and our children acquire it as we develop within this culture. So I conclude that somehow we can teach our families a better way—admittedly a big order if you happen to live among a few feisty neighbor kids—and at least avoid some of this behavior.

Feeling angry and frustrated one day, having to deal with a bizarre example of teasing from neighbor children, I asked a fifth-grade teacher where he thought these negatives come from. "From watching television," he said, "and from parents who encourage a dog-eat-dog, competitive approach to life. They teach their children to be number one, on top of the heap, no matter what." "You mean they teach them consciously or is it just a tacit thing?" I asked him. "Well, I think it's because they feel that way themselves, and then they just neglect the children," he said. "Do you know that I spend much more time one-on-one with some of these children than their parents do themselves? They grow up in an emotional vacuum."

Yet I think that parental neglect may be only a part of the problem. We observed the sons of respectable, moral parents who behaved quite decently when the parents were around, yet who waxed vulgar, crude, and blatantly mean when the adults were gone, blasting their rock music against the family rules and teasing younger children. This behavior would become doubly obnoxious when their peers, their friends, would visit them. These young people had been socialized in the school mode to get away with whatever you can but to play the obedience game if there were danger of getting into trouble.

The bad behavior seems so deeply etched in the American life that I despair of any other kinds of relationships. I don't think there is any real way of handling it, except to try hard for good attitudes and behavior in ourselves. "Don't say anything negative," I tell the children when a problem arises. "Don't tease and don't fight yourselves. Just come home without saying anything." An excellent schoolteacher friend said, however, "If he did such-and-such to me, I'd bash him in the face and run home as fast as I could!" I keep dreaming about how it will be in a Zion type of society, where children feel good enough about themselves so they don't have to tease and hurt each other. For now, I guess the only option is to struggle for proper attitudes ourselves, and perhaps the time will come when we can enjoy these kind of relationships.

One mother, homeschooling most of her ten children, commented that those children who went to school one year—by choice—begged her intensely to be allowed to come home to school, while those who had homeschooled the entire year asked to be allowed to attend school! This family lived in a city neighborhood without the rural advantages they longed for. In addition, the mother wryly noted that the school-attenders felt compelled to go play with friends—or have friends visit—every day, while the homeschooled children were content to visit more moderately, happy to pursue their home projects. (One teenage boy instructed his mother not to wake him up during a nap should any friends call; he felt annoyed by friends interrupting his personal space so much!)

This mother concluded that living in a neighborhood made homeschooling more difficult; neighbor ladies were always dropping by or phoning just after the housework was done and the homeschooling beginning; children came over by threes and fours at all hours in the afternoon; and teenage friends descended in hordes at any hour, even in the middle of the night. She liked her children to have friends, she averred, but felt that a city situation could impose too much on her and her family.

Jean Liedloff points out in *The Continuum Concept* that children are inherently sociable. They wish to behave correctly, and they study the family around them to see how to act. I have noticed this in my younger children. Sarah at fifteen months constantly watched her brothers and sister to mimic their facial expressions, gestures, words. Liedloff, from her observations of the Yequana Indians, suggests that children need for models calm, confident adults who go about their own work but who include the children as it might be appropriate, never stopping to adapt their own maturity to the lower level of the children. Thus the little ones learn early a correct mode of behavior.

Over the years I have adopted this way of living with children. Though I appreciate it when others contrive little games and conversations especially for the children, I rarely do it. I read to them out of good children's literature, talk to them at a level just a little above their comprehension, play wholesome games with them, but it is always within my adult sphere rather than within their child's reality.

The children are free to be children of course, although I expect them to talk without affected babytalk or undue silliness (we get plenty of undue silliness anyhow). It is sort of a contradiction, for while I love to see competence and responsibility in children and young people, I still hope for them to remain children even into their early teens. Young people are capable of so much, yet so many are robbed of their childhood. I mourn at the tremendous capabilities for doing interesting and important work that are cooped up in classrooms until the young folk, eighteen years old, are released into the working world on graduating. They spend precious years regurgitating lectures and texts while they might have been experiencing firsthand some work that interested them. The spirit of the adult that should emerge can be killed in those tender years.

But even though we expect our children to live maturely and responsibly, I hope we can avoid the "premature maturity" that seems to be a plague in our society today. I once read an article about a young model, aged eleven or twelve. The photograph showed an elegantly clad and madeup young lady you might think to be eighteen, not only from her dress, but from her expression and demeanor.

We press puberty on our young ones in our society, giving them makeup, training bras, discotheque dances, dating, suggestive movies, and so forth at extremely young ages. We pierce their ears; we paint their fingernails; we tease them about girlfriends or boyfriends in the romantic sense. We let them dress—in response to media images—in immodest and suggestive clothing. I don't know why this is so; perhaps we do not trust our own wholeness in sexuality, so try to prove ourselves by forcing our young ones into that role too early. Maybe we do it unthinkingly, unaware that our society has programmed us to do so. However we should clearly sense the child in our children, and let them be that child as long as they will.

This doesn't mean that we should limit their experiences when these are safe and appropriate. I like the point of view of one mother who said, "We are here on this earth to gain experience—the more the better. As long as my children are safe, I hope they will experience lots of things, good and bad, so they will grow." We let our children read almost anything they can read, as long as it is decent and wholesome. Even young readers can vicariously experience mature conflicts, the despicable Murdstones in Dickens' *David Copperfield*; Anna's apparent success yet complete failure, because of her adultery, in Tolstoy's *Anna Karenina*; and so on.

Reading about these things and discussing them expands our children's souls into maturity without their having to experience adulthood prematurely. They see, they feel various ways of being grown up, experiencing them through literature without the risks and pain to themselves. They acquire the words to express what they experience; and the elegant and polished language of literature permeates their thoughts about matters of maturity. When a young girl reads Eliot's *Adam Bede*, she lives vicariously an experience that is very close to home for many teenagers, yet the morality of the book creates for her an appropriate response to Hetty's fall.

Allowing our children to work independently and knowledgeably while avoiding cutesy, self-conscious prematurity seems to me to be one of the great advantages of homeschool, perhaps a soul-saving one in a number of instances.

How do my homeschooled kids fit into situations outside our home? In peer situations they seem to fare as well as anyone else, and they seem to be following typical social development for their ages. Recently at at all-day Scout-o-rama, our family stayed for the entire event. The older children saw me now and again, but most of the time stayed with their own age groups; in particular, David, thirteen, having spent the entire afternoon and evening before with his friends, hardly saw us during the day. The little ones touched base more often, but Sammy and Yoni played independently most of the time. After the activity, they all came home with other people; we just transported the littlest ones home.

If there are any children in the vicinity, Yoni will always find his way outside. Once, meeting some children who didn't seem friendly at first, Yoni thought up various activities to win them over—bouncing on tubes, swinging together, building a play hut. Soon they got along beautifully. And Chava, socialite that she is, would live twenty-four hours-a-day with friends if she could. A neighbor once described her playing with four or five girls her own age, jumping on the trampoline, making sand sculptures, playing house. as "right in her element." Our children don't have television or popular music to talk about, it's true, but they are full of ideas of interesting things to do.

In the world of adults, we have had some feedback about how they fare. At church, Sunday School teachers often seek us out to compliment us on the behavior of our children. They usually tell us how cooperative, communicative and loveable they are. "We just love Yoni," his teacher beams. "Avi is such a well-behaved child; he certainly is intelligent," says his teacher. During the periods when the children have been at school, teachers paint us the same picture. "Yoni is so well-socialized," his third-grade teacher commented during the few months that we sent him to school. When we left New Zealand, Sammy's teacher hugged and kissed him—quite unusual in a fourth-grade classroom environment! His schoolmate later wrote, telling of how the teacher had begun to cry when she inadvertently read his name on the roll after he had gone. Later, when the two older boys attended school half-day, I met at parent-teacher conferences with their various instructors. Some were incredulous that the boys had been raised in homeschool. "Usually homeschool kids are introverted, antisocial," they said, "and your boys are so gregarious."

What makes things work for our children is the strength of homeschool socialization; the developing children grow up feeling and looking natural and behaving simply and unaffectedly. Without the heavy burden of having to compete and tease, without the unease about adult relationships, they behave pretty much like themselves.

As we have spent time with our grandparents and honorary grandparents (those to whom we are bound not by blood but nevertheless by a bond of love), we have grown into a strong awareness of the extended family. Although our society structures the family into strictly a nuclear unit—father, mother, and children—I would love to see it return to the preindustrial extended family unit. We observed it in Rarotonga; families routinely accepted nieces and nephews into their homes, and the older generation easily fit into a family's activities. Whenever a family planned a wedding or had a funeral, everyone pitched in to provide food and make the arrangements. Families went so far as to give one of their babies to a barren relative; of course we can't condone this practice, as we have to accept the responsibility of raising our own children, but it lets us feel how families can erase the boundaries between themselves and their loved ones.

Being with grandparents eases the friction that might develop between parents and children. In nonindustrialized societies, grandparents freely discipline the children of their sons and daughters, and often the grandchildren respond better to this discipline than to parental direction, especially when they become adolescents.

Being with extended families can add enjoyment to everyday occurrences. Even doing mundane chores becomes special when we do them together. Older relatives can teach us many things, but I think their greatest contribution is their gift of themselves; all that they have done and become over the years is present in their reality, and it speaks to us and makes us love them and them us. Nothing can replace their presence; without it we and our children are bereft of an essential portion of our lives. When we arrived in New Zealand to a ready-made extended family of Avraham's parents, his five brothers and sisters and their children, we were full of delight just to be with them; we loved every one of them, most especially his parents, to whom I felt bound by emotional and spiritual ties, though we had never been together before. And how the children loved their cousins!

Although I have spoken at length about socialization, I am sure that there are plenty of other facets of becoming socialized toward a Zion society that I have neglected to discuss. Still, directing our developing children toward a Zion point of view—while we move in that direction ourselves—seems to me to be the important basis of our socialization, and I am confident that we will keep learning along the way.

DISCIPLINE

One year, I went through a major genesis regarding discipline, which had been a source of frustration and even contention in our family. Although both my husband and I agreed that the best discipline—really the only discipline—amounts to self-discipline, we wrangled over how to achieve this.

I felt that loving, considerate treatment, trying to understand the child's nature and enhancing his good points, allowing free conversation and self-expression, and encouraging considerateness and pleasant interaction from the heart, rather than having to be forced, would bring good behavior. Avraham felt that certain standards should be required, and that no one should cross the line, while I would make excuses when the child did cross: "He is tired; he is getting sick; he has been feeling pressured; he's going through a stage."

Through it all I tried to maintain the attitude often expressed in articles in *Mothering Magazine*, being willing to give my whole soul, all my patience, understanding, and help to reach the inner child, facilitating him out of bad behavior into good. Only it didn't always work. To be sure, our children possess the gift many homeschoolers seem to have, of conversing naturally and intelligently with anyone of any age. But often, they would quarrel, complain unpleasantly about chores, tease each other, tattle, or, in the case of the younger ones, whine, cry, and nag.

Trying to be the ever-patient mother, I absorbed all these negative things and helped each crisis work itself out. But every day this process could exhaust my emotional reserve, and the slightest criticism or disagreement with my husband could send us into a quarrel far beyond the magnitude of the issue at hand. He could not understand how I could be so defensively volatile, while I felt that he cruelly pushed me over the brink—after I had poured myself out so much during the day!

Of course, the homeschool routine itself demands an inherent discipline: we must groom and dress ourselves, read scriptures and pray before breakfast. We must order and clean the house before schoolwork. Young siblings need tending when we would rather curl up on the couch and read. After lunch, during rest-time, we have to be very quiet so as not to wake the little ones who nap. (In one very large family, the parents require a silent hour after lunch.) We have to keep the house tidied; we have to care for the animals; we must mow the lawn, rake the clippings, weed the garden; we must care for our clothing and belongings; we must practice our music. When we work on projects, we are responsible for putting away materials and caring properly for our tools. We have to pick up the scraps. If we don't put away a finished product, a toddler might likely destroy it.

When we go shopping or swimming or hiking, the younger children require attention and care. Intuitively growing into these roles, the older children often help the little ones without being asked. When three-year-old Avi wanted to bear his testimony at church, Yoni, then eight, just walked him up the microphone and whispered help into his ear. On a forest walk to see some huge, two thousand-year-old New Zealand kauri trees, toddler Sarah called for twelve-year-old David to hold her hand; on that excursion she became "Dadid's girl." How often our children curl up on the sofa, books in hand, reading to each other—sometimes because I require peace while I cook, but often spontaneously. When Sarah, at two, would wake crying in the night, six-year-old Chava would give her a drink, pat her, and murmur comfort till she went back to sleep. Before Yoni read fluently, Sammy would often take pains to read long books to him; over several days they went through one adult book on the universe together.

Seeing these happy behaviors, I wanted to think we were moving in the right direction with discipline, considering deviations merely as the children's personal search for managing their emotional lives. But the whining, quarrelling, complaining, teasing seemed to worsen the year we travelled, coming to a head when we returned to the United States. Of course I could make some excuses, perhaps valid, for that: disruption of schedule, tiredness, new environment, stress.

When we stayed with friends on our return to the U. S., the husband of this family, a school psychologist, observed what was going on between me and my children. After a while, reluctantly, and with hesitation lest he hurt my feelings, he expressed his observations: by giving 100 percent, as I was trying to do, I was doing everyone a disservice—myself, because each day I endured a great deal of emotional wear (he himself felt exhausted after being in the house several hours with the bad behaviors); my husband, because he could not deal with situations that were out of his control; and the children, because they were being trained to demand, not to give, to drain, not to build; to manipulate me and pull out all my energies.

After hearing this, I felt very depressed and discouraged; I felt as though the foundation of what I was attempting with homeschool—love, understanding, consideration of each child's inner self—had been knocked out from under me.

In further discussions, our friend explained that you don't stop giving love when you eliminate bad behavior. He taught the concept of "high law, high love." Everyone in the family should be expected to live a high law, that is, to restrain bad comments, to forego whining, to get what we want without manipulation, to stop from teasing, to work willingly and well—to give back the love and consideration that we receive. Parents should simply not allow the bad behavior.

I kept trying to get him to tell me specifically what to do, but he never did. He suggested that I model myself on and get help from his mother-in-law who lived with us, who exemplified this concept of "high law, high love." After I decided what to do, he proposed, I didn't have to commit myself to a lifetime of it. I should just try it for two or three weeks, and then I could observe the fruits of it and determine for myself.

So I decided to give up my former approach. For a couple of weeks I would not allow the bad behaviors. If the older children complained about a chore, they would receive another chore to do. Sometimes the children would get a whole string of assignments before the words would stop; one morning David had to bring in several loads of firewood, go to the store for some needed items, tidy up all the toys from the floor and vacuum it, and tend Sarah for an hour before he stopped complaining. When Sammy complained about doing a big load of dishes, he had to dry and put them away, then clean all the counters, sweep the floor, and wash the table—all the tasks we normally divide up between us—before he stopped his noise.

If one of the younger children whined or persisted in teasing or mean talk, he sat in isolation for a short time, in a large room with the light on but the door tightly shut. I would also cage a child who would swear for dramatic effect. Amazingly, the champion whiner, two-year-old Sarah, checked herself almost immediately in order to leave the time-out room. She understood why she was being punished. Emerging quiet from her time out one afternoon, she confided to Avraham, who had just entered, "No whining, no crying, no nag, nag, nag."

This confirms our friend's observation that even these very little ones were manipulating me in order to draw out every bit of attention and energy they could. Of course, we had used this time-out technique before, but never consistently.

I also withdrew privileges. One evening when the family planned to see a special movie, we had sat down for a meal, and Yoni and Sammy commenced to grumble about the menu. I told them to stop immediately, but they continued. I said, "If I hear one more word about this meal, whoever says it will not be allowed to see the movie." The two growlers continued on with several sentences each, and they were excluded from the family treat. Similarly, I have withdrawn dessert from children who disobeyed or persistently talked back.

As elemental as these withdrawals of privilege seem, they "get the kids where they live," to paraphrase a popular way of saying it. Our children love to listen to tapes of literature stories before they go to bed, but sometimes they would delay preparations for bed until the tapes would keep them awake late, causing fatigue and temper in the morning. I made a simple rule: if they were in bed by seven o'clock (winter hours), they could listen to a complete one-hour story tape; if by 7:15 p.m., only one side of a tape. After going to bed in silence a couple of times, they leaped to their beds so they could enjoy the stories.

Trying these simple but strict rules turned out to be easy for me. And the first day was so successful, I felt elated. The whining almost completely stopped, as did the teasing. The complaining and tattling never disappeared but were reduced to a tolerable level. In fact, the whole emotional level of the household has become almost normal again, even pleasant.

Surprisingly, I didn't consider it an irrevocable loss when I found myself less involved in the inner, emotional lives of the children. These new techniques put a little distance between their feelings and my own. But instead of grieving over this, I found it a release. Perhaps I saw myself too much in them and wanted to protect them. The children's emotional realities nonetheless continued quite well without my entering into them all the time. I realized that I was using the children as an emotional crutch to support those inadequacies I felt in myself. Now that was a painful discovery, but by looking at it squarely, I was able to accept and slowly deal with it.

This approach also drew the children closer to each other. They spent more time playing games together, talking, doing projects together, and less time trying to vie for my exclusive attention. Even the younger children glued themselves to a varying favorite among the older ones, being careful to maintain the limits of good behavior. I had more free time to think, read, work; I could choose to be with the children, to read to them, to do projects with them, instead of being driven from one compensating activity to another.   (Of course, I might be overstating the actual situation here, as in our usual homeschool the children would undertake projects of their own with only little adult supervision.   But in this interim period the situation was dramatically worsened.   This, however, turned out to be all for the good, because we could now see the discipline problem in a definite focus and deal with it, even though it was not the norm.)

I also felt a release from the notion that my moods were to blame for the children's misbehaviors, a belief I had quietly nurtured all these years.   Instead, I could accept my own and my children's moods in good humor, still expecting conformity with the basic rules of the household.   And, to my delight, I found myself more even-tempered and cheerful living "high law, high love."

Our friend explained that a long-term benefit from this kind of discipline would be evident: Children who expect 100 percent from their mother or father use all their energy in trying to focus that attention on themselves.   Of course they can never get it, but they make themselves obnoxious trying.   When they get older, away from the close supervision and nurturing of their mother, they try to get 100 percent from their friends and acquaintances, with drastically bad effects—giving into peer pressure to drink or take drugs; and, in the case of girls, seeking that strong emotional bond by inappropriate sexual involvement.   By being forced into the situation of disciplining themselves and being subjected to demanding standards, the children learn to supply some of their own emotional needs, and to get the good attention they need by behaving well instead of badly.

Because the older children now babysit, and feeling liberated from too-close emotional bonds with the children generally, I have felt freer to leave the house and attend meetings, visit friends or go out to lunch occasionally, see a movie now and then, take a walk.   Again, it has only made us all happier.

At first I could not believe that this transition in discipline would be so simple.   It must be an operative law in the mortal world: when we obey certain standards, we reap the good character that results, pretty obvious perhaps, but it took this experience to let me see it.   The children normalize and maintain their good attitudes and behavior so long as I stand firm.   Yet, I was very surprised to see that Avraham, my high-law spouse, found some of the consequences severe, and he occasionally tried to talk me out of them!   I was determined, however, and told him that if I was going to do this thing, I would just do it, no matter how hard it seemed.   He nevertheless supported me in my efforts, relieved at some of the results I obtained. As I discussed this approach with a neighbor, she commented, "I am going to try it, too. In my six years of studying Child Development, nobody told me about anything like this!"

So when David, reading at night in a room of his own, persisted in later and later nights in his books (erupting into temper and even tears the following day because of tiredness), I forbade books in bed for an entire week—a severe punishment for an avid reader. He began to obey after that, however. One night he said, "Last night I read without anyone telling me to go to bed. I went at a decent time. See if you can trust me to regulate myself." Most of the time we have had no problem.

Bedtime often means conflicts for families. For us, bedtime always follows a certain ritual. We have dinner, do the dishes, and then have a devotional, consisting of singing, often a hymn, then a spiritual thought given by someone in the family, usually Avraham, and then prayer. Last drinks and bathrooming follow, and when we don't listen to evening tapes, Avraham often will tell a story. The younger children especially like adventures on Peter Pan Island, and the animal tales involving Miss Mousy, Naughty Mouse, Chippy the chipmunk and his friend Munk, Kangi the kangaroo rat, and many others. When we lived in Rarotonga, the bedrooms were situated near each other, and both Avraham and I told stories. I would retell a scripture story and then a fairy tale. If the children dragged their feet getting to bed, they would hear no stories—a powerful inducement for going to bed.

It was refreshing in New Zealand to see that bedtime is not the issue it can be in the United States, where you seem to show your maturity by how late you are allowed to stay up! There, two of our cousins, aged thirteen and fifteen, went to bed at 7:30 every night so they would be fresh for the next day's activities! We have always tried to put our children to bed early. Some other homeschoolers question, "But how do you manage it?" We have just insisted on it, I reply. Tapes and stories are powerful inducements, and we just turn off the lights all over the house, often going to bed early ourselves or using the time to complete work or just relax briefly without children.

Some approaches to discipline are peculiar to homeschool, of course. Many mothers feel they could not undertake a homeschool because their children would not obey them and do their schoolwork. Others add that they don't have the patience to help their children follow through. Before we discuss techniques, I always remind these parents that homeschool work differs dramatically from schoolwork. Most homeschool children really enjoy the academic and research activities that they do; it is not a chore to them. In fact, the parent often has to run to catch up with blossoming interests and activities.

But for everyday requirements, we sometimes use little techniques to help the children undertake a new schedule or add a task to the former list. I would pound five or six nails under each child's name on a nicely varnished board. Each nail stood for something: reading, spelling, math, chores, piano. When a child completed a task, he would slip a wooden bead onto the appropriate nail. This seemed like fun. When they began to forget their beads, completing the work without the listings, I just took away the board. A couple of years ago, I used wall charts and stickers in the same way, these also losing their appeal and being quietly taken away as soon as possible.

Even just writing a list of expected tasks ("read aloud two books; choose five spelling words and write a sentence for each; do twenty problems of addition and subtraction; write a letter or a story; hike up into the hills") for eight-year-old Yoni, who came home for school when the others attended in New Zealand, seemed to give enough structure. Of course he did many other things, especially drawing, turning himself into a fine artist; but also building things, looking at many books, learning Maori crafts, songs and dances from friends or tapes, taking walks with Avraham, tending the little ones, and generally amusing and instructing himself.

Needless to say, we still suffer through, "Do your schoolwork!", tearing someone away from The Hardy Boys or a drawing of a spaceship. Some homeschoolers feel you should allow the children to work on whatever project he is involved with, not forcing schoolwork at all; but I consider the one or two hours of formal work every morning important in learning to regulate and discipline one's life according to the demands that will ultimately present themselves throughout the children's lives. If we don't finish our formal schoolwork first of all, we usually don't get it done. Also, we have found through sad experience that spelling and math suffer if we don't practice them every day; and they provide a good mental stretch, especially the math.

With a homeschool, many of the discipline problems we face may arise from being cooped up in the house together for too long, so that we begin to irritate one another, focus on each other's faults, and get on each other's nerves. A brief trip or excursion, a simple walk outdoors—together or singly—can blow away bad feelings. I have learned that the out-of-doors heals. You can count on shoveling snow or some other exercise to change the children's view of things, and your own as well. With older children, a hike, a long bicycle ride, a paddle in the stream, roaming in the hills, can restore good relationships if kids go out together; or bring a child to a sense of peace and balance if he goes alone (and here I am assuming an improbability—that you live in a community where single forays are safe).

Throughout the years, I have felt uncomfortable with spanking, usually resorting to it only when someone's behavior pushed me over the brink; and at that point it was unpleasant and not very fruitful. Since employing "high law, high love," however, I use the occasional smack on the rear for behavior that really violates the family standard, such as lying, stealing, tormenting a sibling, or deliberate disobedience. If the child misbehaves with a bad intent, we spank. Ideally, we would live better without resorting to corporal punishment, but sometimes the child behaves much better when he's had a smack. It doesn't take hard hits to communicate the message; the meaning of the spank is what communicates. When two-year-old Sarah writhed and twisted to avoid being diapered, I would warn, "I will spank your bottom." Persisting, she would get a gentle pat on her bare rear, and would wail for several minutes, "Spanked! Bum-bum!" We need to be sure, of course, that our spanking doesn't stem from our uncontrolled tempers, and that we use as little force as possible.

Of course, the presence of babies and younger children, as in our family, provides for more regimention in the homeschool. Reading the glowing accounts of successful homeschoolers in *Growing without Schooling*, I can't help but notice that these families so often consist of two or three children, frequently over eight years of age. What miracles I could work with that situation, I muse! Juggling the activities and intellectual growth of older children as well as the burgeoning delights of babies and toddlers makes homeschooling decidedly more difficult, especially in larger families. These extra demands require that every person pitch in and work.

Daily farm work, on the other hand, would serve the same cooperative purpose, as would a family business. I was impressed to read a talk by a church leader, Elder Dallin Oaks, who recommended that families might start a family business in order to work together for the common good; if you don't have a wolf at the door, hire one, he suggested!

Freed by the practice of high law, high love, I can focus on the positive things in the family. Did you ever hear that it takes eleven positive comments to cancel the devastating effect of a negative one? Sometimes parents fall into the rut of constant negativity: "Why don't you do that right?" "He is just like you, untidy!" "What a mess this floor is always in!" "You children can never get along with each other," and so on.

Most of the time, at least, I manage to speak in a quiet, sweet voice and cultivate the positive. One day I was astonished to hear six-year-old Chava playing house with the two younger children. In a honey voice, she was saying, "Oh, yes, I would be glad to help you with that. You are doing such a good job. Here, help me finish this, then we'll look at the toys together." Later she came up and hugged me. "I am a good mommy, just like you." When I do something special for the children, draw them a picture, or complete a difficult project with the older ones, I am often thrilled to hear them tell me, "You have done a good job. Thanks for your help"—an exact model of what I say to them!

Over the years, I have tried to live each moment for the pleasure of it, even if I am cleaning my oven—my least favorite job. Set on enjoying the flow of everyday life, we can perceive so much good: the glimpse of an intent face, a child breaking into smiles in a new book; a snatch of song, the children spontaneously chiming in together; the smell of a little boy's hair, just come from playing in the meadow; a fistful of daisies from a foraging little girl. I believe that we can accept ourselves and one other, even at the same moment that we require a high standard of behavior as we live together, so that a happy, joyful, peaceful flow of light and good feeling permeates the home. My motto is, "Enjoy everything!"

We once hiked through a beautiful canyon, and though we were carrying children in backpacks and navigating, in hot weather, through some difficult soft sand, I found myself happy and full of pleasure. "Wait for us!" cried Avraham, carrying one tired child in his backpack and another in his arms, "I am having a terrible time here; how are you doing?" "I'm really enjoying myself," I answered. "I think you're not supposed to enjoy this," grumbled the burdened hiker.

I think that typifies homeschool. Sometimes it is hard. You can't compare homeschool to doing an office job or almost any other employment. But the joys equal the frustrations, and I think that the discipline it demands from us as parents can provide a powerful model for children as they move into adolescence and adulthood.

LANGUAGE AND ATTITUDES ABOUT SEX

From the first, I decided to relax about my children's language. Whatever they said was only words, and my reaction to them was more important than their short venture into the scatalogical. This approach worked for a long time. If a child swore or tested me on a dirty word, I would just say something like, "Yes, that's a vulgar way of referring to mating. Nice people don't use that word."

Whenever the children have run into double-meaninged words, I have always taught them the clean-minded version. Until David was eleven, "ass" meant primarily a donkey, secondarily a fool. Only when he spent three months in school did he begin to smirk and refer to someone's ass. Fortunately, a quiet talk and a couple of months at home erased the smirk without pain. For this to work, parents have to respond cleanly to language and overcome any dirty-mindedness themselves, because I believe the smirk that we repress still communicates to the children.

This approach failed us in one dismal instance; and from that experience I feel that some children of about four or five years can pick up vulgarity and retain it. Several months before we left an isolated area, our only neighbors, a retired couple, moved away and a large family moved in. Our children began bringing home not just dirty words, but phrases and concepts that were just plain vulgar. When I spoke to the mother about it, she reprimanded the children, but the language continued.

Even though our family moved, our little girl, then four, did not forget those phrases and attitudes for the longest time; she giggled when she saw someone's underwear and would continue to mouth those dirty phrases. Quite young children seem able to forget bad talk when they hear it; and they are able to handle it when they are a bit older. At a younger and more vulnerable age, however, they seem to hold onto it, especially if they have a disposition for that sort of thing, and some children do. Although we can't always avoid these unfortunate contacts, we should do whatever possible when children are at this sensitive age.

As for how to handle the problem once the damage is done, my method has not been that effective; I simply forbid the nasty phrases. To me they are totally unacceptable and I don't allow them. If a child insists on using them, I make him sit on the bed or otherwise isolate himself.

However, when the children giggle about underwear, I simply shrug and say it's just clothing that goes under the outerwear. Most kids feel the logic of this. When they laugh at someone's bottom, such as a naked baby, I casually say that everybody has a bottom, that there's nothing shameful about it—and babies' bottoms are especially cute!

This leads to the related toilet talk. Some little children—some of mine too—naturally delight in using, over and over, the terms for bathroom use and private parts of the body. I just ignore it unless it seems to be getting out of hand (and that's something you have to feel for yourself, when it's too much). Then I say something like, "Heavenly Father gave everybody private parts—all the boys have penises, all the girls have vaginas. We keep them private because they're sacred. When we are older, we will marry in the temple and have children of our own, and our private parts will help us do that."

Since we have often talked about reproduction, and since the children have observed most of this process in our animals, this is very natural talk. (I use the same approach discussing masturbation.) Nevertheless, some young children persist and occasionally we have to say emphatically, "No more ca-ca talk!" (Interestingly, when we lived in the Cook Islands, I noticed that even some adults, with typical primitive humor, teased children with toilet talk—to the evident delight of all!).

In homeschool, the facts of reproduction can sometimes be taught in unusual contexts. Having animals brings the matter out into the open and allows the children to talk about mating and birth easily. Our first discussion, though, took place when we were reading the New Testament. David was six, Sammy, four. When we came to the part about Jesus' birth, the questions and answers began to flow. The children wanted to know everything about it. I took the advised approach of answering just the questions at hand, and stopping there, but they kept asking. I remember thinking how lovely it was to deal with sexual matters in the context of the scriptures.

We have chosen to use the proper terms for body parts. Some writers say it is less embarrassing for guests if children ask them about their ding-dong instead of their penis, but I feel that the whole family should be able to name all parts of their bodies without embarrassment. Of course, children quickly learn when certain subjects are inappropriate; they don't have to be told. One exception to the true-terms rule has cropped up in our home: they know the word for breasts, but they call them "nurses" (I breast-feed all our infants).

We do use nicknames for bathrooming; I chose ca-ca, which is the Mexican Spanish term, mainly because my childhood remembrances of other terms were negative. From a health point of view, evacuating the bowels is very natural, and I have tried to feel positive even when a toddler messes his legs. Diaper-changing time should be happy and cheerful; I don't believe in calling dirty diapers "stinkies," as I've heard some mothers do. Even young babies quickly read their mother's faces at diaper-changing time, and so quite early form opinions about their own bodies.

When you consider that from the beginning of time people have cleansed their bodies by elimination, our modern disgust over the matter is quite misplaced. We do our homeschooled children a service, on the other hand, by helping them feel natural about it.

It's impossible to nurture a wholesome feeling about body parts and functions, about reproduction and sexuality, unless parents feel wholesome about these things themselves. Having grown up among people who did use dirty talk, I assure you that it's relatively easy to eradicate that reaction in oneself. When you abandon the associations, literature, movies, programs, or whatever engenders unclean thoughts, you just put yourself into a reality, a way of life, that ignores them.

If your married life conforms to the teachings of the Gospel—if you're chaste within the bonds of marriage—if you have a clean and pure outlook on these things, your children will pick up your feelings about them. Remember that the Gospel doesn't deny the body or consider it bad. We should rejoice in our physical existence, enjoy every good and wholesome thing. We should learn to understand our body's functions, so that even changing a diaper can be a time of pleasant interchange. Clearly, a homeschool can discipline not only our children but also ourselves into a higher way of being.

THINGS OF THE SPIRIT

We were observing a family whose grown-up children all seemed to have turned out well; their lives seemed balanced and in correct focus. The father of the family answered Avraham's questions about how he had made it happen.

"The most important thing we can teach our children is how to discern things by the Spirit, how to get answers to prayers for all the concerns of our lives," he said. He told about a son who wanted to practice one of the martial arts; the father felt uneasy about it. He just asked the son to go and pray about it. When the son emerged from his room, he said, "No, it's not the right thing for me," and that was the end of the discussion—no arguing, no clashing of wills, no bad feelings. This father also said, "Never neglect your family scripture readings, family prayer, and family evenings together."

Now that sounds very familiar and very simple, doesn't it? This successful father learned the simple lesson of mortality: doing the right things in the right spirit, consistently, brings the desired outcomes.

Homeschool gives us a very good chance to learn things of the spirit. We can include the scriptures as a central part of the curriculum. Our children read a few chapters of scripture before they get out of bed, following that with prayer. Later, at the breakfast table, Avraham or I read a few verses of scripture; we started with the Old Testament, moved to the Book of Mormon, and then went to the Book of Isaiah, all of this over quite a long period of time. We read exegetically rather than just scooting through the text, discussing the meanings of what we read and asking the children for the interpretation. We are always delighted and amazed at how much the children really understand, the insights they are developing as they interpret the scriptures.

When the children were a little older, we divided the scripture reading into two parts, a half-hour of analysis with Avraham and the older boys, and a shorter session with him and the little ones, often with illustrated stories of the scriptures.

During our formal schooltime, the children write in their journals as part of their daily routine. Although they sometimes grumble about this ("There's nothing to say!"), what fun they have rereading their entries months and years later. For writing assignments they sometimes retell and interpret a scripture story, or write a segment of their personal history. The older children might be asked to read a book about biblical history and write a report about its chapters.

As a part of our scripture reading, we have yet to launch a good memorization program. I like Reed Benson's suggestion of taping choice quotations on the bathroom mirror, without comment or assignment. Soon everyone has memorized the text.

With large sets of the illustrated scripture stories, we often cuddle on the sofa and read together. I try to withhold my astonishment that the four- and five-year-olds often choose these volumes in preference to the many storybooks we have in the house. I sometimes wonder if the dramatic pictures in the Book of Mormon series attract them, but they like the more sedate Church history and New Testament books as well!

In the evening, after dinner and dishes are over, we get into our pajamas and gather for evening devotional, when we sing together, sometimes hymns, sometimes Primary songs, sometimes folk songs. I have taught the children all the verses to special hymns that I like, such as "How Firm a Foundation" and "The Spirit of God." It does me good to hear those piping voices produce eight verses so confidently; and what fun we have in church when the congregation sings one of the songs they have memorized.

Sometimes a child chooses the music and leads it, or sometimes we just sit and sing and sing. After that, either by assignment or by volunteer, we have a spiritual thought, usually something that has come up during the day or something that has struck us from the scriptures or from our experiences. These can be pretty mundane ("We must always obey our parents and not argue"), but sometimes we enjoy some deeper thinking ("Everyone has his own talents, and we should refine and develop them, and learn to cooperate with one another so that we can share them together; if a community shares its talents, we are so much better off than if we try to struggle and do things all by ourselves")—both of these from the children.

These spiritual thoughts can sometimes turn into fault-finding sessions, so we try to emphasize positive things or at least the positive aspects of the problems we are trying to solve!

We hold family home evenings on Monday nights—usually. (When we adults slip and neglect our Monday meetings, we meet a storm of protests.) The children generally volunteer for their family home evening assignments, sometimes insisting that they give the lesson or supply the activity instead of the adults. Often a younger child conducts the meeting—with some aside prompts—and another chooses songs and leads the singing. The older children like to contrive games—physical activities, quizzes, dictionary games, activities from the family home evening manual.

They may also give lessons from the manual or from their own ideas. They often choose scripture charades, acting out scripture stories for the family to guess. We enjoy special fare like puppet shows; recently the three older boys produced a shadow-puppet show, using a textbook story for the narrative, crafting their own shadow props and characters that were very artistic. Frequently Chava, at six, laboriously produced a crafts activity, one item for each member of the family.

We also enjoy our variation of "Win, Lose, or Draw," a charades-type game where you draw hints to elicit the correct word or phrase. How we laughed at two-year-old Sarah's pantomiming actions as she scrawled a little circle on the paper and then silently, wildly, gesticulated over it. Once in a while we go for a walk—not always so much fun with expecting mama and easily-fatigued little ones—or for an evening at the park or an ice-cream at the local dairy. Most of the time we enjoy each other at home, with treats such as home-frozen popsicles made by the children or pudding or cake from Mom's kitchen.

Every first Sunday of the month, Avraham interviews each child separately. He begins interviews with the youngest child, who takes the face-to-face time very seriously. The older children spend more time with him, and he takes notes of their feelings and aspirations. I notice the children emerging happy and at peace from the bedroom; and Avraham feels that he accomplishes more in these sessions than in many whole-family situations.

Sammy, who had fallen into a habit of teasing and tormenting Chava, responded to Avraham's interview challenges to leave her alone—to build her up instead. Recently, hearing Sammy sincerely compliment Chava on a project she had done, Avraham patted him on the back and gave him plenty of praise for his changed behavior. Sometimes, having dealt with a difficult neighbor-child situation, Yoni just needs the emotional nourishment of being with his Dad, feeling his love. (Because Yoni is such an open and giving child, he makes himself vulnerable, and tormenters often see him as an easy mark.)

Avi gave his first talk in church when he was four years old. His age group doesn't usually perform very well during these first efforts (the little girl ahead of him just burst into tears and couldn't speak). However,

Avi, in his usual foghorn voice, stood close to the microphone and gave a little demonstration about how the spirit and body work together, and how they separate at death, joining together in the resurrection—complete with paper and see-through visuals. I shared amused smiles—mine perhaps a little embarrassed at his volume.

In addition to these formal spiritual activities, we use lots of opportunities to talk. Sitting together at meals, praying before we eat, and sharing our feelings gives us a chance to talk about spiritual things in a natural way. When Avraham and I discover something especially interesting in the scriptures, we often talk it over. The children usually listen intently if they are around. One evening, as I shared a discovery with Avraham, I turned and found Yoni, supposedly in bed, lying in the doorway, propped on his pillow, following the discussion! The children enjoy hearing these things, and it is a good informal education.

We want our children to understand the promptings of the Spirit and try to emphasize this in our everyday work and play. When we need to decide about an activity or employment, or a financial matter, we say, "How do you feel about it? What do you feel in the Spirit?" Children have a natural gift for this kind of discernment.

When we were trying to rent a beach house in New Zealand, Avraham and the children drove to a prospective residence; the location was good and the price was right. But the children said, "I just don't feel good about it. I didn't feel a good spirit there." When they found the right place, they all knew it together. Sensitive to these communications, the children know that they can consistently make good decisions and keep themselves out of trouble. One time the older children were hiking far up into the hills, and evening came on all of a sudden. I got worried and went out to call them; in moments, they emerged from the trees. "I just felt in the Spirit that it was time to come home," said Yoni, then seven. "I had to convince the others; they wanted to go on at first, but then they felt it, too."

When our family makes major career or moving decisions, the children can get their own witness of the rightness of our choices. And, closer to their hearts, when we change their schedules or study requirements or work loads, they can feel whether it's right or wrong. This again takes a burden off the parents, who can simply say, "You go and pray about it and then we can talk."

Once, during a chapel dedication in New Zealand, we enjoyed a series of talks by local church authorities and the mission president. Then the stake president rose to speak, and commenced to talk on the teachings of

Jesus. Yoni and Sammy, sitting close to Avraham, one after the other dropped their heads on his chest, whispering what an overpowering Spirit they felt during that talk. Because of the maturity of the spirit within the little child's body, he is capable of feeling and experiencing so much more than we might give him credit for. That is one good reason to follow Dr. Dennis Packard's advice to center on the scripture texts themselves rather than on tapes or retold stories. The children can experience what is there, even if they don't understand every detail intellectually.

We are sometimes amazed at the spiritual maturity the children show. Once Yoni, then seven years old, walked up the microphone during a testimony meeting in church, and began talking: "I was sitting in my seat, listening to the testimonies, when I all of a sudden knew that it was my turn to speak. I couldn't sit in my seat any longer; I had to stand up here and bear my testimony." This startled us adults, who become so used to hearing a child's stilted sequence, "I love my parents, I love the Church . . ."

Many homeschooling parents ask me in worried tones how to convince their children about such decisions as staying home from school or going to classes or to school for a time. They feel that the child should follow their decision, but the child resists. I recommend the procedure of praying and feeling by the Spirit if it is right, simple as this is. That way both parents and child can check to see if they are moving in the right direction, and there are no arguments. It smooths not only the decision-making process but makes everyone feel good about what is decided. It also forces us to humble ourselves and seek and accept answers that we might not have looked for otherwise.

After we returned to the United States from the South Pacific, struggling with morning sickness, a move, and some far-reaching emotional and spiritual challenges, I was letting my homeschool slide for months, accomplishing the basic work in the morning, but not providing sufficient stimulating activities, crafts, outings, and points of view that the older children were needing. They found themselves bouncing around the house, arguing, wasting time. A friend, observing this, commented, "I think your children would be better off in school for a time." School? My children? In this culture? Here I am, the homeschool championing mother—what would it do to my ego to send my paragon children to school? But, praying about the situation, the answer came that a few months in school would be a good experience for those who went, and would give me the space for accomplishing what I needed to do. I had to humble myself and accept that answer, and the children accepted it too.

During those months of school, the ones that attended had a good time, enjoying the experience because it was so different than the routine at home. They had the opportunity, too, of finding out first-hand those negative aspects of school that I felt so strongly about; they could see for themselves that there were few unknown delights schoolchildren enjoyed.

For myself, accepting the promptings of the Spirit in this matter showed me that we can live with many different options, that we mustn't hedge ourselves into one reality. Even while three of my children went to school, I hometaught the others and still felt myself very much a homeschool mother. The children in school were just undergoing another and a different educational experience. By the time school was out, we were all ready and grateful to start the home routine again.

As we are consistent in our spiritual training of our children, we need also to monitor our own spiritual life. The feeling that radiates from ourselves dramatically influences the growth of the children, as much as any formal work we do. During the past year, I have been striving to radiate the charity of Christ, the unconditional love and good feeling that emanates from Him. Not only has this made me happier, it has improved the emotional texture of the family. Not merely seeing but feeling this reality heals and matures the children, providing a peaceful center at home from which to perceive the world.

Parents need to maintain their spiritual growth, read the scriptures, pray together, and always seek the Spirit in their own lives. Just being around such parents educates children in a powerful way. It makes the older children seek out their parents' company instead of shunning it, as adolescents sometimes do.

We are educating our young ones for a very different society than the one we live in now. They will face challenges, decisions, feelings, situations that neither we nor they can now imagine. I am not alone in sensing that these changes will occur during our lifetime, not in some distant, unforeseeable future. There is only one sure way to prepare ourselves for these new realities, and that is to train our spiritual sensitivities so that we can ever make the right decisions when difficult times present themselves. This in itself justifies the efforts involved in homeschool, and it helps us not to lose sight of the important work that we are doing.

READING

Just as "What about socialization?" is the main question newcomers ask, so "How shall I teach the children to read?" is what beginning homeschoolers worry about.

But this is asking the wrong question. Children learn to read in many ways, perhaps no two exactly alike. Once, while attending a weekly class to construct learning games out of cardboard, paper, and found materials, I heard the instructor, a successful elementary schoolteacher, comment, "You can teach a child to read with anything. He can learn to read from magazines, cereal boxes, anything. These games just make it a little more fun."

The question we should ask, then, is "How will this particular child best learn to read?" We answer this by observing the child, through trial and error, and with a basic idea of the ways teachers approach reading instruction.

When I set out to teach my first child how to read, I was convinced that phonics instruction would make him into an early and successful reader. At eighteen months, he could sing the alphabet song and point out which letter was which. At two he knew many of the sounds. By three, he was blending sounds together, using homemade letter cards that I had made. Yet he didn't seem to transfer our learning games to the easy books that I kept checking out of the library. He loved for me to read to him, and I doggedly did it, though sometimes I fell asleep on drowsy afternoons when I was expecting our third child. I remember certain occasions when I would spout all sorts of nonsense words instead of the story, dozing through the pages of the books. Through it all I kept asking myself, "How do we make the transfer from sounding out to reading?"

I made word puzzles, with a picture on top and the severed word on the bottom, mixing them up so he could sound out the word and put the puzzle pieces together. I pointed to words of very familiar books, reading them over and over and having him repeat the memorized text along.

I got frustrated, even angry. Nothing seemed to work, even though I persisted as well as I could with the phonics approach. I would sit on the couch with him (and his younger brother) and write a sound. They would suggest words using that sound. When they came up with a word with a variant spelling, I would put it in another column. Sometimes we would illustrate the words, and often we would giggle over them: "Cat, mat, hat, sat (who sat on you? Was it me?), fat, gnat (silent g, isn't that odd?, g-nat, really), spat (oh, no, please!), brat (who's a brat?)" and so on. As they grew older, they would suggest ever more complicated words, and I would present the more complex phonetic rules, e.g. aught, ough, igh, tion; I used the charts in *Word Attack Joy,* a book filled with learning games you can construct.

By this time David was close to six years old, Sammy close to four. David was at the age that children often learn to read at school, and suddenly, one day, without any particular forewarning, my wonder child started to read.

At about this same time I noticed Sammy sitting with a *McGuffey's Primer,* looking at two facing pages containing alphabets, one upper- and one lower-case. My first impulse was to swoop down upon him with, "Ah, now, that's the big letter and that's the small one; see, big A, small a!" But I didn't. Instead I sat down quietly close to him. He began singing the alphabet song, pointed to each upper-case letter. Then he sang it, pointing to each lower-case letter. He observed, "See, that's big A, that's small a," pointing out various pairs. And from that time on, he never confused the two alphabets, though he continued writing in upper-case (which is the first alphabet I taught) for some years to come. By the time Sammy was four and a half, by participating in reading sessions with David, he was reading himself.

Midway in my struggle to find the right way to teach reading, I happened to chat with a teacher of elementary education specializing in reading. In her Ph.D. dissertation, she had tested Bill Martin Jr.'s *Sounds of Language* series, which utilizes the whole-language approach. She gently tried to explain that phonics are a good tool, but that reading itself is not a phonics procedure; when we read, we take in whole words, phrases, lines.

Bill Martin provides a series of stories with natural, memorable texts and varied pictures. His pre-primer, for example, contains the following story, delightfully illustrated: "Daddy is home, Daddy is home, Daddy is home! Look, Mother! Daddy's home! Hello, Mother! Hello, children. I brought you a surprise, children, Where, Daddy, where? Look in my pocket. Oooooh, look, a surprise. Thank you, Daddy, thank you. We love you, Daddy" (*Sounds of Home*).

Emotionally powerful for the chosen age group, it uses simple language, but natural (in what other pre-primer would you find the "difficult" word *surprise*?). The series advances through grade seven, sometimes including two volumes for one year. I was particularly impressed that in no volume did I find anything that offended me in subject matter nor in illustration, and that the simple, appropriate, natural style was maintained throughout. The usual faults you find in reading textbooks—too much text on the page for the child's age, low-quality illustrations (this series employs famous artists, and each illustration and piece of writing is credited with its creator), tedious typesetting (Bill Martin believes in a variety of experiences with print, and provides a delightful variety of typefaces and styles, including some poems and stories that are printed in circles or other meandering patterns around the page), and hidden sociological messages, such as feminism or materialism, are all missing from the series. It is in good taste throughout, rollicking and light-hearted though it may often be. It also can be poignant and quiet.

In the total-language approach, Bill Martin promotes the use of patterns that help the child determine meaning from context rather than being accountable for every syllable and word: "In the first month of the year, I found 1 little pony, and he followed me home. In the second month of the year, I found 2 white kittens, and they followed me home" (*Sounds of Numbers*). He also uses songs and familiar rhymes for children to chant together as the printed variation of the words becomes more and more familiar.

I was very suspicious of this whole-language approach at first. Bill Martin Jr. was years before his time with it, as it is only now coming into vogue in reading instruction around the world. (While in Rarotonga, I met a professor of reading instruction from Canada who explained this to me; New Zealand leads the rest of the countries because it has championed the whole-language approach for some time, producing superior readers much earlier than their counterparts elsewhere.) "What about phonics?" I kept asking my friend. Patiently she explained the use of phonics to me (to attack unknown words, but not directly in the reading process), and just encouraged me to try the readers on the children.

She gave me a complete set of them. My children fell in love with the *Sounds of Language* series, and I keep the entire set out on the bookshelf. They select volumes from all age levels and read them for pleasure. How often we sit on the sofa, all crowded and cuddled together, reading, singing and chanting. I doubt that Bill Martin, Jr., intended just this use, a family swaying together, singing, "K- k- k- katy," or "Just a spoonful of sugar." Another surprise, during a supposedly humorous poem

("Five Little Monkeys," in *Sounds Around the Clock*), at the conclusion: "Wicked Uncle Crocodile, to gobble up our brother"—we were all in tears! I am certain that this whole-language approach leads to early and accurate reading, and though we have never met, I feel tremendous friendship for Bill Martin, Jr.

However, along came child number three. Proceeding as I had with the other children—with doses of phonics, much reading aloud (as I consider this important to develop a large speaking vocabulary, so that the child owns many words, ready to recognize them in context; also because they need the soul-enlarging experience of reading before they can read), and much work with the *Sounds of Language* and other similarly constructed books—yet Yoni did not know how to read at five. Nor at six.

Nor at seven! He got tired of our sofa sessions, and resisted any and all attempts to help him sound out the simple stories in our favorite beginning readers such as P. D. Eastman's *Go Dog Go* and the Berenstains' *Bears in the Dark*.

At this time I helped Betty Teela, author of *Teach your Child to Read at Home*, prepare her manuscript for publication. Having tutored many children who were thought incapable of reading, bringing them to a point of reading easily and well, she maintained that thorough phonics instruction helped children previously unable to read. Her book, beautifully hand-lettered with big letters and words, presents the best and most systematic approach to phonics I have ever seen.

Here was the key to help Yoni learn to read! He struggled through many of the lessons, but still could not read. Finally, I decided to keep reading to him (and to the other children, as Chava and Avi were now of the book-gobbling age) as much as I could, but not to worry about him nor press reading to him anymore. We were travelling during the year Yoni was seven. He played outside passionately while in Rarotonga, and I rarely pressed the issue of his sitting down and reading to me. However, Betty Teela had mentioned in her work that *The Book of Mormon* is not too difficult for children to read, and that it is one of the most important books they can read. She starts her early tutees on *The Book of Mormon* as soon as she deems they are ready to handle it, using the large-print version. I mentioned this to Yoni, and on occasion he would sit with me and struggle to read out a few words, without much success.

Well, I decided, he would not grow up an illiterate adult in our household, where everyone disappears into books many hours of the day. I recalled the study where the fathers of nonreaders were asked to sit by a lamp and read to themselves a half-hour a day. If they couldn't read, they were to sit and turn the pages. Being paid for this, they complied, and the non-reading children, led by this powerful, silent example, all purportedly began reading! So I commenced to say nothing more about it, and though Yoni felt left out and sad each afternoon when the little ones napped (Mother, too), and the big ones read, he still didn't start reading himself.

Then he turned eight years old, and was baptized in the lagoon in Rarotonga. He found it a thrilling spiritual experience, describing his moment under the water as being one of perfect peace and spiritual harmony. Then and there he decided that he would read *The Book of Mormon*.

So every night he read several verses to me, pausing for help only on hard words like "knowledge." Quiet on the outside, I was leaping around with joy inside. Yoni was reading!

Admittedly, his intense interest slacked off, Yoni-style. But when we went to New Zealand, he, along with the other eligible children, went to school. There he found himself in the very easiest readers, most of the other children far ahead of him. The teacher worked with him quite a bit, sending home regularly some of those delightful "little readers," small paperback books using the same approach that Bill Martin, Jr., takes. Before long, Yoni was reading steadily and well, and I saw he would never look back. I continued to check out from the library books that would be on his level and would interest him. One night we opened *Arthur's Star*, a New Zealand primer, a gentle and very simply written tale about a young star that visits a boy during the night ("One night/ when Arthur was asleep/'Sigh,' sighed a star."). Yoni amazed himself by reading the entire book, and confided that this was the first book he had ever read for enjoyment.

Then I began to use many of the early-reading techniques that had worked with the other boys. He tackled road signs as we drove along, especially the names of stores and traffic directions, and also advertising signs. I wrote a list of chores for each child to do each day, matter-of-factly including a slip for Yoni ("Bring in wood and pine cones, plenty of them. Walk up to the shop for milk. Sweep the kitchen, laundry, and bathroom floors."). We devised treasure hunts, with a small surprise at the end. When the other children were small, I wrote up these hunts, but now the children do them for each other. In fact, Yoni himself wrote up many of them, reading them over and over, and providing the little treasure himself. We also checked out books from the library with riddles and jokes—a favorite all around.

All during these years of waiting for Yoni to learn to read, he kept up his writing, asking me how to spell various words. One would think that eventually he would learn to recognize the ones he kept repeating, but strangely he couldn't do that until he was about eight. Then, memorizing a list of the most commonly used words (the, it, and, and so on), he seemed to be able to retain them, and once he knew them, he didn't lose them again.

Our fourth child, Chava, began writing words and stories when she was about four, though I didn't press to teach her reading during the year we were earning our fare to travel to the southern hemisphere. During our four months in Rarotonga we did little in the way of formal school, both as we adjusted to the new and absorbing culture, and also as we came down with tropical sicknesses. Chava had what they said was rheumatic fever. However, when we went to New Zealand, we decided to send her to "infant school," as the first year of schooling is called. There the children learn reading from the small paperback booklets with color photographs and a patterned text: "She went up the path," "She went up the stairs," "She went up the ladder," etc. Evidently each school there has a multitude of these little books, which teachers slip into "journal covers," secured with loops of string, and send home for parents to hear. The parents must sign and comment on a slip of paper! I was impressed with the effort to involve the family.

In addition, the children colored and decorated large sheets with a capital and a lower-case of various letters, and learned songs about each letter; in particular we loved the one set to the tune of "Skip to My Lou"; "Jellyfish Jumping, J, J, J," or "Umbrellas are up, U,U,U," The children learned some sight words, such as the, am, are, but mostly concentrated on the total-language approach.

The total-language approach is very different from the look-say method most American schools use. So as to avoid confusion about these two reading approaches, here are the basic differences. The total-language approach presents a text of emotional interest to the children, accompanied by exact photographs to give contextual hints. The texts in the early levels are patterned, often only with one word or phrase varying. The children follow the text with their finger, guessing from context when needed. The actual vocabulary is not limited by graded difficulty, as in the limited-word books you sometimes see; the words are chosen according to the meaning in the pictures.

On the other hand, the look-say method assumes that children will learn various words by memorizing their shapes. (Some workbooks I have seen even give a game with the boxed shapes on one side and the words on the other, requiring the child to match the shapes to the words.) Providing textbooks with limited vocabularies, which also contain usually peurile and boring texts, they expect the children to memorize the words they need to know. Phonics proponents consider the look-say method ridiculous, because there are about 80,000 words in the average person's reading vocabulary, 80 percent of which can be attacked phonetically. Some proponents of phonics say closer to 90 percent of English can be analyzed phonetically. The look-say method also encourages guessing, but not so much from the text as from the shape of the word. I was taught to read using the look-say method, and to this day I recall the gut-level dread I felt on finding an unfamiliar word, groping around for what it could possibly be.

Observing Chava learn to read, I still maintain that some phonics instruction makes it easier for children to analyze unknown words. Chava knew unerringly the words and phrases she gained in the whole-language method, but lacked the skills to sound out new words. Rather than interfere very much with her school experiences, I gave occasional phonics lessons ("you know *look*; this is *book*, this is *cook*," and so on), but mostly I concentrated on life-skills such as cooking and sewing when we were together—also a lot of just plain talking, which Chava loves (she talks at least twice as much as any other child in the family). Later, when Chava was six and seven, she eased herself into reading without much help or encouragement.

At the same time, I noticed that Avi, at three, was already extremely fond of books. He strongly insisted that I sit and read various books to him, easily memorizing the texts and using phrases from them as he worked and played. I often ran my finger under these familiar texts as I read, and little by little he acquired familiar words. We also worked on writing the various letters in a large-lined copybook. But my feelings about this early reading have totally changed.

With my first child, I wanted an early reader. I felt that children would be richer if they could enter the beauties of literature for themselves at an early age; and there is truly much to commend this approach. But as I have watched my little ones grow, I concluded that babies should be babies in a totality. They should enjoy reading only as much as they desire, and if they do early-reading or -writing exercises, these should be only for the fun and interest they offer, and not in the hopes that mama is going to produce a prodigy. No tension should accompany the lessons. You should stop them before the child wants to, so that he will ask for them again soon. You must avoid any hidden agendas that you might have to push the child into early reading, because little children can "read" your emotions better and more easily than any book!

At four, Avi seemed ready to leap into phonics. I pulled out the worn magnetic board and moveable letters and began with the short *a* sound. That day we made plenty of words, and he insisted on making a word book of *a* words, illustrating them.

We did errands and yard work in the following few days, but soon we returned to the magnetic board. The short *a* was old hat by now. He had been experimenting with spelling *yes* and *no*, so we naturally pursued the short *e*. Interestingly, in these sessions I taught no consonant sounds formally; he knew many of them, but the ones he didn't, such as the sound of *h* and hard *c*, he learned incidentally as well. In the short *e* session, we were driven to using blends: *spend, sled*, etc. Interestingly, too, he kept coming up with the multiple meanings of words; for *sent*, he commented, "That's a smell (scent) too." I didn't correct the difference in spelling at this point, but certainly enjoyed the intellectual activity that was going on! Short *o* followed soon, with another word book, and not long after the *i* and *u*; the "sometimes *y*" introduced itself during the *e* session and stuck. As with the other children, I generally gave a space of time between learning these short vowels and introducing the "when two vowels go walking, the first one does the talking, and he always says his name."

All of these vowel sessions include a great deal of hilarity: "Peck, I'll give you a peck; pet, are you my dear little pet?" Indeed, when things get too tame, Avi suggests, "Do a funny one!"

Probably the greatest lesson I have learned from teaching my various children to read is that every child learns to read when he is ready, in his own personal way. We congratulate ourselves on producing an early reader, and go through agonies over a late reader—though the latter might be as intelligent a child as you could find. One of our family friends, a literary man and a poet, learned to read as late as nine or ten; his family and of course he himself took this late reading very hard, thinking he could be retarded. He still carries around the emotional scars from trying to be forced to read.

I learned much from letting Yoni begin to read when "his last chromosome clicked into place," as we jokingly say in our family. Babies learn to walk and talk when they are ready, and children, in the same way, learn to read. Of course we continue reading to them and gently supply lessons, but we must relax and let the reading emerge at the right time for each child.

An interesting sidelight, however: some educators relate the eye-hand coordination gained in crawling to reading success later on. Sammy, our earliest reader, crawled longest, walking at fourteen months; Yoni, our latest reader, got up on his feet at eight and a half months.

Once the children have unlocked for themselves the secret of print, we can do much to help them improve their reading. First of all, we can sit close to them on the sofa, listening to them read. Sometimes I read one line or one page, and they read the alternate one. I rarely force them to analyze words for themselves, unless I am positive they can do it easily. I just supply the difficult word and let them go on.

The best reading builder I know is to check many books out of the library just below the child's reading level. Most teachers continually try to make children read just above their level, forcing them upward. But supplying many easier books builds tremendous confidence and enjoyment. Following this course with Sammy, I was chagrined when he came home from the library with *The Star Wars Story Book*, a book which I considered far above his level. No, he wanted to read it, and read it he did, mastering "Artoo-Detoo" and "Droid" along with other, more common vocabulary. I consider this book his quantum leap into complex reading; it happened to him at the age of five.

Perhaps the following suggestion sounds like a mean trick, but we have used it successfully, as have other homeschool families. You cuddle together, reading an easy, high-interest book, such as one of the *Little House on the Prairie* series. Just when the Indian points his gun at Ma, or the dog vanishes beneath the surging stream, you smile, stretch, give the child a hug and say, "That was a good session. I've got to cook dinner now. We'll read some more tomorrow," and put the book up on the mantlepiece or on a prominent bookshelf. Unable to stand the suspense, your fledgling reader will often sneak the book from its place and work his way through the pages until he finds out what happens.

We often purchase workbooks to build reading and spelling skills; I especially like the School Zone "I Can Do It" series, because it presents skills simply and provides practice without the tedium of drill. But if you can pick up workbooks of any kind at garage sales or used-bookdealers, most of them are cheerful and give good practice. When the older children work on their math or spelling, the little ones enjoy using these workbooks. How often I have stationed myself on the sofa, flanked by little children with workbooks in progress, calling out the answers to questions my older children, working at desks in the adjacent library, throw out to me:

"Mom, what is a permutation? What shall I write in my journal? Who were the first inhabitants in England? Do I have to do all the problems on this page of math?"

Once Dr. Bill Hoyer, whose dissertation compared education in industrialized and nonindustrialized societies, commented, "If I had a 12-year-old son who couldn't read, I wouldn't worry about him, and I wouldn't push him." By this he was referring to the many important skills at which the boy might excel—as did the finely tuned members of "primitive" societies, who could identify by name and habit and use a multitude of plants and animals, who could provide a comfortable and happy living from materials in the environment.

Despite the credence I give to this kind of thinking, I consider competent reading a lifesaving skill in today's society; not, as you might think, to get a good job and compete for higher salaries, but to escape the mundanity and immorality of modern life. If you reject most of the popular media, as we do, you must have something to profitably amuse yourself. In former times, people often worked together, perhaps telling stories, singing, talking. Today we are isolated into nuclear families and often separated from a sense of community, so reading can amuse us, teach us, and help us spend our time well. Dr. Arthur H. King commented that when he grew up in the early part of this century, it was the common practice for boys and girls to spend much of their time reading; my children do the same, in addition to playing games, making crafts, etc.

Having experienced a somewhat late reader in our family, I recommend this course for a tardy starter: first, eliminate all entertainments that will entice him or her from the delights of reading. That includes television, videos, computer games, etc. Then supply an ample sampling of tempting books from the library and bookshop, making yourself available to read aloud and to listen. Continue daily lessons of friendly phonics, always cuddling close on the sofa. Weave reading into the daily schedule, cooking from recipes, going on treasure hunts, writing notes to each other, writing to relatives, doing projects from crafts books, writing away for free gifts (we once found a book, *Freebies for Children*, that provided many hours of reading, writing, anticipation, and delight in receiving the materials, which generally required even more reading to assemble or use).

Your attitude can make all the difference to a beginning reader. How often I have heard parents say, with an irritability and criticalness you could tangibly feel, "You still aren't reading! When I was your age, I had read *Treasure Island*! Why haven't you tried any reading today? You haven't touched a book all week! I don't know what we are going to do with you!" These are the kinder comments—I have heard worse. They make the child feel two things: misery in his inability to do the thing everyone else does and that he really wants to do himself; and a growing determination not to try the thing that his parent is so negative about. Somehow you will have to let go of all these negatives and, still working steadily with the child, turn your feelings into joy at his achievements, however small they may seem to you at the time.

It really is a big step when a child realizes that t-h-e always spells *the*, and that someone is in error by leaving his car near the "No Parking" sign. Without being silly, we need to show our true happiness at these achievements. When Yoni read his first verses in *The Book of Mormon*, I felt like leaping off the bed where we were cuddled and dancing around the room. Restraining myself for his sake, I just hugged him and said, "You read it! What a good job! I am so proud of you!" There is nothing wrong with offering rewards for reading a book during the day (or for real problem readers, even a page a day): a walk during the evening with Dad, the privilege of making peanut-butter balls, a small notebook or pencil. If your child is weaned off the flashy media, these quiet rewards will be enough. And you can offer something really major for a series of books being read, such as the purchase of a particular book of his own, or a picnic, or lunch out. Sometimes just a series of stickers—or stars or home-drawn symbols—will delight a child.

If the child strongly resists your efforts, I would withdraw to the point that he finds acceptable. You might continue the short phonics lessons without requiring any reading for a time. You could even drop the whole thing for a while, still continuing to read aloud to him every day for a couple of sessions. Sometimes another person can make the difference; for example, a friend of mine brought her child to me for tutoring in reading. I merely sat with her on the sofa and had fun with the *Sounds of Language* series, much as I did with my own children. Soon she was reading well on her own. Hiring a tutor, whether in phonics or the whole-language approach, could stimulate the child to read. Yoni felt peer pressure to learn to read when he attended school and began memorizing common words on his own, though his scripture reading began before that.

If you are really worried about the child, I would suggest praying about his reading. You may likely feel that there is nothing to worry about, that he is growing up fine, that his reading will commence at the right time for him. Because reading is measurable and because it forms the foundation for most other classroom work, we tend to push it; but there are many other things a child can be learning if he isn't reading early.

More important is our positive feelings for each other—and about reading. As I learned in waiting for Yoni to read, the day will come that he picks up a book and commences reading for pleasure.

Parents with kids in and out of school often worry that their child is dyslexic, or has dyslexia. This term refers to a person's inability to perceive letters and words the way they appear on the page. They reverse letters or the positions of letters in words: *saw* for *was*, for example. More and more reading specialists, unable to teach a certain child to read using the usual look-say methods at school—and creating more and more of a vicious emotional cycle about reading—label the child dyslexic.

Experts in reading instruction, however, insist that these diagnoses are incorrect; an M.D. specializing in the area asserts that he has never seen a true case of classic dyslexia. Some children tend to reverse letters quite far into their reading career. If you look at it from their point of view, *b* and *d* really do resemble each other, and it may take a bit of practice to consistently read them rightly. These experts recommend large doses of good phonics instruction. I would add a very positive attitude, resisting the temptation to force and harangue, and accepting the fact that just as some kids learn to read early, some learn later. It may make us feel better to say of a late reader, "Ah, he's dyslexic, you know," but I don't think it makes children feel better, and I don't think it helps improve the situation.

If your worries continue, you can consult with a reading specialist in the school or community, but beware: they judge by grade level standards rather than letting the child proceed at his own pace.

Perhaps more important than these issues of how to teach children to read is what you provide for them to read. When homeschool parents beg me for reading lists, I simply say, "Read to your children every day. Have your beginning children read to you. And only choose books that you truly enjoy."

This last makes all the difference. So many children's books today are paltry in text and illustration. With monsters and silliness they perhaps attempt to simulate the thrills of television and entice modern kids into reading. I detest their poor taste, and refuse to read any such book that happens to ride home with us from the library (if the child wants it, he has to read it for himself, and then only with the knowledge of my disapproval!).

And there are many truly beautiful books that I enjoy reading for my own aesthetic response that I do not mind rereading for the thirtieth or hundredth time with the children. We were given a lovely edition of *The Wild Swans*, illustrated by Susan Jeffers, and I gladly read it yet again to my children. Any book with her illustrations delights us. Books with good humor and clever illustration, such as those by Bill Peet, never wear out, either. We always like Margaret Wise Brown, though I feel her texts are far superior to her own drawings. Some people dislike Richard Scarry or the Berenstains, but I enjoy both (though there is too much incidental violence in Scarry, like cars shooting off into the water or falling apart on the roads).

Whenever we are browsing at the library, we always check for books by Mitsumasa Anno, the Japanese children's artist, that pack incredible detail into each page. Most of his books are visual rather than textual, and they teach an amazing amount in a small amount of space. Else Minarik's *Little Bear* books, intended for beginning readers, have rather more words per page than my beginners like; yet the tales and pictures are so endearing that we can't resist them. I read most of the text and the children read what I point out. The same goes for the *Pippa Mouse* series by Betty Boegehold. Pippa is the perfect model for a good child; she loves her parents and is quite obedient, yet she is very curious, inventive, and daringly courageous at times.

We love Frances, the little girl badger in the series by Russell Hoban, for the same reasons; though Frances is not so daring, she is a tremendous poet. *Bread and Jam for Frances* has to be one of the most intimate favorites of our younger children—the story of Frances' rejecting of all food except bread and jam, and how her clever parents deal with the problem. We love the Robert McCloskey books, especially *Make Room for Ducklings*. We love the illustrations of the classic fairy tales done by Paul Galdone, looking for his name on the shelf whenever we can.

After feeling absolutely distressed at the mess caused by *The Cat in the Hat* and the general silliness in other books by Dr. Seuss, I rarely let his books into the house, though we do like earlier ones such as *The Lorax*, which have a good moral message. Similarly, I dislike books with cute monsters á la Sesame Street; in the same category are books that capitalize on some television character, like Strawberry Shortcake. The tone and presentation are demeaning, and I feel put off by them whenever we read them. In some libraries, you really have to filter through the books the little ones choose to avoid the cheap and distressing.

My particular love is poetry, and the children can tempt me to the reading sofa with poems quicker than with anything else. We have a classic Mother Goose volume, and we sing the ones we know the tunes for, make up melodies for others, and read the rest. I use different voices and accents, and we all have a rollicking time. As the children memorize the poems and songs, they can follow along as you point to the words together. I like to read aloud Robert Frost, John Ciardi, Emily Dickinson, Ogden Nash, Lewis Carroll, some things by Carl Sandburg, and some of Shakespeare, especially the sonnets and various songs from the plays. There are so many children's poets that we like; Aileen Fisher, for example, never fails to hit just the right image and feeling. *The Oxford Book of Poetry for Children* is an excellent collection; Childcraft's *Poems and Rhymes* is pretty good.

When it comes to the older children, like all families we have our favorites. If you want a superior booklist to choose from, the catalog from John Holt's Book and Music Store, Holt Associates, 2269 Mass. Ave., Cambridge MA 02140, is a grand list to work from. In *The Abundance of the Heart*, Dr. Arthur H. King suggests a reading list for all ages, including many books young people should know. He particularly refers to Dickens, Kipling, and Arthur Ransome as good for growing children. I have tried to guide our children to the classics, including biography and adventure (*Kon Tiki* and *The Ra Expeditions* are current favorites) and classic science fiction, such as books by Jules Verne and H. G. Wells.

I have been very disappointed with popular science fiction, though if you browse through volumes ahead of time, you can find worthwhile works. Recently we have been entranced by the science fiction works of Orson Scott Card. However, I particularly dislike what I call "witchy" volumes, books that cater to the modern mania for magic and witchcraft, where children's problems are solved by mysterious powers and peoples from nether worlds. I strongly discourage the children from reading this type of book.

It is impossible to list all of the books that the children deeply loved and which have made lasting impressions on them. Wherever we go we have accumulated new favorites that might not have meaning in other contexts: for example, in Rarotonga we read much Pacifica that had seemed quite meaningless before. We fell in love with the books on Rarotonga by Ronald Syme, and bought some to help us remember island life.

Nevertheless, you might be interested in certain of our favorites. By far the most frequently-read books in our home are the *Chronicles of Narnia* by C. S. Lewis. Because they deal with the supernatural world, these might at first glance seem to break my no-witchy-books rule; but they are very different. They have a strong Christ figure in the character of Aslan, the gentle and yet terrible Lion who is the spiritual guide of the stories, as well as an always-reliable morality that is never preachy. *The Last Battle*, the final volume, presents a last-days plot that comes very close to how the scriptures foretell the last days; but because it is given in narrative and images the children experience the feelings without having to be preached to. Our boys pick these up and reread them cyclically. The reading level is not difficult, so early readers can handle much of it. Our younger children love to hear the dramatized taped versions of *Narnia*.

The children began early with the Louisa May Alcott books, too. I remember David and Sammy, at eight and six, debating whether Father Baer's punishment—having a miscreant strike the kindly teacher himself, instead of the other way around—was fair and effective. The older children have become fond of James Herriot's books, and, having bought tapes narrated by the veterinarian author himself, we all have found Herriot a firm favorite.

We love the Pooh stories and poems, though to tell the truth I sometimes tire of the stories myself; and also the *Jungle Books* and other works by Kipling. Lewis Carroll has been a steady favorite, early and late, and we have loved E. B. White (*Charlotte's Webb* etc.). After reading The *Secret Garden* by Frances Burnett, we looked up all the other volumes we could find by the same author. She is consistently good. We read and reread the Arthur Ransome books for children; they stand alone as wholesome adventure books, again with completely trustworthy morality, exciting yet believable plots, and—a rare plus—strong girl-leaders in the stories.

Pinnochio, original version; *Swiss Family Robinson*, same; *Treasure Island*, *Sherlock Holmes*, *Black Beauty*, *Peter Pan*, *Incredible Journey*, and authors like Mark Twain and O. Henry, and most of Jules Verne (especially *20,000 Leagues Under the Sea*, which Sammy started reading at about seven and has reread perhaps six or eight times)—in fact, almost any young people's classic you can name is dearly loved here at home.

It is very important to avoid abridgements or watered-down versons, in my opinion. You can miss much of the flavor and delight in the descriptions; in homeschool, time is not the critical factor in reading. The Disney adaptations, in particular, mutilate the spirit of many fine classics, e.g. *Swiss Family Robinson*, *Bambi*, *Pinnochio*. The Disney version of *The Jungle Book*, especially, is a distressing travesty of the original. If certain descriptions become too unwieldy, most children, like most adults, will skip over them themselves; but most often they read them and absorb their richness.

Sometimes children balk at attacking certain classic volumes because of their covers. I have some sets in matching covers, which the children would not touch at first, but after finding Bunyan's *Pilgrim's Progress* in another, colorful library version, they read it and other similar books happily.

Cassette tapes of classics, although they are invariably abridged (we have, however, an incredibly narrated rendition of *Pinnochio* which is nearly intact, and some companies produce the full texts of some classics), give a good enough foretaste of the books to tempt the children to read them, as well as being happy entertainment themselves. Many nights, after our evening devotional and a story-telling session from Avraham, the children go to bed with these stories in their ears, or perhaps scripture tapes, or classical music. We bought many tapes cheaply when a lending library went out of business, and we have also bought quite a few from the bookstore; we have plunged a fair bit of money into our cassette library. We listen so much that phrases from many books—and intonations from narrators—weave in and out of our conversations and jokes.

In addition to reading the classics, the children build the foundation of their subject areas with personal reading. As you will see further in my chapters on science and social studies, I actually teach very little in these subjects, instead buying and borrowing from libraries good books on the subjects, which are left on the library table with the other books. The children choose to read them, often several times; sometimes I read aloud books on a younger level. You would be amazed at the factual matter that children amass with such seemingly casual reading. When the children have taken the standardized tests, they always score in the 99th percentile in these subjects where they receive so little instruction.

When they wake up in the morning, all who can read, read from the scriptures. In this way, David and Sammy read the *Bible* and *The Book of Mormon* several times during the year President Benson first emphasized the *Book of Mormon's* importance. The scriptures have thus become the standard by which we can evaluate all other books.

It is interesting that, again without very much formal instruction, the children soon become adept at criticizing books properly. In one instance of Sammy rejecting *Jaws*, the book's problems were obvious, but I have been delighted to hear something like the following: "Tolkein is different from C.S. Lewis. They both write about other worlds, but Tolkein emphasizes the darkness and magic in his books, while the Narnia books seem to have more light. It's like Tolkein uses the darkness to attract his readers, while Lewis uses his books to teach his readers about the light."

We love Mother Goose, using a reprint of an old-fashioned volume; we have actually worn one out and bought another as the children have grown. We also like the originals of the fairy tales, favorites being Hans Christian Anderson (we received a large volume of the complete tales, to our delight, for a birthday) and Grimm.

I disagree with educators who advocate changing the frightening or violent parts of the story, so as to avoid nightmares and fearfulness—the worst example of this, I think, being the two little pigs who did not get eaten, in the Disney version of the story, but escaped to live happily ever after with their provident and hard-working brother in the house of bricks. Certainly children have fears and we should not play on them; but by experiencing the terrors in the tales and overcoming them, children can work out their own frights in a safe and positive way. However, if we expose them to the senseless and sensual fears on television, where people are routinely battered and bashed and shot, and where cars crash into walls and off cliffs and into water, children can develop a very uneasy or hopeless feeling about the safety of the world around them.

Despite their ability to recognize good books, the children nevertheless are tempted to read inappropriate books, mostly of the "witchy" variety. But they know when the books cross the line (once David spent quite a bit of time explaining how such a book was essentially wholesome after all!). Again, unless a volume is grossly inappropriate, I do not forbid it, but express my feelings about it.

You may find, if you use some of these methods to develop good readers in your home, that your children choose reading above other pastimes. Once a neighbor smiled at how our children came to visit, and then draped themselves all over the furniture, wrapped up in books. When our crew visited some relatives who are very active in sports and outdoor interests, only Yoni was invited right back because he threw himself into riding horses and seeking out rabbit dens; the other nestled into books. Admittedly I get cross and repeat what I remember my mother once said to me, "Why don't you put that book down and go outside to play!" Yet Dr. Arthur King recalls, as a child, walking from place to place, book in hand, and I can only hope that our children might grow up to be much like him!

WRITING

For as long as I can remember, I have been writing—poems and stories, letters and songs. Along with reading, writing has been the stuff of my life. You would think that with such a bent I would produce writing children. For a long time it wasn't so; only at ten or twelve have the older children begun to blossom as consistent writers. Our writing experiences in homeschool have not followed my pattern, yet they seem typical of many homeschools.

Except for Sammy, who plunged into reading almost instantly, my children have taken "the writing road to reading," that is, having learned to write the letters of the alphabet, they station themselves near to where I am working and endlessly ask how to spell the family's names, the animals' names, friends' names, and words that have caught their fancy: beach, sled, swine, cicada, jersey, tua tua (a type of New Zealand shellfish)—whatever! I spell the words letter by letter for beginners, who at first scatter the letters all over the page and need to be taught to draw lines, to write the words from left to right, leaving a space between words. Older ones get words whole; or in halves for long ones. Yoni, for example, at eight, usually requested the spelling for captions to attach to his drawings. Helped with phonics lessons and my reading aloud, the children sooner or later take the plunge into reading and can spell more and more of the words they want themselves.

When children begin writing letters quite young, say at three or four, I generally start them on all capital letters. Some Montessori teachers and other specialists disagree with this, rightly pointing out that most of our reading is printed in lower case; the capitals only rarely occur, as in proper names or at the beginnings of sentences. Yet to me the lower case letters have such a similar appearance one to another, and the capital letters such striking differences. The little ones seem to make emotional friendships with the initial letters of their names (Avi, at three, forbade anyone to use a capital *A*!), and they internalize the other capital letters more easily, I have noticed. At late four or five we begin games of connecting the capitals to their lower-case counterparts. In some cases this speeds along effortlessly; as Sammy at four poring over two adjacent pages

97

in McGuffey's primer.

Yoni, on the other hand, from the beginning resisted my proffered reading/writing lessons. He seemed to tire almost immediately when we would sit down together. And he continued mixing his capitals and lower case until he went to school for some months in New Zealand. It took him only a short time to develop conventional writing, producing a lovely hand that his teacher used as a model for the other children.

Chava, attending infant school, learned the correct relationships between the caps and lower case by copying words written by her teacher, taken from lovely "little books." They also colored big caps and the lower case of each letter. At home after school, she continued her requests for the spelling of many different words—almost as an activity apart from the structured teaching she was getting at school; but I noticed a more correct use of the lower-case letters!

Avi, at three, invented a classy way of learning capital and lowercase letters. He absorbed the capitals from his brothers and sisters, quite surprising me one day by saying, "H, yes, that's two up-and-down lines and one across," and so on. Looking at books that presented all those confusing lower-case symbols, however, and my ABC chart with both sets (Aa, Bb, etc.) didn't solve the problem. One day he was experimenting with the typewriter, seeing his familiar cap ABC's on the keyboard, but noticing the elusive lowercase as he typed. So he began to type from one of Bill Peet's books, identifying the printed letter, locating its keyboard capital, and typing it in lowercase. In a one- or two-hour afternoon session, Mother standing by, he memorized both sets together.

Some teachers like to begin with cursive rather than manuscript, while others like Denilian, a sort of modified manuscript that leans toward cursive and helps ease young writers into cursive. In England, the students all learn Denilian, very elegant. I have taught the conventional manuscript to begin with, starting with cursive from store-bought writing books at about age eight. I post a cursive chart near the child's desk that he can consult any time. Occasionally I have to correct the formation of a letter, but usually the children move into cursive easily. They often shift from one to the other, sometimes writing journal entries for weeks in cursive, then switching to manuscript for some reason, and back again. However hard I have tried to press good handwriting, our children's remained pretty awful until they attended school in New Zealand, where penmanship was emphasized, and then they all strove to conform and eventually produced lovely hands. Unfortunately, they don't retain a commitment to good handwriting unless prodded by school experience; I haven't insisted, either.

I teach them how to form the alphabet when they are young, but then their writing may take a turn for the worse, mainly because saying what they want to say, have the vocabulary to say, takes too much strength and endurance from the small hand muscles. They get tired. The children have used unorthodox pencil grips to overcome this fatigue, and I have not pressed too hard for them to correct their grips; David to this day holds his pencil oddly compared to the conventional grip, so much so that a kind schoolteacher at church brought him over some of those triangular pencil attachments that force the fingers into the correct grip. Sammy and Yoni adapted their grip to my gentle demonstrations, and when they went to school in New Zealand they conformed completely. Interestingly, Chava and Avi began using their pencils in the conventional way from the beginning. I myself use an unconventional grip, being double-jointed; and from observing other adults who deviate from the standard grip and yet who write quite nicely, I don't feel that it should become an emotional issue.

With a typewriter especially for the children to use, they write letters and stories more easily. I don't allow them to use our quality manual typewriter nor our IBM Selectric (unless with permission and some supervision for the older ones, as when they begin to learn to touch type), because I have found that children invariably break the machine and that repairs cost. I know that the late John Holt, that great and gentle proponent of homeschool, strongly recommended that little children be allowed to type with electric machines, but six children and many dollars of repairs down the road, I must loathfully disagree.

Our children's typewriter, a plain and sturdy manual given to me by my grandmother, sees plenty of use; and we have only had to repair it once—so far. Until I require an older child to make his way through a touch-type manual, the children use the peck-and-find method. They produce some nice stories and letters with the typewriter. Computers encourage composition, and it is an easy way to write and edit. When we finally did obtain a home computer (see chapter on "Technology" for details), the children often wrote long stories or essays, facilitated by the machine.

A favorite purchase from *Learning at Home*, the homeschool catalog from Hawaii, was "Keyboarding Skills," a typing course for elementary and junior high students, Chava was the first, at six, to begin. She made her way through the alphabet, in correct position, with ease.

Next, we sent the course with Avraham and the three older boys as they went to study at BYU. Each learned typing quickly and easily as can be, Yoni surpassing all with his facility. This surprised him—and delighted me—because he had proclaimed an aversion to typing or reading or writing or anything related. He turned out to be one of the best at composition, studying with the tutor, as well.

We had purchased other typing manuals, but we found "Keyboarding Skills" more accessible and certainly more effective.

For a long time the only writing I consistently required from the children was daily entries in their personal journals. They sometimes resisted writing so much that I had to specify a three-line minimum; though occasionally I discovered them entering long complex observations. More and more they also write poems or stories.

Every so often one of them isolates himself to play with pen and paper and composes a long story or essay that has been brooding in his head. Sammy has written some about taking trips to the moon, riding around in spacecraft, and other fantasies. The boys have written some surprising and delightful poems:

Poem
by David, at twelve

Softly a light begins to shine,
The dark shape of the mountain
Is exposed from the clouded sky,
A beam of light shines through my window
And onto the bedspread.
As the moon rises above the horizon
And illuminates the clouds.

Poem
by David, at twelve

One day I had just woke up
And got out of bed,
And out of the window
to greet my sleepy head

Was a blanket of white,
On the houses and trees,
And little white jewels
Were dancing on the breeze.

All of the mountains
Had pulled down their caps,
And the dark forest trees
Lay huddled in their laps.

I let out a yell of joy
And clambered down the side,
Had my breakfast, bundled up,
And went for a sled ride.

I also made a snowman,
And told him he was Joe.
And rolled in, and played in
The very first snow!

Snow
by Sammy, at ten

I walk outside; falling jewels glisten in the light.
My feet are crunching
Like a monster munching
A bone
While seated on a slimy throne.
A sudden chill runs through me
As I take a breath of air.
I throw a snowball at the porch,
As if I didn't care.

When Yoni concocted stories too long for his endurance, he would dictate parts of them to me, though he was unable to read them himself; members of the family had to read them aloud, much to his pride and enjoyment. Later he began to write and type long, nicely illustrated narratives. The older boys steadfastly resisted my attempts to involve them in learning composition until David was eleven and a half; then he suddenly was ready, and began writing with delight in response to my assignments.

That was in Rarotonga; when he began attending school in New Zealand, he wrote copiously, page after page. "What are you doing in writing?" I would ask, "Writing process," he would explain, using the New Zealand long *o*. "And what is writing process?" "Well, you write anything you want to. You have to decide what you want to write, and how you're going to write it. Then you do it double-space, and the teacher corrects your errors. Then you decide if you want to copy it out again correctly to keep." "Does she grade your work?" "Naw, she just marks it with a check-mark." (This is the method I noticed there in all the schoolwork. The children did the work and the teacher checked it with a red check-mark—no grades. I could tell the teachers really looked at the work though, because they caught any errors or even malformations in letters. And astonishingly the children seemed to feel excited to receive those check marks.)

I was taken aback by this "writing process" because it was just the easy-going approach I had strived for years to use with the boys! I noticed that Sammy and Yoni as well wrote much more in school than ever at home. Hopefully their willingness there would carry home when we began homeschooling again. They both reported that they were considered to be the finest story writers in their classes (which sat around on mats and listened to each other read their stories). Every few months the school published all the stories submitted, without a teacher judging which was best. In addition, children wrote news items and editorials to publish in these journals. What an excellent way to stimulate good writing.

One day Sammy suggested a suitable writing course. "If your child is interested in reading, he can write his ideas about a story he's read. If he likes sports, he can map out where he's going to run and what exercises he will do. If he wants to do mechanics, he can write out his projects and list all the materials he needs. You just need to suit the writing to a child's interests" (this is a ten-year-old talking!).

In order to ameliorate the problems I have experienced in having the children write, I think the above advice might help somewhat. A short stint in school, provided the school available to you is suitable and provides a good writing program (two big ifs), can break the emotional barrier to writing. A correspondence course for writing, with a teacher's comments on a child's efforts, may work well, if you can afford it.

Have the children write letters to missionaries, grandparents and other relatives, friends in distant locations. Perhaps you can write a family letter and each child can contribute a paragraph.

Write some "silly stories," where each person is assigned the beginning, middle, or end. Decide on the characters you want, write the sections independently, and then read them together.

Teach some of the basic forms of poetry: haiku, couplets, quatrains, ballads. If you are fortunate to live near a college or other source for resident poets, run some of your best productions past them, being certain to choose real poets and not dilletantes.

Some of our best writing burst forth when we were making books. Using directions from Wiseman's *Making Things*, we cut, sewed, and bound some real books. David especially got into this craft, but the others have all produced books as they felt the need. With your own book in hand, you are almost compelled to write, and we enjoyed some nice illustrated stories that way.

At school in New Zealand the children did SSW, sustained silent writing. "We get to write anything we want!" they gloated (didn't they get to write anything they wanted at home, I silently wondered!).

In the style of the *TinTin* Books, the older children enjoy making comic strips, garnished with conversations and captions. This is real writing; it communicates, has to be spelled correctly, and requires organization. It's a lot of fun to read aloud.

I like to use the children's journals as the receptacle for all their creative efforts; they, however, prefer to write stories and poems in separate booklets, retaining the journals only for their proper use. A school exercise book, bound, lined paper with a sturdy cover, can store their work just as permanently as a journal; you might title it "Yoni's Writing Book" and let him decorate the cover if he wants.

Bill Martin Jr., in his *Sounds of Language* series, encourages imitative writing, using patterns you have previously read to create new ones of your own. So long as the children understand this as an exercise in thinking and creating, and not stealing someone else's things, it's a good practice. At the highest level, poets do this: the sonnet is a very standard form, and we use it as a pattern to create our own expression. Using other writing as patterns gives young children tools to work with, and we can delight in the ways our creations differ from the originals. Fractured fairy tales always make us laugh, like Sammy's, included here:

The Ugly Bugling
by Sammy, at ten

Once there was an ugly bugling. When he was a grub, his parents nearly vomited (bugs can't really vomit) at his manners. So when he hatched, they were astounded because he was SO ugly and his manners were getting worse. So his Mom and Dad turned him out of house and home, and all he said was, "I ain't care, and the reason I ain't care is 'cause I hate yer yellerin' at me for these manners!"

But he soon found that instead of "ain't care," he did care, because there was no food at all, and soon night came. With no shelter he got very cold and to top off all, it started to rain. So he crept under a leaf and made the best of it till morning.

Then he got up, ate his temporary shelter, and hopped onto the road, when all of a sudden, a huge growling machine came and stopped right by him. A huge Beast came and enormous hands picked him up and put him in a glass jar. Plonk. He fell into the jar. It was full of mint leaves, a particular dislike of the poor bugling, which his parents used to force him to eat. "Alas," said the poor bugling, "I'll have to eat it."

So weeks passed by and the bugling grew into a handsome staghorn beetle. They let him out of his glass prison and he went straight to his parents. They were astounded to see him so handsome, and they apologized to him, and so he lived happily ever after.

Moldylocks and the Three Fairs
by Sammy, at ten

Once there was a girl named Moldylocks, and her hair was very curly. It would have been very nice but it was very moldy, despite the fact that she used the very latest hair tonics (the reason it didn't work because she bought some old chemicals from a gypsy and mixed it with the hair tonics; these chemicals grew mold.)

Then a fair came to town with two rival fairs tagging along. The gypsy decided to sell her mold-growing tonic to the fairs saying that it was a hair tonic, of course. So she did. Moldylocks decided to look for some new hair tonics at the fair. She did. After buying some "Fancy Fangled Frilly Fruity Fizz Tonic for Hair," and some "Slushy Silky Sleek Slicky Stuff for Hair," she was suprised to find some of the gypsy's hair tonic!

Now this moldy girl was not such a nice and kind girl as you would expect. She thought to herself, "I can steal some of that hair tonic. They wouldn't miss a couple of bottles. I know! I can steal two bottles from each fair! Then I'll have six bottles and then I'm sure my hair will get clean after all that." So she walked home around the fairgrounds to plan her scheme. Then she went home.

Late that night she crept into the fairgrounds. There was no moon, and it was raining torrents. The first fair was easy to get into, and so was the second. Then she went to the third, which was actually stationed in town hall (with the Mayor's consent, of course). It was two stories high.

She got in through a window and sneaked up the stairs up to the top story, where the tonic was. She got to the top and grabbed two bottles, when all of a sudden BRRRNPOOW! The burglar alarm went off! Immediately crowds of people wearing night gowns rushed up the stairs.

They were yelling, "Stop, thief!" So she hurriedly opened a window and jumped out, just in the nick of time. She landed head first in the mud, which had accumulated there because of the rain. She ran home, vowing that she would never again steal anything.

And they all lived happily ever after. Well, not so happily, because she kept on using that hair tonic.

Although not written, the children indulge in various word games that certainly sharpen their awareness of language. We house one of the worst assemblages of punsters in existence. Leaving home the other day for a shopping trip, David said, "I've got my list," tilting himself over sideways. In addition, they fool around with language a lot: "If Abba (our name for Father) brought a watch to class, it would watch the students. If he brought a baby to class, it would baby the students; if he brought a stick to class, it would stick the students; if he brought a match to class, it would match the students," and so on (and on).

Another completely self-initiated activity, but which surely qualifies as writing, is Sammy's scientific lists. Observing the different kinds of rocks or shells around, he looks them up in the guidebooks and lists them in categories in his little notebooks, sometimes commenting on where he found them or facts about them. When he was ten, I found him making this list:

Facts About Kiwis

1. They are nocturnal. 2. There are three kinds of kiwis—brown, great spotted, and little spotted. 3. I have seen all three kinds. 4. There are hardly any left. 5. The kiwi is the symbol of New Zealand. 6. The kiwi eats grubs. 7. They used to live in the bush. 8. Kiwis cannot fly. 9. Their nostrils are at the end of the beak. 10. They only occur in New Zealand. 11. The Great Spotted and the Little Spotted live only in the South Island.

If I were really acting the schoolteacher, I would offer to help him with these lists, showing him how to place the items logically and write them completely and correctly. But I feel that these skills will come as he matures, especially since he's an avid reader, and that the important thing now is the thinking and the enthusiasm. I feel sure that my intrusion at this point would dampen his efforts. And his work never stops delighting me, as when during a general conference of our church he noted the names and interesting points of each speaker, all without being asked. As we were viewing in a local chapel, many people commented on such mature behavior in a ten-year-old. Later he shared his notes with the family during our evening devotionals.

In this category of self-initiated writing fall various creations that I don't really like, but that certainly take a deal of work. David began writing variations on Dr. Seuss when he was ten, illustrating them and typing them up in booklet form. I dislike them because they seem pretty silly; I let David know, but he persists in creating them. After reading Carroll's "The Hunting of the Snark," he redoubled his efforts, producing a baroque take-off on Carroll. He found himself in good company with his light-minded verse! I happen to have at hand his *The First Airplane*:

> Long ago in the days
> when things always went wrong,
> and axle-wheels broke
> like the hammer-and-tong;
>
> Long ago in those days
> when the axle-wheels bent,
> I had a big brother
> who liked to invent.
>
> He had a small workshop
> where he kept his tools,
> and to go past the door-stop
> was breaking the rules!
>
> Some said he kept gold there,
> some said he made beer,
> and on certain dark nights
> strange noises you could hear.
>
> Well, the noises went on
> and people kept wondering,
> till at last he came out
> dragging some kind of thing!

It was tallish and fattish
with millions of pipes;
it had four blades on one end
and made smoke of all types!

Well, big brother got in
with all reason and rhyme;
and he slammed closed the door
as he counted the time.

Well, he got down to one
and he pulled down a switch;
and from somewhere inside
came a muffled chir-ich.

The thing trembled once
like a tree in a rain;
and it rose with its blades
going like a hurricane!

Well, my brother was proud
as he rose through the air
but as he circled his shed
something raised up his hair!

The engine went put,
and it started to sag;
and when it finally gave out
he fell down like a bag.

Can you guess where he fell
and took several hard hits?
Well, he fell on his shed
and he broke it to bits.

Well, my brother has stopped
he'll make nothing more;
and to top all of that,
he works in a store!

Similarly, after reading some of those peurile "choose-your-own-adventure" books, he spent long hours creating some of his own, the initial stages of which resemble a large genealogical chart. Some of the commercial books center around haunted castles and dark deeds—other discouraged themes.

I don't make the children feel guilty when they write or draw items I don't like. I just let them know my feelings, and they understand they are free to go on with it if they like. They don't seem to suffer from coersion: they usually keep writing what they want anyway! We draw the line at vulgarity, of course.

Although the daily journal supplies much of the need for personal-history writing for children, sometimes a major experience produces some longer writing. Encourage this, if you can, if only because the children love to look back and read it. Of the hurricane in Rarotonga, David wrote:

One day while we were in Rarotonga we were playing outside. In the sky there was a gray mass of clouds and strong winds pushed them across the sky. My mother had just been to our neighbor's house, and when she came back she said that a hurricane was coming. Soon my father, who had been out, came back and put boards on the windows, while my mother chattered on the phone. Then it began to get dark, and we all went to bed. The wind was getting stronger all the time.

Some time later in the dark of the night I woke up. I saw a glow in the kitchen so I got up. In the kitchen there was my dad and my brother Sammy up with the flashlight and some candles. They said the power was off. Outside there was the sound of the whistling wind and the banging of things on the house. Soon we were made to go to bed, while my dad stayed up. After a while I went to sleep.

In the morning it was calm. Our place was strewn with rubbish. Our house was lucky. We only had a fallen solar heater which hung on its pipes and unbelieveably still worked. My mother went to visit our neighbors and learned that we were still in the hurricane. We were in the eye where the air is calm. We stayed in the house and sure enough, it began to blow again.

It blew most of the day and when it finished we began to look at the damage. Besides the heater, we had a fallen tree (large) another (small) and lots of bush strewn around. Our power and telephone were off, and we had to use our neighbor's phone. Besides that we only had our water pressure *down*.

In a while we went for a drive in our friend's car to look at the damage. There were roofs off everywhere and the social building was totally collapsed. As we drove past the waterfront there were boats and buildings collapsed, and a restaurant called Trader Jack's was reduced to a skeleton. Stores had windows off and they were covered with wood.

Later my brothers, my dad, and myself were busy cleaning up rubbish. We cut apart branches and hauled them to the heap. The tree that had fallen we cut apart all except for the trunk, which is still there.

People said there hadn't been such a bad one in 30 years. Shortly afterwards another hurricane came, but it was not as strong. It just pulled more rubbish down.

A word here about grammar and conventions. Many people gape at me when I tell them we learn only the basic terminology of grammar, not entering into it with memorization, tests, etc. In recent years, universities have taught many different kinds of grammar in addition to conventional, Latin-based grammar: structural, transformational, rhetorical analysis, etc.

Children learn to speak properly from their parents (my little ones have never erred using lie/lay, because we adults use it correctly). They need grammatical terminology to improve their writing (as in "Use the active rather than the passive tense!"), but they do not need to be quizzed from an early age on grammatical terms. If they come to the age where they want to take exams for college entrance, they can easily memorize what they need from a grammar book. Why do high schools teach and reteach the same boring grammar year after year? Why don't the students seem to be able to remember it? If they want to learn it, they can and will do so very quickly. I would say, concentrate your efforts on the writing skills of your children, for good writing is good thinking, a skill worth working on.

Using punctuation, capitalization, and other conventions should also grow out of the writing experience. They are not difficult for children to remember, even differentiating between the use of the dash (—) and hyphen (-) or the mystery of the slippery semi-colon. As a freelance editor, I routinely correct plenty of such errors, the children casually observing my work. Imagine my surprise one evening to return home with my husband from a dinner with friends, finding that ten-year-old David had corrected the essay the babysitter had written for homework, not only locating and rectifying every mistake, but also correctly finding and putting right problems in the paper's organization and content! I had both copies (she left the flawed version as well as a special copy for the children) to make the comparisons.

Spelling is a different matter. Using copies of an excellent but now out-of-print series, *Spell/Write*, I tried to teach spelling as an outgrowth of learning to write manuscript and then cursive, and then of expressing one's views on paper, as well as using crossword puzzles and other writing games. But I found that the children didn't really learn to spell words this way. After David had attended school for a while, he preferred to memorize spelling lists, complete activities using the words, and take spelling tests at the end of the week! Sammy's spelling improved dramatically when he began school and used the same technique. From now on I will use spelling lists in my homeschool. Surprisingly, the children seem to enjoy the excitement of learning to spell the words in the list. Spelling bees can be fun when all the children are spelling near an equal par. My notion that correct spelling will grow out of reading much and writing has not fully proved true, although I still believe that reading a great deal can enhance one's spelling.

Reading good books certainly does improve one's writing, however. Arthur H. King pointed out that our grandparents and their progenitors wrote very much better than we do, because they were immersed in the scriptures and other worthy writing. We, on the other hand, are doused in the media and in an onslaught of very loose and casual prose. By choosing very carefully what books come into the house, and by centering our children's reading first on the scriptures and then onto other quality books, we can improve their writing.

Reading widely and well certainly builds a fine vocabulary effortlessly. Friends of the family invariably comment on how intelligent our children seem, how well they express themselves; but most of this results from good reading rather than innate intelligence. The parents carry a heavy responsibility here, needing to choose books to avoid vulgarity or commonness. Soon the children pick up the standards and can judge for themselves.

When Avraham and Sammy shopped at a used-bookstore, Sammy asked to buy a popular book. Not knowing its contents, they brought it homeward, but on the way, beginning to read it and finding it full of unsuitable language, Sammy put it away, commenting that if it had just been better written, it could have been a good story!

Most of us fall short when selecting books, allowing silly and unworthy children's books to come into our homes. I avoid books that talk down to children, that promote violence or silliness, or that use monsters or ugliness of any kind to draw the children's attention. This sounds very obvious when you read it here, and yet if you look at children's books generally, you find so many of them do these very things. Choose books whose language delights your soul, that you love reading again and again. Soon you will hear the language of these books becoming the children's language, popping up in their conversations and in their own writing, so it's worth the effort to choose the very best.

Writing—books, generally—is an important part of our religious tradition, right from the earliest times. Keeping a daily journal should be a minimum for our homeschooled children. By keeping your ears open for interesting comments that might lead to writing, you can perhaps stimulate your children's efforts.

And save the good ones. You'll experience such delight reading the old stories and poems together, and rereading the journal entries is a lot of fun too. I include here a small sampling of some recent efforts, just for fun:

The Hill Robbers
by David, at twelve

Walking down valleys, up hills, and through canyons, they came; settlers wanting land, always more land. And with them came the outlaws, robbers, highwaymen, the lot. And this gives us our setting. Three men were coming up the trail, three men on horses.

As they came over a ridge, the leader stopped.

"This is where it is, or used to be, anyway." He was a big man, and nobody was sure of his age.

"What was where?" The speaker was just a boy of about 18, named John.

The other man in the company, a short man, wearing a sombrero, lifted his head. They called him Bill.

"The old Indian village. They say it is buried under all that loose rock."

"So?" said Bill.

"Well, it's said that there's an Indian treasure buried with it," said the leader without heat.

"There is?" said John. "Maybe we could find it."

"Yeah, there's only one problem," said the leader. "The guy who owns this place is not particularly interested in it. He's got *No Trespassing* signs up all over."

"That's never been a problem with us," said Bill.

"Yeah, but the story is that he's got a shotgun that he's mighty fond of usin'" said the boss.

"I know," said John. "We could camp on that ridge, off his property."

"Sure," said Bill, "What good will that do us?"

"Well, you see that the site of the village is right next to the ridge. We could dig a tunnel that would only have to be about ten feet long. The digging would be easy."

"Yeah, but what about the owner?" said the boss.

"We could pitch a tent over the entrance and he wouldn't have to know anythin' about it," said John.

"Will you please start talking about something sensible?" said Bill.

"His plan is perfectly sensible," said the boss. "Why not shut up yourself?" Bill shot an amazed look at him, but said nothing.

"In fact," said the leader, "I think we should do exactly that. If we found it, we could get purty rich."

"There's always that 'if.' What if we don't find anything?" said Bill.

"Who's boss here?" said the leader. "Me, or you?"

Bill started to speak and then fell into a sullen silence.

They headed towards the ridge. When they got there, John and the boss started marking out the hole, while Bill unpacked the saddle-bags. Then they started pitching the tents. They pitched one over the hole-site, and two others for sleeping in. Then John went into town for supplies and shovels, and some boards to hold up the tunnel roof. They started digging as soon as they had lunch.

The days passed, with the usual grumblings you find among outlaws, until the tunnel was about nine feet long. Bill said that they weren't going to find it, and he was not going to help anymore, and that was that. The boss said, "That's fine with me, 'n you just aren't getting your share of the profits." Bill said, "That's fine with me, and who says we are going to find anything anyway?" Well, they got into a big argument and were just about to split up when John, who had been digging, said, "I've hit something!"

The boss came down in and saw that it was a wall made of adobe bricks.

"I've found it!" yelled the boss.

They removed one of the bricks, and found a lantern to explore the insides of the building. They found the room had a door that led to other rooms, but they didn't find one ounce of treasure. Bill was just getting mad when John found a tunnel that seemed to lead to the surface. They crept up until they came to a blockage of soft earth. They figured out that it was just short way to the top. Slowly they pushed their way out until they came to a natural cave with a trapdoor leading to the outside opening. John bumped into something. When the boss held up the lantern, they saw it was a wheelbarrow. And right next to it was a pile of Indian treasure.

"What in the —!" said the boss. "The guy must have already found it," said John, "That's why he didn't like trespassers."

"Well, what do we do now?" asked Bill.

"What do we do?!" said the boss, "We get our bags and start filling them up, that's what we do."

They went and filled their bags, but on the third time round, just as they finished filling their bags, the trapdoor started to open. They took their bags and dived down the hole, quickly packed their bags, took down their tents, and were gone.

They got away fast enough, but their whole adventure didn't profit them any, because in their hurry they left the treasure behind!

A Day in My Life as a Mouse
by Sammy, at ten

I woke up in my cosy nest of lint. I yawned. I can hear Nate, the Humans' Great Dane, sniffing somewhere near. Now I must look for my breakfast, so I peek out of my hole. I find myself staring into the face of a cat named Panther. I use him as my fitness course, and the way I do it is: I attract his attention, so he runs after me, but he can't catch me, and that is how I do the fitness course. Once I tried it with Bandit, his brother, and nearly got caught. He and his mother, who doesn't have a name, are the most dangerous of the cats.

After undergoing the fitness course, I hear Sammy, one of the humans, mixing the chicken feed. Sometimes he spills some, and my relatives and I get some. Today he spills a whole bunch, and my relatives haven't woken up yet, so I get it all to myself! What a breakfast! There is, say, half of it left for my greedy relatives, who hardly let me have any most of the time. So now they are waking up and complaining about hardly any food, and they are fighting over it.

In the afternoon I see a human put a board with cheese on it on the bench. Soon after, my relatives discover it, and one of them, still hungry from the scanty breakfast, bites the cheese. Snap! It shuts on him. Soon my other relatives try. Snap! Eeek! Click! Yeoow! Click! Ahhhh! Eeeoow! Snap! Help! Aggh! Now all my relatives are dead, and the humans are throwing them to the cats.

I shouted warnings, but they took no heed. It was a grisly scene. One of my pregnant aunts got hit smack on the nose and the blood started pouring out. I do not want to say anything else, because it was too awful.

For lunch I sneaked some scraps from the chickens. Suddenly the mother cat sprang upon me. I feel the sharp claws pushing and shoving against me. Now I hear Angel, one of the kittens, cry out. The mother cat lets me go abruptly. So I run off, unharmed except for a few scratches.

In the evening, my cousin, the kangaroo mouse, comes for dinner. It is very nice. Now he is going home. The humans spy him and repeat the words: A kangaroo mouse! A kangaroo mouse! Among themselves they try to catch him but he outsmarts them and gets home safely.

It is night now. I curl up in my cosy nest of lint and go to sleep.

MATH

Some people live and breathe the atmosphere of numbers and logic. I don't. No one but myself would make the hundred-dollar error in the checkbook, or counting up dinner guests, figure on one little chicken to serve seven visitors and our nine family members.

Because math has always come hard to me (except for geometry—easier to conceptualize), I have had to try extra hard to provide superior math experiences for my homeschool.

Most of it I modelled on Montessori. The children played with homemade number games, placing a numeral card next to a card marked with spaces for buttons to be places. Eventually Avraham forbade the buttons, which always get scattered all over the house, tempting the creepers and crawlers to ingest them. Alas, I still pull out the buttons, trying ineffectually to control them, for such activities as the even-odd chart; pennies work here, too, but they also travel into little mouths.

At the BYU College of Education materials laboratory, I cut 1-by-1 lumber into ten-inch lengths, splitting some of these into one-inch cubes, leaving some pieces long, to help learn the logic of our ten-based system. Along with that went a game of counting-by-twos, adding a teen card to each numeral, then a twenties card, then a thirties card, so that the children could easily see the pattern. Eventually I constructed a tens and teens board, where the child slips in the appropriate number, a ten and a one. Bent on doing the thing right, I bought some multifaceted, little amber beads from a craft shop and painstakingly threaded them onto wire, bending the ends over, to replicate the Montessori golden-bead material (I never did make a hundreds cube however—I wore out!).

We played lots of games with little animals and toys: "Put two cows over here in the pasture; now add three sheep—how many all together?" When we cooked together, often we had to double or treble a recipe to feed the whole family. Casually I asked the older children to make the computation and write them alongside the recipe for future sessions; this can be challenging if you deal with many fractions—1/8 cup doubled and then reduced to 1/4 cup, etc. Traveling, we would compute how far we had gone and how far still remained, using maps as well as road signs.

Later we constructed a Montessori multiplication board, so that the children could see just why six times eight makes forty-eight: you place 48 little markers. It didn't take long for the older children, learning their times tables, to make such charts for themselves so they could just look up the answers. Consequently, David never really memorized the tables until forced to do it when he went to school for a few months at age eleven. The other children have to endure drill to get the tables automatically. Recently, in desperation, I sent away for a musical multiplication tape, *Audio Memory* from Memory Publishing, 1433 E. Ninth Street, Long Beach CA 90813, which all the children enjoy; they even opt to listen to in preference to other tapes. At every meal for some months, I dragged out the multiplication flash cards. Not surprisingly, the younger children memorized the combinations as fast—and in some cases, faster—than the older ones.

Plenty of everyday activities build math thinking skills without actually dealing with numbers. In Chava's infant-school class in New Zealand, math consisted of manipulating many charming little toys: placing plastic cups and saucers together to make sets, putting toy trucks opposite or behind or beside the toy cars, grouping classes of miniature animals, patterning beads on strings, fitting together three or five or eight snap blocks. Formally as well as casually, we do lots of that kind of play at homeschool.

Mathematical thinking really pervades so much that we do. When we practice physical fitness, we time ourselves with a stopwatch, trying to improve our daily run. We mark and use a long-jump, recording and comparing distances. We count the books we bring to and from the library—which can turn into a sad sort of subtraction: "We brought home forty-two, but here we have only thirty-eight. How many are we still missing?" How many quarts of milk did Nellie and Bess give today? How many quart jars of tomatoes do eleven dozen make? How many eggs did the hens give over the last four days? How many cups in a quart? How many quarts of juice do we need for everyone to have one cup? How many quarts in a gallon—are you sure? How come there seems to be a little bit more to add? (Inaccurate measurement!) How hot is it today? The newspaper said that last year, it was three degrees cooler; how hot is that? What is the average for this time of year in this area?

When Sammy, at eight, got into rainfall measurement, having made a rain collector at Cub Scouts, he recorded the rainfall every day for weeks one spring, making a nice little chart of it.

How far is it from Utah to Sabta's (Grandmother's) house in California? From Los Angeles to Tahiti, from Tahiti to Rarotonga, from Rarotonga to New Zealand? The children made lovely little maps chronicling all of that during our South Pacific trip. If we get on the plane at twelve o'clock and get off at four-thirty the next day, how long have we been in the plane, allowing for a two-hour time difference? (Of course, a ten-year-old might feel the time differently than the two-year-old, and the mother!)

What time does the sun rise? We wrote on the calendar the daily time, calculating the differences over several weeks. How much sleep do we get if we go to bed at seven-thirty? At eight? A dangerous fever begins at perhaps 102° F. How high is the baby's temperature? After we give him herbs and a bath, what is his temperature? How hot must the milk be to make yogurt; how hot is too hot, which kills the culture? Same with yeast for bread: What is the ideal temperature? How hot should the oil be to make homemade french fries? How hot must candy be to solidify properly? How hot is boiling; how cold is freezing?

We have bought several clocks with various features, including one with removable numbers in puzzle-shaped pieces. I have stuck to my duty in teaching children to tell time, remembering the lackadaisical homeschooler I once met who commented, "Ah, well, most clocks are digital these days, anyway"; the nine-year-old hadn't the faintest notion of using a clock-face. School people consider six or seven the appropriate age to know how to tell time, but usually the children develop a keen interest and immediate skill at about age eight. We play with the clocks, then, and I always answer precisely when someone asks me what time it is—"seven thirty-two"—but defer the detailed learning until the child seems ready.

Without a doubt, math does require some drudging hard work, but by bringing the children into the many facets of real life that require math logic and computing, you can help them feel competent and natural with numbers.

Having babysat for a friend who worked at a school-supply shop, she traded with me, giving me a big set of math workbooks, along with other things. From the School Zone series, these seemed to work fairly well, but lacked consistency and adequate practice. *Math Matters*, by Dr. Randall Souviney, features a complete and structured approach to math, using both homemade and purchased materials, specifically Unifix cubes, tiles constructed into strips of tens as well as in ones, and Base-ten blocks. These tactile aids give a concrete experience with a concept. Next, a representational experience follows, using paper and pencil or a similar method. Finally, an abstract experience follows—which is what most students receive first and last in schools! The approach is very good, but it became difficult to pursue with many different children who were all on different learning levels. I still think it good to support the abstract concepts that most math programs offer.

After an interval of working through the activities in *Math Matters*, I decided to look for a text that would progress each child without involving me so much. Especially when I have to balance babies into the equation, the work sometimes doesn't get done. School texts seemed to cram a great deal of busy work into not much actual learning. Pages and pages of David's school text hashed over adding and subtracting decimals, which is a very simple concept not requiring so much ado. Finally, examining a friend's books, I settled on the Math texts in the Beka books. These books are provided for the children of Christian missionaries who live abroad and cannot obtain an adequate education; Christian homeschoolers also use them.

I did not particularly like Beka's complete program, finding in the science and social studies texts the same problems as school texts, rendering the real, interesting subjects dull and lifeless. I did not like the English and grammar texts because of the moralistic tone and quotations inserted; I like scripture in its own context, not slipped by bits into other things, and I like literature that compels us to be moral by its own morality, not by didacticism.

But the Beka math program, interspersed quotations notwithstanding, seems to me to be excellent. Providing a good deal of drill and practice, it also progresses at a good, steady pace. The only drawback is that you need to know how to divide fractions or apply the rule of nine in case the child doesn't understand the directions, which are at times a tiny bit confusing. The books themselves cost about $10 for a year's course, minimal compared to home-study courses. You can also buy the teacher's text for another $10, which includes all the answers as well. I check each day's work by eye. I also like the math materials from *Learning At Home* in Hawaii.

Despite my weakness in math, I feel delighted when my children excel in the subject. When David was seven and Sammy five, I gave them the *Stanford Achievement Tests*. They excelled in everything but math and spelling, and so I decided to regularize our study of these subject, which seem to require constant practice. Our efforts paid off. When tested with the Stanford Tests two years later, they placed high in the 90s; and some of their highest marks in school in New Zealand were in "maths," as it is called there.

I happened to find a used copy of BYU's Pre-Algebra course, a remedial class. David at eleven was just the right age for it, and I look forward to exploring some of the other basic university courses for the older boys. They have a no-nonsense accessible approach, with just enough practice. Later we were delighted with Harold Jacob's *Elementary Algebra*, a thorough, comprehensive course extremely well-written, with lots of challenging and clever exercises.

The ongoing, real-life experience with math, I think, gives confidence to learning and remembering the concepts. When we were working with stained glass, David wanted to make a triangular prism using special glass to be purchased, instead of the random scrap glass by the pound we normally bought. We could estimate the cost, I figured, if we knew how much glass he needed. Unfortunately I did not recall how to compute the area of a triangle, so I telephoned some homeschool friends, both of the parents having graduated in the sciences. They didn't remember either, but knew where to look it up: in *World Book of Math Power*, containing nigh about everything you could want to know about math computations. So we had the formula: $A=1/2$ (height x length). Having computed the area of the triangles and added them together, we figured in a bit of waste, and, selecting the desired glass, determined the cost of the project, including the copper foil and fixings. It didn't add up to all that much—but it was a super math experience.

By far the most beguiling of casual math experiences must be counting money. Off and on we give allowances, but usually we operate on the idea of giving workers their all when needed, and getting our needs on request. Of course, often I slip 50¢ into the hand of a valiant babysitter who voluntarily sweeps the babies away while I cook or type. And Avraham occasionally pays bigger money, a dollar to two, for large projects, like deep-cleaning the entire house, helping when moving house (something we seem to do often), or mowing and raking large lawns.

The children work out the interest on their missionary savings accounts. They compute how much baby chicks will cost, how much for their feed, and how much the eggs will bring. They juggle costs versus available funds for coveted items, along with a lecture from mother when they want to buy something plastic that will break within the week. They converted U. S. funds to N. Z. and back again when comparing costs of different things they wanted to buy.

The children hoard their savings, then blow them all on gifts for each other, one notable Christmas nine-year-old David spending his all, close to $25, on his brothers and sisters. When the family decided to replace our twelve-year-old stereo, which had not worked for four or five years, each child handed over $5 or $10 to complete the cost: they worked out again and again what it all added up to, their portion included. They always compute tithing, although our peculiar banking system renders this payment irregular: when a child earns a dollar, we sometimes keep it in hand and he adds it to a mental running sum, payable on demand. Usually the children pay a big lump sum tithing once in a while; this works especially well when we are on the piggy-bank system, each person guarding his own.

Recently we bought a bigger set of the Cuisenaire rods and a few of their books (*Cuisenaire Roddles*; *Hidden Rods, Hidden Numbers*). This exploded into a great interest in math games, with everyone from Avi at five to Sammy at 12 getting caught in the wave. Yoni began to construct Cuisenaire rod sculptures, using the logic of the rods to make pyramids and pagodas. Chava at seven needed some review of place value and regrouping, and the rods worked wonderfully here.

We had sent for some workbooks from *Learning at Home* in Hawaii. The second-grade *Basic Math* suited Chava exactly; and I liked the approach, utilizing some algebra and emphasizing the commutative properties of numbers. She sat on the sofa, working page after page, asking for instructions when needed. At the same time, Avi, just turned five, picked up a second-grade Holt Mathematics workbook. It takes a more conventional approach, and he began working side-by-side with Chava. He skipped the kindergarten and first-grade materials we had around, but somehow the second-grade work suited him precisely. At the same time we bought another *Little Professor Math Game* (the first had broken some years ago) and everyone began intensely on that. What a joy it was to see Avi on the floor, Little Professor and Cuisenaire rods at hand, adding 9 + 7. He had no problem at all with the teens, although some children struggle with that. One day he sat for over two hours working out math problems.

Sammy had been feeling inadequate in math, so we bought *Problem Solving* from *Learning at Home*, a word problem approach for the sixth grade. After he finished that triumphantly, we went on to BYU's Pre-Algebra course, and he found he was doing fine, after all. However, Yoni at ten still rarely chose to read, so he had a hard time accepting the word-problem workbook at his level, finally agreeing to work through it quickly with Avraham's help so he could get onto something he liked.

The most important thing about homeschool math, it seems to me, is to keep at it. If you slacken in math practice, you lose ground that you must regain by hard work. Almost like the physical body, it improves if you keep it in shape, but you regress to square one when you neglect it.

And an added benefit—if you, like me, muddled through school feeling an absolute zero in your math classes, homeschooling math gives you another chance.   Suddenly algebra reduces to some manageable concepts, and I like it! Inept as I am, I enjoy the math games requiring long strings of computations; and when a textbook offers a muddling explanation; I work through the problems until I can explain it better. Another barrier crushed for the homeschooling mother—a chance to learn what we missed years ago!

SCIENCE

The staff of one elementary school, its children going on to middle school without having studied a science curriculum, was astonished that these children scored highest on their standardized tests in the areas of science! Similarly, my children, without a regular science curriculum, always score in the 99th percentile in science on standardized exams, and they display amazing general knowledge in the subject as well.

It shouldn't surprise us. What a pity that we learn to despise science subjects in our high school and university training, for science makes up all the interesting stuff in life! I always enjoy Brigham Young's enthusiasm: "Go to school and study; have the girls go, and teach them chemistry, so that they can take any of these rocks and analyze them. . . . The sciences can be learned without much difficulty. . . . I would like nothing better than to learn chemistry, botany, geology, and mineralogy, so that I could tell what I walk on, the properties of the air I breathe, what I drink, &c" (*Journal of Discourses* 16:170).

The questions little children ask almost always deal with science: "Why does the river flow this way and not that way?" "Why does the wind blow?" "Where does the snow come from?" "What is the name of that bird (or this rock, or that flower, or these mountains, or any number of things)?" "Where does the sun go at night?" "What are those bubbles in the bottom of that boiling pot of water?" "Why does the bread rise?" I could go on, but if you have little ones, you could likely supply pages of questions from your own home.

It's fun to find the answers to these questions, and in doing so, we encompass a formidable science curriculum. We use encyclopedias; we check out books from the library; we use textbooks accumulated over the years; we search in Nature Guides for names and habits.

Take, for example, our Year of the Cicadas. One spring, we noticed all these little holes appearing in our back lawn, and where was the grass disappearing to? And what was that clicking in the trees, increasing day by day? At last we caught one of the culprits in the act of shedding its skin—a harmless-looking, brown, fly-like creature almost an inch long. In our books we found the answer: it was a cicada. The brief encyclopedia entry informed us that cicadas vary in their life cycles, but the basic pattern was as follows: Cicadas come in two different varieties—dog-day and periodical. Ours were the periodical kind. They take either thirteen or seventeen years to develop (so that is why there was no grass in the back yard!).

The female lays her eggs in the lilac bushes near our back door, sawing a hole in the twigs and placing the eggs in the little holes. In a few weeks, the eggs hatch and the nymphs appear, falling down to the ground and digging themselves in. There they eat roots for years until they are full-grown, whereupon they crawl out, climb part-way up the walnut and Chinese elm in the back yard, shed their skin, and fly away to live for a few weeks, mating, laying eggs, and beginning the long process again.

Now this caught our imagination. Those bugs crawling over our hands, that the children sometimes helped off with their coats, had been in the ground for many years. We began to notice different colors and sizes among the cicadas, so we called the Bean Life Science Museum and talked to the entymologist there. Yes, these were periodic cicadas, some with a thirteen year cycle, but some with only a five or a seven year cycle. The children separated the different kinds into cans crawling with cicadas and then let them go, to fly into the trees and click like mad to attract their mates. I didn't mind losing my back lawn to them.

By now we were clearly focused on flying insects and their larvae and it didn't take much time to notice the monarch butterfly larvae on the milkweed. We collected several of these fellows and jarred them safely, feeding them milkweed until they turned to chrysalis and eventually emerged. I recall the wonder of these bug births. Yoni in particular tenderly coaxed the damp-winged monarch onto his finger, gently helping it unfold (I know you're not supposed to interfere, but Yoni proceeded undaunted) and then "teaching" it to fly, with a bursting heart letting it soar away into the sky.

But where did it go?

By now all the children had to know, so we dug out a National Geographic article on monarchs and went to the library for books on their habits. How surprised we were to find out that monarchs migrated. We read a story about a Canadian scientist tagging specimens and then, after many months, receiving a letter from southern Mexico that the tagged specimen had come to rest there. In the text of the book, the scientist postulated the different stages of the journey, the dangers the monarchs must have endured, the changes in climate and scenery.

From monarchs we predictably leaped to butterflies in general, and we devoured encyclopedia articles, nature guides, and books on the subject. The children chased after samples, books in tow! Collecting and mounting the specimens, labelling them, drawing them with their appropriate larvae, seeing their distribution and habits all consumed days of happy labor. Specimens we couldn't collect we drew and labelled anyway. Butterfly study soon included moth study; there were many more moths around our place than butterflies.

Soon Sammy cut, sewed, bound and wrote a book in the shape of a butterfly, about the flutterer who migrated to the moon, and finding life unsatisfying there, brought himself home again. We also enjoyed butterfly stories, poems, and songs.

Did these children need a test on insects to see if they had learned "everything they need to know?" Did a teacher have to force them to utilize proper format and techniques for scientific accuracy? We had so much fun with the cicadas and butterflies, and forever after have kept a sharp eye on the creatures flying about us. Supplying materials and looking up answers, I learned more about the subject than I had known before, and enjoyed it as much as everyone else.

To be truthful, most of my formal science lessons have fallen flat. Using Julia Waxter's *Science Cookbook*, I have attempted to plod through regular lessons on the coagulation of protein, congealing of starches, and all related information. The children worked with me on the experiments, but never showed the excitement they generate when they pursue interests of their own. Wondering whether honey dissolved faster in cold or hot water, they devised their own experiment without me, and amassed much more information than I could have administered, including observation about the swirling patterns of water as it heats.

When the children set their own science course, facilitated and encouraged by the parent, they absorb correct techniques, proper terminology, and thoroughness. So instead of trying to teach things, I spend all my science energies on providing good books and tools and materials, and guiding the children in their own interests.

When we lived at the beach in New Zealand, for example, I showed the children how to mount shell specimens on cardboard and label them properly. Those whose names we didn't know we looked up in library books. We learned plenty of interesting sidelights as well: the small, curling macaroni-looking shells we found scattered prolifically after rough seas formed on the tentacles of a deep-sea octopus, rarely observed!

Using the library to locate good books and then purchasing the ones we like best, we have accumulated a decent library on science subjects. During the last decade many superior children's books on science have appeared, as well as much other excellent nonfiction, and we can be sure that a selection of the library will delight us. Word Book and Childcraft also supply a foundation of information, though we usually find that, looking into a subject that has caught our fancy, we must go further than encyclopedias to get any satisfying information.

Nature Guides, especially the classic Golden Guides, have absorbed my young scholars for many hours, though you might not consider this children's reading material! Self-propelled, the children learn about the distribution of various minerals, or birds, or fishes; and they astonish us by remembering a lot of it. Again in New Zealand, a whale was beached near our neighbor's farm. Avraham casually mentioned that it could have been a right whale. Oh, no, corrected Sammy, right whales don't appear in this ocean. It probably was a small blue or a hump-backed whale.

Sometimes our Guides can't give us enough information, either, so we utilize BYU or other schools, or museums. I remember taking a big plastic sack full of fossil rocks that we had found in the foothills to BYU campus, trekking along the pathways with a baby on the hip, passing the heavy bag of rocks from child to child to another, so that someone in the Geology department could help us identify what turned out to be mostly corals, though we did locate one rare kind of sea worm.

Sometimes experiments result from books themselves, especially forays into electricity or physics. Scientist friends, who have a homeschool themselves, guided us to an excellent set of books: *Physics Experiments for Children* (Muriel Mandell), *Electricity Experiments for Children* (Gabriel Reuben), *Chemistry Experiments for Children* (Virginia Mullin), *Biology Experiments for Children* (Ethel Hanauer)—all published by Dover Books. Our copies are well worn. The children ask me for D-cell batteries, light bulbs, wire, buzzers, switches, and then construct their own door bells, lamps, railroad signals, microphones, even radios.

Sometimes we don't keep a careful enough eye on things, though. When David was six, in the midst of electric exploration, he tried putting the ends of a pipe cleaner into an electric socket, burning it up, scorching his fingers, and scaring everybody else! Perennially favorite, the chemistry experiments use real chemicals and test tubes, and every so often a serious researcher pulls out these items and conducts his own experiments, perhaps noting down his results.

Freely available as toys are magnets and iron filings and a variety of metal materials to experiment with. Cellophane viewers give opportunities to mix colors. Every couple of days a little child is filling a sink with water to see what will float and what will not, whether liquid from a small container will fit into a larger (with vocabulary from Mother about cups, pints, quarts, gallons), and to find out what will dissolve and what won't—salt, honey, pepper, chili powder, poster paint.

Graduating to another dimension of bathtub play, twelve-year-old David constructed a model of the Nautilus that would sink and rise with air pressure. We have magnifying glasses, a small, cheap, but usable microscope, and magnifying mirrors that leap into occasional popularity, children roaming together avidly throughout the house to examine this or that. I remember Sammy's excitement at age ten as he rediscovered the microscope, putting in fly wings and wool fibers and hair and leaves. The children run through a shameful amount of batteries experimenting with the light from the flashlights—how it reacts in the mirror, around corners, under the blankets, in one's mouth and—unfortunately—in someone else's eyes!

And again in this category of casual science, we receive a never-ending succession of rocks, some of them unusual and lovely, feathers, leaves, flowers, twigs, and small creatures such as toads, insects, and sometimes little birds or baby animals, for us to classify, observe, enjoy.

We reserve the finer microscope for more formal situations, such as gathering pond water and looking at the creatures therein, or sitting outside during a snowfall, waiting until the glass slides and 'scope reduce in temperature enough not to melt the flakes, and then watching the wonder of the beautiful crystals. We always enjoy looking at purchased, prepared slides; what memories we have of passing around the microscope, everyone eager for his peep at a flea or diatom. We have followed our way through the standard microscope experiments, such as looking at a dyed onion skin and at the linings of our cheeks.

Weather always fascinates, and during our stay at Rarotonga we had a first-hand experience with an extreme: a hurricane. At first we found it incredible that moving air could work so much damage, uprooting trees and dismembering houses—and destroying all the ripening fruit and garden crops. We checked out books from the local library to find out all we could about hurricanes and cyclones, predictably diverting to Dorothy and the Wizard of Oz. The children also like to follow the more usual weather, putting out cups to measure rainfall, constructing anemometers to measure the wind, discussing the origins of storms, and comparing temperatures at different localities, such as in the hills and in the town and by the mouth of a canyon.

Living by the sea or out in the country, children who spend time outdoors can learn to know when a storm is coming, or compare the qualities of wind from different directions. They can walk outside in the rain, stand in the falling snow, watch the irrevocable onslaught of a mudslide. We endured one right in our driveway one year; and during a previous year, we drove to a very large one in a nearby neighborhood, one that even moved a house that stood in its way. In the spring and fall we chart the time and location of the rising sun over the mountains, amazed by its rapid progress once the seasons start to roll.

Living by a river, we observe and comment on the fluctuating level and force of the flow and enjoy all the wild things that live there. When we lived in the hills, every year a shallow pond nearby would fill just for a few months in the spring, when it would come alive with tadpoles and then little frogs. Where did they come from? Where did they go? We raised tadpoles and let them go into another pond. We also tried raising salamander tadpoles, but the children did not feed them consistently; and so they went home to the pond prematurely one day when I awoke to find that one had devoured his brother!

Every year, the children, alive with spring, love to experiment in the garden. I am learning to be a good gardener myself, having had plenty of failures before; carrying babies and tagging along toddlers has worsened my record. Avraham, on the other hand, gardens superbly, and when he puts together a garden, what joy the children have planting the seeds, watching them sprout and grow, develop, and bear. When Avraham doesn't garden, I put in small, intensive plots, which the children always help me with.

Some of them, such as Avi, are natural gardeners. He doesn't mind digging, pulling weeds, or watering, and how he loves to plant! At four, he painstakingly cleaned a lot of squash and pumpkin seeds that were destined for the compost heap, dried them carefully, bagged and labelled them for the garden in the coming spring. "There's lots of dirt now," he commented during a freak February thaw, "let's plant!" His sprawling pumpkin vines, begun in February, covered a front flower plot and produced a large crop.

We sprout alfalfa seeds, and mung beans, and occasionally try an avocado tree. In Rarotonga we tasted the surprising delicacy of a sprouting coconut!

Because of my own interest, the children can identify many of the edible and medicinal plants growing in different localities we have been in.

While in New Zealand, we admired a completely different set of wildings than we have seen in Utah, tagging along with old women skilled in Maori medicine to try to catch the native names and uses. Every year when a particularly interesting plant, such as catnip, peppermint, or mullein comes into season, we all troop out to gather what I want, helping to hang it to dry. Less skilled in identifying trees and shrubs, I run to the books to help us identify other things growing around us.

In addition to the rocks that we collect and label, we find ourselves often talking about geological formations. How did those layers of rock curve and twist so dramatically? How were canyons formed? How did these metamorphic rocks get here? (The children can usually distinguish between the different types of rock.) Whence this bench, these hills, this valley? Sometimes I know the answers, sometimes not, and what we cannot find in books, we ask from cooperative teachers at the high school or university.

Every year someone wants to make a vinegar/baking soda volcano, and sometimes we vary this with a glass bowl full of marbles and beads, using mothballs to dance up and down. We have also grown crystal gardens with salt, blueing and ammonia, though these never turned out as beautiful as we have hoped.

Having had guinea pigs and goats, chickens and cats gave us the opportunity to observe reproduction in a natural way. We watch the goats mate, gestate over a long time, and give birth to beautiful, perfect little kids, who nurse avidly but still leave us enough milk for our porridge. We goggle over the fluffy, nervous little chicks who nonetheless grow into gangly, awkward teenagers and then into hens; or roosters who somehow become fierce, aggressive, the possessors of piercing voices. Sometimes a kitten dies, and we bury her in the yard, suffering sore hearts for a few days. We like to watch the young calves or sheep nurse from their mothers.

When we slaughter the flock of meat chickens that we raise, we observe the growth of feathers and the digestive systems and eliminative systems, which I was astonished to see the children accept very matter-of-factly—much better than their squeamish mother. We begin to understand that whenever we eat meat, an animal has given its life for us to be able to do so. We enjoy the tactile adventure of finding smooth brown eggs amongst the prickly straw in the hens' nests. And we accept the sometimes unnerving reality that milk squirts out of the teats of rather smelly, warm, and very alive creatures. I feel it is very important for children to connect with the sources of their food, and to see it as part of the life cycle they participate in.

Occasionally I assign a book on science to one of the older children to read, to make sure that they are assimilating and reviewing concepts and vocabulary. Often, however, I smile in delight to see someone independently perusing a volume on physics or chemistry. We have not yet memorized formulas or figured out the relative distances between stars, but when the time comes for that, it will proceed naturally and without force. At the moment of writing this chapter, twelve-year-old David sits in the schoolroom studying a volume on electrical circuitry, preparing a list of materials to buy so that he can make an electric organ. He has advanced in this subject without any encouragement from me.

During our stay in the southern hemisphere, we were awed at the totally different night sky, understanding why many astronomers make special trips there to enjoy the different constellations, the Southern Cross, Scorpio, Sagittarius. We would like to get a flexible star map, Night Star, a dome that helps you identify formations at any time and anywhere.

We are studying science when we read about the development of the baby in the womb, and branch off into genetics, a subject of great interest to children of all ages. The older children checked out a book about clones to augment this study! We all find it fascinating to compare the stages of growth of different kinds of fetuses, in addition to human: dogs, goats, cows, pigs.

We have been lucky to live a half hour from Brigham Young University, where we can enjoy a superior life science museum, with ever-changing displays and a superior room prepared for children with touching fingers. We also like to visit the Ossuary, the dinosaur museum, recently renovated, again with tactile displays and interactive videos about the past. Each of the science departments features interesting displays, and if we are fortunate, we will run across a graduate student or faculty member with time to answer our questions.

Recently we bought some science kits and boxes through *Learning at Home* in Hawaii—a primary and intermediate box of science experiments, and some kits for studying light and going backyard science. Once a week, each child produced an experiment to show the rest of the family. So far our favorites have been the classic of putting a jar over a candle sitting in a pan of water. As the candle uses up the air in the jar, the partial vacuum sucks the water into the jar—drama! We also loved the experiment of boiling the water out of a gallon honey can, quickly lidding it, and watching the partial vacuum crumple the can.

We worked with insects, sand, snow, leaves, rocks--on and on.

The older children found some of this old hat, of course, because of their reading and previous experiences; but they followed through to teach the younger ones. These little ones really loved choosing a card and preparing each his own experiment.

We bought an inexpensive microscope from *Learning Things* (68A Broadway, Arlington Mass. 02174), which provides a super catalog full of things you may never have thought of (or that you may not even know the uses of!). Their prices are fully retail, but we think the stuff is worth it. The microscope (which *Learning Things* claims is nigh-indestructible) opened up pond water, hair, bugs, skin, and (ah!) snowflakes to us. We also bought others things--a pantograph, for enlarging and reducing pictures; a simple adjustable camera, black-and-white film, developing tank and chemicals; a couple of geoboards to make geometric experiments with rubber bands, a prism, and so on. There was plenty more there to buy if you had the resources; I would have loved to purchase some solar materials. These science materials make science (and math) activities so much more accessible, particularly the photograph--even contact printing and developing without a darkroom.

With a Ph.D. friend in science, David began a high-school biology course at age 12, working through correspondence (the friend lives in New Jersey). In addition to guiding him through the text *Modern Biology*, our friend provided interesting question and lab activities. This course proved to be pretty rigorous, but absorbing and expanding for David. Unfortunately, however, family activities and later half-day school enrollment and half-day correspondence school enrollment cut off this productive correspondence.

I point this out because people sometimes worry about providing in-depth experiences in certain subjects--usually math and science--that they feel inadequate in. I think that there is a world of helpers ready to teach children things you may not feel skilful at. The older children went once a week to a Ham Radio course--as the youngest students there--and worked toward getting their radio licenses. I also found that the Boy Scout merit badges expand their skills and interests in many subjects. Our particular area provides lots of resource people that love their subjects and want to help kids excel. A retired engineer for General Motors Corporation taught the children computerized automobile design. Another friend, a retired schoolteacher, helped them construct a model airplane.

The larger picture here says that even though the children are at home, we are not limited to the resources of home. In fact, with a little ingenuity, we can provide much more depth and breadth by ranging out of the home into neighborhood and community resources.

When you encourage children to thoroughly enjoy and explore their interests and to find the answers to their questions, you don't have to worry about   scientific method. They want to be sure that they understand things correctly; they want to miss nothing. When Sammy attended school for some months in New Zealand, he was amazed at how much he knew. He attributed it to the good teaching of the New Zealand instructors, because he had not been taught any of this (formally) at home. We had to tell him, laughing, that you don't have to be taught in order to learn something, and that he had received a first-rate education indeed before he ever stepped foot into a classroom.

As the children's intellectual capacities and interests mature, they move naturally to more and more complex scientific studies. The parents' job remains the same, to provide suitable materials and to put books in the children's way to facilitate their studies. If someone seems to come to a standstill, I may assign a book to read or a set of experiments to do. Usually, though, the young person patiently does the assignment, and then branches out into some other study in another area!

Quite apart from the superior science education a homeschooler can receive, this happy approach to science makes a lot of fun and interest for the parents and the whole family, leading them to enjoy and understand the many things about the world they might not have known. I enjoy that particular thrill of looking into the books, "Let's find out." Always on the watch for something new and interesting in nature, we sharpen our love and appreciation for the world around us, which I think should be the meaning behind all science study anyhow!

SOCIAL STUDIES

As with our science explorations, one might be surprised at our lack of formal work in social studies, with such high performances on the standardized tests.

When the children are small, we sit together reading Childcraft and library books about other lands. They like these sessions, and enjoy preparing some tortillas or tofu or mutton stew. Once in a while we make flags from these different countries, and we also locate them on the globe and in the atlas. We were once given a textbook series by Bowman-Noble treating some basic social studies concepts in an attractive and intelligent way, and sometimes we would read parts of these together and perhaps try some of the many interesting projects suggested there. And we frequently visit the post office, police stations, business offices, industries, and factories and fairs to understand firsthand some of these doings.

As the children begin to read, the spine of their social studies must be the Landmark series of books. Written by a scholar in a particular speciality, each volume discusses some personality or segment of history on about a third- to fifth-grade level of reading. We don't let the simplicity of the text fool us though; this is real history or biography, full of exciting and authentic detail. We bought dozens of these Landmark books through a used bookstore that acquires them in the East, where they are very popular. Even as the children grow older, they reread them for enjoyment. Typically, crafts projects shoot off from these readings: someone made a Monitor and a Merrimac, stream-worthy, while someone else branched off into coonskin caps and World War I battle maps.

We also buy older copies of *National Geographic* from the thrift shop. Although these might be only slightly out of date, perhaps a year or two, perhaps older, they only cost a quarter each. The children read them freely, the younger ones studying the beautiful photographs, and both their science and social studies knowledge are enriched.

At the homeschool conferences held annually in Utah, a used-book salesman makes available some excellent materials. We bought many volumes of the Life World Library at 50¢ each. Full of wonderful photos, graphs, charts, maps, and a very readable text, these volumes too receive frequent use.

Because of Avraham's and my own interest in American Indians and also in the Soviet Union, we have purchased many paperbacks on these subjects, rereading them now and again, discussing them, drawing the children into the books out of curiosity. We cannot match the young homeschooler of our acquaintance, however, who, fascinated by Indians, educated himself thoroughly on the subject, able to identify tribe and location when observing an artifact or hearing of a cultural practice.

Perhaps the best of our social studies has been born from our travels. Whenever we plan a trip, we check out every book we can find on the area we are going to. We try to understand something about the geography, the language, the cultural practices, the point of view. Prior to our trip to Mexico, the children were tutored in Spanish and customs for some months; though when we actually lived in the place, few of them ventured to use the language! While in Alaska, we used the library to learn all about early explorers, geography, history of place names, migrations, and so on. We could not read anything local while we were in Mexico, but we spent much time talking to people and getting their points of view.

Prior to our trip to Rarotonga, we looked everywhere for information about the island. Encyclopedias yielded almost nothing; some of the Time-Life books featured articles, but I kept feeling that we were missing the essence of the thing. Only when we actually arrived in the place were we able to experience and learn what the social reality was. Basically typical Polynesian islands, happily living on a subsistence economy, the Cook Islands were changed forever when the first Christian missionaries arrived in the 1900s. They clothed the almost-naked islanders in modest gear covering ankles and wrists and necks, and drew them into an avid religious practice that has remained extremely active to this day. They brought goods and tools which transformed the island life radically. And they brought liquor, still a source of tragedy; one neighbor lost a son, newly married and full of bright promise, in a motorcycle accident! He was struck by a drunk driver, a common occurrence.

Nowadays the essence of what is Polynesian is nigh-obliterated by the overflow of western culture: vehicles, foods, clothing, alcohol, incessant videos (most homes have a VCR, even if there is little else, and the machines run from dawn till late in the night, without much discrimination about what is shown). Although people have little money (most work for the government at a median income of NZ $6,000, worth about two-thirds that in American dollars), they are ever drawn into the imported foods and goods of western culture. Gardening and gathering, heretofore the staple of the country's economy, have dwindled alarmingly.

Little of this reality appeared in any of the books we read, but we found ourselves absorbed in it and caring very much about it. We discovered the writings of Ronald Syme, a British author who early settled himself in Rarotonga, eventually marrying a local woman, writing passionately and well about these changes. We also worked ploddingly through Rarotongan Maori, though it took a couple of months before I could even distinguish words and place names and family names. We learned to dance, tried to learn some of the songs, and by necessity absorbed the customs of eating and celebrating.

Every wedding, missionary farewell, or other occasion included a feast, where all food, standard and predictable (boiled taro, kumara, certain salads, fried fish, boiled arrowroot, papaya, as well as purchased cookies and some other imported foods) was placed on a big central table. After speeches and a prayer, everyone shuffled around, filling his plate, sometimes enormously, because some families don't get a great deal to eat at home. No forks or other utensils are used, and people scrape up sauces with their fingers (finally I began carrying forks in my basket to distribute slyly to other *papa'as* who were as uneasy as I was).

So many cultural practices colored everyday life. In Polynesian culture, status and rank play an important part, and this transferred into the Church. Working in the women's church organization, which is called Relief Society, trying to help branch Relief Societies reorganize themselves, we ran into it. After listening to a president explain that her counselors never attended meetings and never helped with anything, we recommended that she release them and allow other sisters an opportunity for leadership. Here she burst into tears and said that she would give them another chance; for being released from a position carried dishonor, as it would in former times for someone to lose rank!

Similarly, there always seemed to be some pulling and pushing for rank and power among the different local leaderships, a source of puzzlement and frustration to the missionaries and outside leaders trying to improve the Church situation. But on the positive side, at missionary farewells, everyone would give generously to the departing elder or sister in typical fashion. And sometimes people would come over to our home and casually visit, relaxed and comfortable in a way that eludes most of us westerners.

Every week we would go the library and check out books on the Pacific and on Rarotonga, and there were plenty of them. Local people also gave us a good rundown on their feelings about the current situation and how it had developed. Even when neighbor children came over to visit, without knowing it we were busily assimilating language patterns and cultural points of view. When we arrived in the island, seven-year-old Yoni could not yet swim. An older neighbor boy found this impossible and not a little funny. "Why didn't you just go down to the ocean and learn?" he queried, not able to visualize the fact that the ocean in America was located almost nine hundred miles from our home!

During our stay in New Zealand, we followed pretty much the same pattern of study, although there our school-age children attended school, where they absorbed much more of the culture, the language patterns and accent, the mental set and point of view, as well as cultural practices. Also, the schools actively taught some Maori culture, consisting mostly of singing and dance, but language and culture as well. In particular, five-year-old Chava brought home many songs and dances.

At home, we eagerly read everything we could about Maori culture and history, bought some tapes and began learning by assimilation some of the songs, and quizzed our Maori friends at Church whenever we had questions. The cultural pattern in New Zealand followed the typical tragedy of native peoples in many places. The Polynesians came to the land, settled it, and lived successfully there (we cannot say peacefully, because these Maoris were traditionally fierce warriors). Along came white explorers, who by force and bloodshed demanded the land for themselves, eventually dominating the culture as well. Soon all Maori children were attending school, for many ugly years forbidden to speak their own language and in all ways made to feel awkward and inferior, a feeling that persists to this day. (A recent renaissance of Maori culture is restoring some pride.) Most people lost their Maori language and skills, and modern-day efforts to reteach them are only partly successful. At some point, however, many people have drawn the line. "We have come halfway," commented one Maori friend, "and we can go no further."

Because I felt that many traditional Polynesian practices, such as the life-style of the extended family, the warm social kiss and embrace, the open-handed generosity, the nurturing of babies and children, and many other small but important ways, were more positive than their *pakeha* (western culture) counterparts, I felt the poignancy of the Maori situation. In contrast to Rarotonga, where the negative influences of the West are accepted pretty much universally, in New Zealand we met intelligent and articulate people who are striving to restore the good things and eliminate the bad. Unfortunately the predominant culture makes change very difficult.

I detail our social studies in these new cultures to show you how we have tried to make other cultures and countries real to ourselves. I have always felt that the tragedy of social studies in American schools was the "we and they" attitude that we often adopt, assuming that our ways are superior and others' quaint but inferior. Even at home in the United States, I try to help the children see other cultural practices as just as valid and important and useful as our own. Reading about the histories and cultures of other peoples, we try to feel with them, to put ourselves into them. I consider my goal part-way met when we get together with folks from other places, and the children talk to them and accept them naturally, not overly reacting to differences in appearance and dress.

As for the more particular studies of geography and history, I use that same technique for making maps and globes and interesting books available, using them myself, discussing them, and allowing the children free access to them. Predictably, children such as Sammy soon amass plenty of precise information about these things, and though I am sure that we have plenty of gaps, the children fill in many of these as they continue to read and study. When I observe a particular weakness, I will sometimes explain things myself, such as when some of the younger children were faltering in their understanding of civil boundaries. We drew big charts of towns, cities, counties, states, countries, until they began to conceptualize these arbitrary borders.

Similarly, when legislative sessions bring up controversial subjects, we spend some formal time reading and explaining the Constitution, discussing the reasons that certain proposed laws violate or fall within the limits of that document. And sometimes we have to correct certain misconceptions about early leaders of our country, pointing out that some historians like to emphasize the negative without seeing the whole, positive picture of historical personalities.

Our boys have always loved war history, and though I don't like it much myself, Avraham has made sure that they get the books they are interested in. Feeling that they might be facing war-like situations when they are grown, he thinks that reading about war history when they are young will help them understand. Certain of the children really get into this subject: for example, Avi, at four, would sit through a half hour or more of detailed history about Genghis Kahn or Napoleon Bonaparte, sometimes exceeding my own interest in the subject! He seems to intuitively understand and appreciate stories about military campaigns and conquests.

The children who already read pore over the thick war-history books with great interest as well; I am sure these are at least better than the senselessly violent programs many other children watch on TV!

As in our science studies, I occasionally assign a book on American history or other subjects when I feel a child needs more background. David, at twelve, and deeply interested in Egypt, was assigned a thorough-going study of an excellent book on the pyramids, writing chapter summaries as he went along (much better than just answering questions at the end of a chapter). Sometimes we play board games asking questions about American history. Although the children don't receive precisely the same information about the subject as the schoolchildren do in their textbooks, I feel they are getting a good background, and I am certain that they retain at least as much as their peers!

We have yet to maintain a successful language-study program, though we have ventured into Spanish, Hebrew, and Maori. As the children enter adolescence, I may initiate a formal study of Spanish for all of them, considering that an important language to have. Certainly if our family lives in Israel for a time, as we may someday do, we will launch more thoroughly into Hebrew and perhaps Arabic. Realizing that young children learn languages best, we have nonetheless lacked the consistency and discipline to work at bilingualism in the home—though both Avraham and I have something to offer. We seem to be following the more traditional path of having the adolescent children learn languages.

Recently, however, we have found a delightful language course for young children, "Willey's World," published by The Lyceum, P.O. Box 66, Payson UT. With an ear-training approach, young children absorb new language as they did their own. The young children especially love the tapes and books.

As with our science studies, homeschoolers need to distinguish between this open, facilitating approach and neglect. Interested in the subjects myself, I make sure that lots of books and materials enter the hands of the children, and we discuss issues and history and stories all the time. I insist on certain books being read if a child seems to be slacking off in his own pursuits. We often experiment with foods from other cultures, and we enjoy good visits with people from other places whenever we can. In addition, because Avraham's parents are Dutch, because he is a citizen of Israel and New Zealand, because my forebears were English, Irish, German, and Russian, we continue a lively study into these subjects so close to our hearts. "What part of me is Russian?" muses Yoni, pondering the fact that several of my Jewish lines go directly to that country.

In contrast, I have noticed homeschool families with many children just letting go of these and other studies. The children might continue to read on their own, but this uncaring attitude doesn't produce the consistent excellence that should characterize our homeschools. Above all, our social studies should help us appreciate, understand and love other peoples and cultures; we fail if we do less than that.

CRAFTS

"Why are you teaching that boy weaving when he's not even reading?" asks a neighbor.

"Well," I answer, perhaps somewhat defensively, "I can cite some good, sound educational reasons. Weaving goes from left to right, as you know—the other way, too, of course—and it demands planning and executing patterns that repeat themselves; that relates to reading. It lengthens the attention span. You have to follow directions."

My friend is impressed, and perhaps convinced. But these are not the real reasons that seven-year-old Yoni would spend the morning weaving, or why the rest of my children pass much of their days weaving, sawing and sanding, painting, sewing, sculpting—creating. Our reasons reach deeper into an educational philosophy that has formulated much of what our homeschool is all about.

For us, crafts help shape the study in our homeschool. When David, at ten, began to admire the Statue of Liberty, he read everything in the house on the subject, including some poetry, and then got a hunk of wood and his (sharp) carving tools. To scale, he made a lady-with-the-light that now sits on his dresser. What's the point of all that? Well, he studied from his own interest, giving the history of the Statue of Liberty a special life for himself. As he sculpted, what he learned formed images in his muscles and in his mind. Woodcarving takes time; during his work he told the younger children all about his research, and everyone now feels something about climbing up to the statue's head, about the restoration of the park, and the oxidation of the metal. They all long to visit her, though I tell them that the Big City would tire them out physically and spiritually. The children, especially David, won't forget what they know about the Statue of Liberty, and I have been able to discuss the founding of New York City, emigration, the incredible economics of Manhattan, and other such subjects with them.

After our morning schooltime follows the real learning of the day. I set the children loose and have available lots of crafts materials, and usually they get to work or ask me, "What can I make?" or "May I use the sewing machine?" Sometimes the readers read all day, sometimes for days

139

on end. Sometimes they all play in the sandbox using water and homemade boats. This is such a popular activity that visiting children cannot resist it. Once, when a family with teenagers happened to be here, their big boys couldn't keep away from it!

You might like to know what kinds of crafts we do. I'll mention the ones we repeat the most, and then explain why I feel they're so useful.

Sewing

I read in *Mother's Almanac* that, while children can very definitely harm a typewriter (alas, we have found that is true. . .), they can't do too much damage to a sewing machine. I start my children with embroidery thread, decorating a hooped fabric when they are just three or so. They continue to demand this for years; my older boys still like it, and at ten David designed a cozy fireplace with a "Home Sweet Home" curling over it. As soon as the children can understand that they must lower the pressure foot before sewing (and not mess with the tension knob), I let them use the sewing machine. Usually they just scroll lines of stitches all over a plain piece of material and admire their wonderful designs. Sooner or later we make a bag and I show them how to run a cord through the turned-over hem at the top.

Bean bags follow, and after that the children make stuffed animals. Although I have bought a book on the subject, and occasionally check similar ones out of the library, they also like designing and making their own animals. Sammy, at nine, had a bedful of creatures he sewed and stuffed. He related to these creations; a gift of one of them to another child is a special gift indeed. Making a grid and enlarging patterns, following instructions, visualizing parts-to-whole, and long-suffering and patience are the fruits of these sewing sessions. And, as you can guess from a gingham dog and calico cat, they can also result from the child's reading.

After the stuffed-animal period (which can go on for a long time), the children sometimes want to make clothes for dolls or for themselves. Doll-clothes we design and sew together. Real clothes we cut out of patterns; I help the child piece together the garment, and I draw ballpoint-pen lines for the seams. Usually the hems are not too straight, and if a child insists on using navy-blue thread on a white T-shirt, he can see for himself that something isn't quite right (especially if the seams waver, as they always do). But what can compare with the pride and joy of a child who says, "Yes, I made it myself!" When David sewed as part of his Intermediate School Curriculum in New Zealand, he was perhaps the only boy showing expertise to do it.

And—though perhaps today it need not even be said—our boy whose beloved stuffed toys and homemade flannel blanket adorned his bed is perhaps one of the the most masculine of the lot.

Wood

About five years ago my husband Avraham put together a long-nagged-for workbench, heavy and sturdy with space for tool storage and a heavy-duty vise bolted on. With scraps from the lumber store, the children mass-produced various kinds of boats for a long time, graduating to cars and trains when I purchased wheels from the crafts store. Although we had a variety of saws available, most of the children chose to cut (even straight cuts) with the coping saw, which has a good sharp edge; however, it didn't cut really straight, and most of the contraptions produced with it were slightly wavy. A prison-bar mousetrap, a marble-rolling maze, and various folk toys, such as climbing bears, typify what rolled off that workbench.

One year, however, we purchased a scroll saw, a light-weight, relatively inexpensive electric saw that is bolted to the workbench and sports a rotating sander attachment. The children's working-bench world changed forever! No one cut his fingers on the machine, though we got it when Yoni was six and he used it frequently, along with his two older brothers. Interestingly, Chava, then four, and Avi, then two, wouldn't attempt the saw; they seemed to know that they were too young. With the power behind that machine, plus an electric drill we got second-hand, you would be amazed at the creations my children have made.

David, at eleven, crafted a Revolutionary War chess set, regularly in use between the three boys. He painted the pieces gray and blue and somehow they learned to play chess. (I didn't teach them! David finally taught them.) Although we don't have a television, the children somewhere learned about transformers (as in the cartoon show and toy store). David crafted many different transformers, smoothed and painted and very clever—a camera, two dinosaur-types, a gun, and so on.

Sammy has cut and sanded some old-fashioned-type guns (although I don't forbid guns, I insist that no one points them at anyone else). He invented various wooden board games with teeny pieces all smooth and painted. He also did some nice free-form sculptures. Yoni, at seven, not yet skillful and patient in using wood, yet sculpted some very nice boats and, one remarkable day, a beautiful space shuttle with removable module. As you can imagine, the children's friends delight in coming over so they can use the machinery and produce objects d'art of their own; David's transformers are particularly in demand. I listen with delight as he uses that old technique on his friends: "You can do it by yourself; you don't need me. Sure you can do it!"

The vise and hand tools, too, don't lie idle; the children still nail and file with them. The younger children use them frequently. Until Avi, I had never seen a baby eighteen months old hammer a nail. He never made anything that you can identify, but he was great at filing and hammering.

When we took off for our year in the South Pacific, we thought we would rest the woodworking for that year, and took no tools along (we couldn't haul any with us anyway because of luggage restrictions). But during our stay in Rarotonga, David fairly itched for woodworking. For Christmas he begged for a coping saw and a hand drill, so we complied. He created some interesting animated figures, some heads with movable eyes and mouths, some foot-high marionettes that supplied happy dramas for us all. Chess sets and other games rolled off the bench, especially after we supplemented the tools with a small, screw-on vise.   He also created a threading toy from a branch of the aromatic ti tree for baby Sarah, and he made, with two large cross sections of ti tree, a decoration that astonishingly revealed a map of New Zealand in the wood's grain.

Before long, David knew that wood was his best medium; he felt confident that he could produce anything he wanted, though for a long time he stuck to the miniature rather than to full-sized, utilitarian projects. His nickel hockey and table soccer games, finished with detail and care, amuse us for hours, especially tantalizing young visitors. He crafted and tole-painted a lovely toothbrush holder when we lacked one—much nicer than a two-dollar plastic variety! His kachina dolls to scale contain the immaculate details of the originals, including feathers and fabrics. He made wooden toys and boomerangs and, with Marion Millett's *Working Wooden Toys* for instructions, some marvelous action toys, men sawing wood, acrobats balancing, horse-back riders, ducks quacking, and so on. He designed and built a useful wooden clock, decorated with cartoon characters from *Footrot Flats*, a New Zealand fad. For a Christmas gift, he crafted an aesthetic coatstand for our friends, and just now he is designing a pantograph, figuring out the calibrations to reduce and enlarge the different proportions. Writing this, I am sure that I have neglected to mention the majority of his projects!

Following David's example, the children consider wood a natural and easy medium to work with. They throw together toy helicopters or tops or game pieces without any trouble, and when the Cub Scouts made wooden stools, Sammy proceeded with nonchalant confidence. Having regarded woodworking with awe as I grew up, I am grateful for these self-assured projects, especially since they develop skills that can prove useful all life long.

Paper

Some people shake their heads at our profligate use of paper—about a ream a month. This costs about $5 to $9. We also use quite a bit of end cuts of printing stock (free) and roll ends of newsprint (also free, at least at our small-town printer's). Paper serves many more purposes than writing, however; it is for painting, planning never-before-seen machines, sending missiles to Grandma (illustrated) and missiles around the house (paper airplanes). It is the stuff of homemade books and stories and poems and origami (we have a couple of good books on this subject; I especially like *Origami, The Art of Paperfolding* by Robert Harbin) and paper-cuts.

To let you visualize the impact of paper, I remember a grand trip our family made to California one year. We spent a couple of days each way at a hot springs, we visited the beach, and we even went to Disneyland. The children seemed to enjoy themselves, but only came to a sense of peace when we arrived home. They all rushed in the house, pulled out pencil and paper, and silently set to work. Nowadays we take paper and its paraphernalia camping.

So our small monthly investment pays its way. I cannot begin to describe the creations that come out of the paper consumed in our household. The children create incredible robots, rockets and flying machines, complete with power systems and gears and landing arrangements. They plan their wood projects on paper, often in parts to be assembled. They paint (in watercolors and acrylics; they use poster paints on the larger sheets of newsprint). They practice typing; Chava, at four, steadfastly produced the names of her family and friends and the guinea pigs. They enlarge grids or create patterns for stuffed animals.

When we checked out from the library a book of Chinese papercuts, David and Yoni reproduced most of the scissor-cuts (we didn't have an X-acto knife sharp enough for the knife cuts); they were exquisite. When birthdays come around, the children paint gift-wrap for their homemade presents. Once every few weeks, each may become inspired by something they've read and create a poem or story on paper (I encourage them to write these in their journals, but usually only a blank sheet of paper suffices). I remember the gusto of this wry creation:

> G-g-gorilla,
> Ugly gorilla,
> You're the only chimpanzee that I adore.
> When the baboon shines,
> Over the monkey house,
> I'll be waiting at the c-c-capuchin door.

Several years ago we really got into book-making, a passion that reemerges every few months. Using the directions from Wiseman's *Making Things*, we stitched books the traditional way and covered them with wallpaper from a big book of samples we scrounged from a paint supply store, or sometimes covered them with bought fabric. David made endless books of various sizes and shapes, used as gifts and vehicles for long, complicated stories and illustrations. Sammy still has his butterfly-shaped book from that era, with the story of a butterfly who flew up to the moon but decided that home is best after all. Chava created a sweet volume entitled *The World*, decorated with hearts and flowers, telling about birds, nests, snow melting and spring coming, all precisely illustrated.

Wiseman also supplied directions for paper-making. Our children like to produce homemade paper from time to time, although instead of mushing the pulp with their fingers they've graduated to blending it in the blender. They use their hand-produced sheets to write pirate letters mailed to their friends miles away.

One of the nicest inventions of our family came one winter with our two woodstoves. The children took two sheets of paper, one as a pad and the other for the creations. On the woodstove they drew designs with crayons, which melted into translucent beauties. Visiting children got into this one! As you can imagine, this used up a lot of paper, but it was worth it. The children also made wax paper by rubbing candles onto paper on the top of the woodstove.

What else they do with paper I can hardly begin to describe. They make themselves good-deed charts with it—Sammy's contained commitments to do jumping-jacks and to read to Chava. They line their animals' cages with it. They list their I-wants on it (Sammy loves to peruse the baby-chick catalog and make lists of what he'll buy when we get a small farm). They design alphabet robots with the typewriter. They love to light fires in the woodstoves or in the fire-ring out by their homemade playhouse, where they make toast. They construct flashcards out of it to test each other. They make paper money. They design complex cities with roads for toy cars. They make treasure hunts for each other. They write notes to each other and to me—Avi at four, gave one addressed Avraham: "Buy me a flashlight!" As they grow older, they create scripts for puppet shows or homemade movies and write adventure stories. They contrive so many uses with that necessary staple, paper, I cannot possibly recall them all.

Clay and Wax

Not far from our little house in the foothills, the children found a nice bank of natural clay. Trooping excitedly home, they carted plastic bags and spades to the site, hauling home big lumps of it. They didn't sieve and clean it in the prescribed way (I recommended it, but they were not interested); they just started sculpting. Yoni made a traditional pot, which fell apart when drying because of the high sand content in the clay. David made a hogan which dried okay; he fired it in the ashes of the woodstove, and there it fell apart. Sammy made animal figures.

Whenever I bring home a ten-pound bag of clay, the children work fiercely until it is all gone. We try to contain the mess on newspapers, and the creations dry on the children's bureaus. A nearby art shop has given classes which some of our children have attended, learning how to control the shapes so the pieces can be fired into permanence. Clay releases tensions and helps the children see three-dimensionally.

Sometimes we make play-dough or even buy it, but it is not as satisfying as real clay. We have made cornstarch play-dough, very elegant and smooth. One year we created lovely Christmas tree ornaments from this dough, painting and varnishing them afterward.

That year we also made tin-punch ornaments out of aluminum trays, coloring them with permanent markers. These made delightful, lasting ornaments. Each year we save a few of these homemade treasures, setting up the tree and spending the weeks before Christmas creating new ornaments, such as Ojos de Dios, paper twirls and twists, cookie ornaments (which never last until Christmas), as well as the usual popcorn strings, etc. We often check out books containing patterns for ornaments from all over the world, spinning off from our creation studies into Japan or Sweden or Mexico. One year we made kikuchi dolls from Japan. We also ate tofu and plum candy, listened to some new and surprising music, and read Japanese stories.

Sometimes we paint greenware like the crafts classes recommend, but these decorations nearly always break. We haven't gotten into decorating poured ceramics yet—though the children want to try—because I have felt it paralleled coloring in coloring books. Likely I'll give in and we'll have a go at that too.

Perhaps into this category falls bread-dough sculpting, which often happens when I bake. The children model fanciful sculptures, decorated with nuts, seeds, and raisins, which they eat for lunch.

We have always liked candle-making, but the usual method of melting the wax, pouring it into the molds, inserting the wick, and letting it harden has seemed too tame.

Instead, the children melt old candles in old tin cans over hot water (or sometimes over the woodstove, or sometimes, with great patience, in tin cans directly on a stove burner!), extracting the old wicks as they emerge. They add crayons to color the mixture, and then remove the can from the heat. When the wax is cool enough to touch (which they sometimes facilitate by pouring it out on to a paper plate covered with plastic wrap), they roll it into shapes. All of the children, even the two-year-old, participate in this activity, usually without my help.

The older artists sculpt complicated shapes, usually busts and heads, which they contrive to do interesting things: often a skull is shaped in red wax and covered afterwards with white, so that when it melts, it looks like it is bleeding—often through the eyes, I am horrified to report. We have enjoyed a passable George Washington bust, though when it melted it was a bit disturbing. Sometimes the children arrange for the melted wax to come out the mouth, under a large, pointed nose, a cause for much laughter. And the little children enjoy watching their cones and balls lit up at mealtimes, just as much as the older ones revel in sophisticated creations.

We have never had a fire—though we have suffered some burnt fingers—and the children burn the candles at the dinner table themselves.

This year we bought some candle decorating wax, thin colored sheets of beeswax which you cut and shape into decorations for plain candles. As usual, the children used the material passionately till it was all gone. We were especially excited to craft a person with his arms wrapped around the candle, as well as the usual repeated patterns and shapes.

With crayons we have also made some crude experiments with batik. Someday I would like to advance to the more sophisticated methods using wax and dye.

Glass

One year I yearned to try stained glass. My mother had collected all the gear for it and decided the craft didn't suit her, so she sent her tools, and we bought a few things as well. Using scrap glass purchased by the pound, we scored and broke glass, a bit frightening at first but easier as we gained confidence, and learned to fit the shapes together using the copper-foil method, which avoids prolonged contact with lead—better for children and for expectant mothers too. The children all enjoyed cutting the glass, even the very young ones who could not make anything out of it! The older children made several lovely light-catchers; since it was Christmas time they peddled them to the neighbors, earning about $20.00. This special craft, like papier maché, required my complete attention and so usually consumed entire mornings at a time. We must admit to more failures than usual, because getting all the shapes to fit and getting the foil to stick challenged us! David did all the soldering, acquiring yet another skill which has served us when repairs are needed.

As a kind of finale to our stained-glass year, David, disdaining my mother's multitudinous pattern books, designed and made a good-looking bed-lamp, featuring a crown on a cushion, which has held together through several moves and which we still have and use.

We keep the tools and scrap glass in a desk drawer, always at hand. Although we don't often attempt full-scale glass projects, someone is always slicing off a bit of glass to put a window into a homemade wooden house, to provide a mirror lake in a woodland scene, to tape together for a free-form creation.

Taking off from our glass experiments, we studied the history of glass, how it is made today, unusual uses for glass (it is sometimes spun). We visited a glassblower at Brigham Young University. And we discussed some archaeological mysteries about glass; some scholars assert that the ancients did know how to make glass, but it is never found in digs because it disintegrates so readily!

Yarn

I love crocheting and knitting, though I am not very good at them. Whenever I pull out the wool and needles or hooks, a flock of little ones demands each some for his own. The older children can crochet in double and single stitch fairly well, though they soon get tired of it. They do like to produce long, thick chains, which they lovingly carry around for a time.

Yoni, on the other hand, conceived a powerful desire to knit properly. A visiting friend, crafting a beautiful baby blanket out of champagne wool, cast on for him and taught him the basic knit stitch; but he soon dropped stitches and got lost, and I was not skilled enough to help him.

Later, living in New Zealand, we discovered a whole new world of knitting. There, in the land of 85 million sheep, everyone seems to knit, including many men! If you visit a doctor's office, five or six women in the waiting room will all be busy with their needles and wool. The aunts and grandmother all produced beautiful sweaters, and Yoni's (and my) passion for the craft reemerged. Fortunately, we found good help among friends, and then discovered a delightful child's kit, *Knitter-Bugs*, with explicit and clear directions on all the basic ways of knitting. Patiently Yoni mastered the knit stitch, but got tangled up in purl—not unlike his mother. We persisted and produced a few squares of admirable knitting.

Ann Wiseman reflects this comfortable, natural approach to knitting in her *Making Things*, providing instructions for projects that both boys and girls can enjoy, including a large hammock knitted on needles made of dowels that you sharpen yourself!

We choose wool or cotton yarns for these projects, using acrylic for yarn paintings or Ojos de Dios or bead necklaces or doll's hair. Again inspired by Wiseman, we have made popsicle looms to weave lovely yarn belts. We also bought a good-quality plastic loom, learning to warp it ourselves and make crude but satisfying beginning weavings. If we get into weaving again soon, we may follow Wiseman's patterns for an inkle loom, made from a cardboard box or from wood. At one time or another, everyone gets into spool knitting, both on smaller, wooden spools and on larger machines made with cardboard tubes and nails. Admittedly, we don't usually produce enough coil to make a rug or anything big, but the neat, even rope is a pleasure to the hand.

Perhaps our perennially most popular yarn craft must be ropemaking, a technique again supplied by Wiseman. You can begin by twisting many strands of yarn, tied to a doorknob, holding the tension tight, and then, when the yarns are twisted tautly, dividing in half and letting go! Amazingly, the yarn spins together in a double reverse twist that holds in a rope. You can repeat it several times for a thick one. And if you really get into rope-making, as Yoni did, you can create a rope winder out of wood and coat-hanger wire to twist your yarn easily and almost magically.

We still have many more adventures left to do with yarn. A friend of ours described their homeschooling forays into fiber. They watched a neighbor shear the sheep, and took home the shearings, washing and carding and spinning them into homespun, which they then knitted into (small) articles, a wonderful experience of one of the world's basic crafts.

Leather

When the older children were two, four and six, I went through a shoemaking phase. I had thought much about home storage, and could mentally envision my ability to provide many things should there be shortages, but shoes baffled me. After some research, I found a Tandy booklet on sandal making and a wonderful book, *The Make It Yourself Shoe Book*, by Christine Clark, that gave me the confidence to try making some. I made a pair of leather sandals for each of the three children, finding it not too difficult, gleaning lots of compliments wherever they trod. In the process, I obtained the basic leatherworking tools I needed. I also found myself with lots of leather scraps.

The children over the years have utilized these scraps and other leather I have bought to make knife sheaths, belts, home-imagined boots, arrow slings, and many unnamed items. Soon, also, I had purchased a leather tooling kit, with a few basic projects included, such as leather coasters and a wallet. At eight, David took over this kit, making up the projects (he gave the completed wallet to our honorary grandfather), subsequently designing many tooled objects of his own. The other boys have made their own wallets, as well as decorated leather objets d'art without discernable purpose.

Now we feel comfortable enough with the medium that whenever someone wants a knife sheath or a Scout tie slide, he just goes to the leatherworking stuff and knocks one out for himself. I have yet to come back to my shoemaking; but recently at an Emergency Preparedness conference, I happened to attend a session on making your own footwear. Imagine my delight to see Christine Clark's book cited as the best do-it-yourself manual on the subject!

Papier Maché

Not high on my list of favorites—but certainly high with the children—papier maché requires many steps of work, involving Mother most of the time. Any birthday produces a piñata, usually a simple process of layering newspaper strips and flour paste into a balloon. We have made masks as a variation on the theme, layering the maché on just one half of the balloon, cutting and decorating the creations when they were dry, usually painting them with poster paint which rubbed off on all little fingers when the masks were handled!

By far the most demanding of papier maché crafts we ever attempted were the dinosaurs. We came up with some astonishing creatures, including one two-foot brontosaurus. These fellows were created amidst astonishing mess, beginning with rolled-up newspaper and wire armatures, a nice lesson in real sculpture. Sticking it out over several days (and the double entendre is very much intended), we finally and joyfully displayed our poster-painted and then varnished creations, which bumped around the house for a year or two.

To tell the truth, I put the children off as much as possible when they want to papier maché. Despite their struggles toward neatness, they make a horrendous mess when using papier maché—especially when (not if) the toddlers want to join in. And again, despite their struggles to help, Mother usually ends up mopping up the mess.

Plaster

A close rival to the mess of papier maché, plaster of paris nevertheless offers some fascinating lessons. Mixing it up can be strange, because it sometimes absorbs water so unpredictably; and when it dries, it gets warm, a curiosity for everybody. We usually made the hand-in-the-paper-plate with the little ones, poking a hole in the top for hanging just as they do in nursery schools.

In the sandbox we have tried sand casting, dampening the sand and carving out shapes, including different textures and designs using sieves, silverware, and burlap. To be truthful, these sand-castings never turn out as well as we imagine them, but the process is interesting.

We have also poured plaster of paris into wax cartons, stripped off the carton when the plaster was set, and used the block for carving—again, the creation never satisfying the imagination, but a fun experience with the medium.

We tried the suggestion in the *Mother's Almanac* to make birdcage balloons, coating yarn with plaster and draping it in cage shapes over inflated balloons, waiting impatiently for the exciting moment to stick a pin into the balloon. These were not quite as aesthetic as they promised to be.

We have also made medallions with plaster of paris, pouring out a spoonful of the stuff into waxed paper, poking a hole in the top and letting it dry, afterwards practicing plaster scrimshaw in the smooth surface, imitating the Eskimos, or perhaps just painting the medallions.

Perhaps because it involves fewer materials and because the children demand it less frequently, I feel more patience in working with plaster!   And of course, we always tell the story of the Parisian shepherd who legendarily invented the stuff.

Nature Crafts

Although I have no time for nature crafts that mock natural materials, such as sculptures out of nuts or spray-painted weed collections, we have enjoyed much peaceful fun with natural materials.

My favorite must be drying flowers.   What a revelation it was to discover instructions for making one's own simple flower press with plywood and blotting paper, held together with c-clamps! We gathered garden flowers and wildflowers, grasses and weeds, drying them with some impatience, posting them in notebooks with explanations of their location and type, and sometimes using them to make wall hangings, stationery, or just decorated pictures.   After we missed the wild roses during one memorable camping trip, I vowed to take our little press with us whenever we packed the tent.

We also like to dry flower stalks upside down along with the medicinal herbs that we gather during the summer.   We display these dried bouquets for a while, until they get ratty-looking and start shedding seeds over the bureau.

Although we are still far from proficient, we love learning the names of the flowers and weeds around us, and find out some of their uses. Predictably, Sammy displayed a collection of common weeds, notating their Latin and common names.   Some of our happiest walks have been with our honorary grandparents, experts at identifying the wildings.

In *Easy Woodstuff for Kids*, David Thompson provides numerous projects for young children, many of them using, simply enough, found sticks. We have especially liked sanding a slice of attractive branch to make medallions or candle-holders, and have also liked making birdhouses from sticks and pieces of wood.   These projects might strike you as overly simple, but they really appeal to little children, and give them a chance to work with wood successfully and aesthetically.

Admittedly in the way of kitsch, we enjoy collecting stones and painting them into creatures; we do not go so far, however, as to inscribe little captions on them. I keep trying to stretch the children into delicate and imaginative creations, as we read about in the *National Geographic*, where a Russian artist chose stones meticulously and transformed them into character sketches. We usually varnish these to avoid rubbing poster paint into our hands; or the older children use acrylics.

We discovered a delightful winter's craft. Using ice-cube trays, jello molds, popsicle molds, spoons, cookie containers, cookie sheets, styrofoam trays, and fancy shapes of all kinds, we filled them with water, sometimes adding a few drops of food coloring, and set them outside at night to freeze. In the morning, we dipped the containers briefly into warm water to release the shapes, and using water in a spray bottle as a glue, fastened the pieces of ice together to make fanciful castles and sculptures. Placing these where the morning light could stream through them, we found these ice sculptures some of the most beautiful creations we had ever made; even when they melted they provided amusement! And of course, this stimulated that classic discussion of the different forms of water, developing into an experiment with condensing steam over a boiling pot.

One year we got into basketry. Using a book on making baskets from natural materials, we taught ourselves how to gather reeds and bulrushes from the marshes, dry them, reconstitute them, and weave them into baskets; most of the other materials in the book we could not forage. Our baskets, wobbly and uneven as they were, gave us so much pleasure, and we look forward to learning how to strip, split, and weave with willow.

In New Zealand, Yoni, our fierce Maori dancer, wanted an authentic costume, so out we went to gather New Zealand flax (a native fiber plant, not related to true flax). We put together headbands, and the Maori dance kilt, a *piupiu*. Again, these efforts produced inferior items, but we learned and had a great time.

Camping in Southern Utah, amidst the beautiful red sandstone, the children ruined several of my serrated knives carving creatures out of the rocks. I remember a snake, coiled in the sun, and a bear that turned out quite well; a visiting artist commented that he liked them too. During that trip the children also scrounged little glass bottles and layered different colors of sand in them. As always, when we are out in the wild, they gathered pieces of driftwood to carve into the shapes suggested by them. And who will forget the hoots of the willow whistles?

Craft Books

Every trip to the library includes bringing home several craft books—crafts from different countries, nature crafts, preschool crafts, crafts in different materials. Sometimes we don't even look at them, but sometimes we try many of the projects, so we have experienced most of the typical crafts of childhood in addition to the ones detailed above. I can hardly remember all the projects we have tried! But this overview demonstrates my firm notion that education belongs to the hands as well as to the head—that it can take place best through the hands as well as through the intellect.

After searching for five or six years, I bought from a used-book salesman a set of *The Family Creative Workshop*, published by Plenary Publications, International, New York. This crafts encyclopedia details a mind-boggling assortment of projects, beautifully illustrated with photos and drawings. That is opening the window onto lots of different techniques, ideas.

Freya Jaffke's *Toymaking with Children* and *The Doll Book* have strongly shaped my philosophy of crafts and play in general. I strongly recommend them to any homeschooler trying to forge a good alternative to the overwhelming mess of the toybox. Jaffke reflects something of the Waldorf philospohy when she says that children need unstructured materials from the natural world to stimulate their imaginations and their senses. *Toymaking* emphasizes making toys out of branches, wool fleece, silk and cotton squares, lumber and fabrics. The toys are simple to make, yet so charming! They take us a world away from the toystore, and they can be easily repaired, added to, and cleaned. *The Doll Book* gives specific instructions for making the Waldorf-style dolls with knit-fabric bodies, wool fleece stuffing (which gives back the warmth of a child's embrace--they are absolute tactile delights), yarn hair, and very simple faces. When we made such a doll for Chava's seventh birthday, she followed the process with wonder, exclaiming that the final results (with the addition of a little wooden bed and mattress made by David) were "gorgeous!"

Through *Hearthsong*, P.O. Box B, Sebastopol, CA 95473-0601, a rather expensive but very stimulating catalog, we ordered some books on celebrating holidays and seasons. *The Children's Year*, though it empha-sizes seasonal celebrations, provided crafts ideas that I had never seen before. Knitting small farmyard animals, making unusual Christmas decorations from felt and fleece, crafting unusual costumes--the book has a comparatively large number of crafts for one volume. Chava and I loved making a "horse" harness, a snap-on vest sort of creation with long reins in the back. One child wears it; another plays driver, the roles shifting frequently. She decorated hers with felt appliques and many eyelets, which made a sparkling and fanciful harness. Simple as it is, this harness exemplifies the liberating quality of the crafts in this volume; each thing opens up a new avenue for imagination and play.

From *Hearthsong* we also bought a most favorite volume, *Earth, Water, Fire and Air* by Walter Kraul. As you have seen from the chapter on "Toys," we have learned that some of the best playtimes come through free experimentation with the elements. This volume presents a wide variety of projects, some of them demanding enough for a young teenager to complete well, others simple enough for your preschoolers to carry out joyfully. The book doesn't shy away from getting wet or dirty, and each project is delightful. It even gives instructions for homemade hot air balloons, with appropriate warnings for safety. I found this a most enabling crafts book.

In addition to books and things you can buy, *Hearthsong* has provided another inavluable service for our homeschool. Since many of the offerings are made simply and well of easily available, natural materials like wood and fabric, we often imitate them to make projects of our own. They sell "Wind Wands," for example, which are sturdy rods topped with a wooden ball, from which flutter several fabric streamers. We constructed our own version of these wands, and found that all the children, young and old, loved running with them and flapping them in the wind.

Steve Caney's *Toy Book* has been a longtime favorite of our homeschool. We frequently make the racing turtles. His pea-and-toothpick sculptures, as easy as the concept is, have been another perennial favorite.

Looking over our bookshelves, I see many favorite crafts books that the children use over and over, books on basketmaking, needlework and sewing, knitting, carpentry. Childcraft's "Things to Do" volume appeals repeatedly to the children, even though we adults may get tired of the same projects. Even that old encyclopedia, *A Bookshelf for Children*, offers many fascinating projects. The recently republished *American Boys Handybook* by Daniel Beard, originally issued in 1882, is often in the children's hands, although some of the instructions need translating into today's terms.

Echoing Ann Wiseman, crafts can lead us into many subject areas, most directly into the world's cultures, but also into mathematics, language, science. Working with the hands gives us a chance to fix ideas in our brains, gives us time, and reinforces the thinking patterns through muscular activity.

Not only that, when you homeschool you can never fill up the day with strictly academic work. Not only would the children reject it, but you yourself couldn't stand it. Crafts pleasurably fill the day with productive, instructive activity that everyone enjoys, especially Mom and Dad, who can't help but admire the prolific results. And the children develop and refine skills that will serve them as they grow as well as throughout their lives.

PHYSICAL EDUCATION

"Your children don't play sports," criticized one relative. "They're not very athletic."

That's particularly true, though given the chance, Sammy and Yoni showed up stars playing soccer and rugby when they attended school. One ineffective part of my homeschooling program has been P.E.

Not that I haven't tried! I devised an individualized fitness program for each child, including timed running, sit-ups, push-ups, jumping jacks, and knee bends. We noted our daily gains on charts.

But as for the expertise gained in playing team sports, that quiet mastery of one's body, the ability to throw and catch skillfully—we haven't always had it.

At one time, David especially appeared awkward and ungainly, partly from inexperience, partly because that was just how he was. The other children performed quite a bit better, but only because of their school experience. The one year that we enrolled the children in soccer, we lived five miles from the practice field, and eight to ten miles from the playing fields. I was expecting a baby at the time, dragging along with me a two- and a four-year-old. That soccer season nearly did me in, and I vowed never to repeat that kind of commitment, running three different boys to three different sets of practice times during the week, along with three different game times on Saturdays. Avraham took his turn on occcasion, but because of his work, I did the lion's share of the running. Now I know that some families pull this off with finesse, but we are not one of those. I need a large hunk of home time each week, and if I run around too much, my householding falls apart and I frazzle. Perhaps without babies and toddlers I could manage better.

Certainly without these little ones I could play sports with the children. As it is, in New Zealand, when our family would run out to play soccer on the beach or in the field, some toddler was always crying, running to catch me by the legs or to be picked up. This quickly dampened my enjoyment in running and dodging the soccer ball. I am not the one to teach the children sports, I think, but so far Avraham has not been able to spare much time from his work to play with the children. And sometimes when they do assemble to play, the older ones throw fits because the younger players can't abide by the complete set of rules, thus souring the fun for all.

In our home, this is how it works: if one of the adults go out for a walk, a run, or an outdoor game, the children want to go too. If I stay inside, they all stay inside too. We *can* boast about our family walks, a Sunday tradition as well as weekday pleasure; my children have become steady, happy hikers. And when I take off for my daily run, if I agree, one or more children bumps along beside me. They are good joggers. And we do own a fair supply of basketballs, soccer balls, mitts and gloves, baseball bats. This year, we acquired a weight lifting bench to go with a set of weights we had, and the older boys consistently work out on them; David won't miss a night. Similarly, we put up a basketball backboard, and not only have out skills dramatically improved, but the neighborhood children find themselves here much more often. In particular, Sammy, whose social contacts have always been minimal, now plays basketball regularly with his friends, both here and at their houses.

Of course, often the children will contrive a hike together, complete with water jugs and snacks along the way. When we lived at the beach in New Zealand, they would climb the cliffs, scouring the place for shells, rocks, nests, and insects. Often they tumble outside for "ball-tiggy," where you throw the ball to tag someone. They love to ride their bikes with friends. They also love to swim and the older ones go regularly to pools or ponds; in the ocean, the younger ones can wade and dip together without much adult supervision.

But often day after day they drape over chairs, reading, or sit at the table, drawing, or hang about the work-bench, making things, without the strong, vigorous exercise that I feel should shape childhood. They certainly get more of a workout at school; and for homeschool I often growl, "You children go outside for some fresh air and exercise!" They like as not resist the admonition, though in the wintertime, when we lived atop the best sliding hills I have ever seen, they quickly agreed to their P. E. up and down hills. Like another homeschool family, we have also done crosscountry skiing for winter exercise.

When Avraham and the three older boys began their three-times-weekly schedule at BYU, which they continued for a little over half a year, they arranged for a new approach to P. E. At noon the boys would jog a couple of miles on the running track, sometimes adding weight-lifting or, when the equipment was out, high-jumping. At 5:00 p.m., they would troop down to the swimming pool for an hour of swimming, some required laps and the rest fun. I was a little incredulous at first, but Avraham assured me that the boys did swim for the whole hour.

Some months previous, we took the plunge and bought a 14-foot trampoline. Everyone quickly grew skilled on this (even I graduated to knee- and seat-drops); but Yoni especially shone, swiftly learning to do flips and combinations of tricks. We did endure one bad sequence, where David, against the rules, got on the tramp with Avi, who broke his leg and had to wear a cast for six weeks. But most of the time the tramp has proved safe, lots of fun, and great sport for all the neighborhood kids, and we adults use it reguarly, too. We enrolled Yoni, Chava, and Avi in a community school gymnastics class. All three of them did well, but Yoni was exceptional; one of the teachers assured him that he could win a college scholarship with his gifts, if he only kept practicing.

Ideally, one would live close enough to community sports, in a community of relative safety, where the children could bicycle to and from practice and games without this incessant driving back and forth. This year, even without such ideal circumstances, we are pursuing T-ball for the younger children, and soccer for the older children, with Avraham providing the main transportation around the demands of his research. Most of my children really enjoy team sports, and so long as we keep the competitiveness in perspective, I think they are good. This is one area, though, where our homeschool has fallen short of what the children can experience in a school setting.

MUSIC AND DANCE

You may be expecting here a happy rundown of music lessons, practice sessions, explorations, performances—and that is coming. But music, at least, creates one of the most controversial discussions in this book.

Most of us grew up immersed in inappropriate music. I remember exactly when the Beatles superceded Johnny Mathis and Elvis Presley, when I was twelve, so I am not speaking as a misty-eyed proponent of the good old days. I grew up in the midst of rock music, and had no way of determining if it was good or bad.

However, during my dating years at BYU, I went to a rock dance with a new boyfriend. In the middle of the evening, I had a strong feeling, "This is not the place for you. You do not belong here." Not always a courageous hero in these matters, I tried to put it off, but the feeling repeated itself insistently. So, leaning over to my date, I asked if he might take me home. He was shocked! As we walked home, I tried to explain my feelings. Then he was disgusted! I never heard from him again.

The semester following—I believe it was in the spring—one of the weekly devotionals, given in the DeJong Concert Hall, featured Dr. Arthur H. King. Among other subjects, he talked about what was wrong with the music most of us listen to. At last, here was an educated, clear explanation of what I had been feeling. I listened to the tape of his talk in the Media section of the library many times over at intervals after that. Years later, an edited version of his remarks appeared:

Radio and television, records and tapes—these allow us to bring music into our homes on an unprecedented scale. Unfortunately, there has been over the last few centuries an inverse relationship between technical expertise in producing, recording, and broadcasting music and the quality of the music being reproduced. Jazz and rock have now become a predominant moral problem for the whole of Western civilization. I find it difficult to see anything in most of the variants of jazz (ending at the moment with rock) except sex and violence alternating with self-pity. This music exploits musical rhythms in a deliberately excitatory way, and the original purpose of that exploitation was to excite to violence and/or sex. The fact that we suppress our inclinations in those directions doesn't mean that the music isn't doing that to us. Jazz rhythms are emphatic, but they are also disturbing and destructive. The spirit of this music is, as a whole, orgiastic; and its mere loudness is one of the ways in which sensitivity is lost (and, indeed, actual physical damage done to the hearing). Jazz and rock produce violent sensations which lead to a desire for still greater violence, still greater volume. This music is demonic. (Arthur Henry King, *The Abundance of the Heart* [Salt Lake City: Bookcraft, 1987), 217)

Dr. King also drew contrasts between various kinds of classical music, showing how Bach, Mozart, and Handel created a wide variety of music within a framework of worship and faith; while Wagner, Tchaikovsky, much of Beethoven (and, in my experience, many of the more modern composers) are full of "self-assertion, defiance, the dramatic gesture, the heroic," as well as eroticism and self-pity (King, 218).

Learning at last what was wrong with popular music, I stopped listening to it, as much as I could, though forced to listen on occasion, such as when I was compelled to chaperone high-school dances while a teacher. The less I heard the music, the more disturbing and even shocking was its effect when I was exposed to it.

Thus it was no surprise to learn of the research done by a California scientist, who created two greenhouses with the same conditions. In one she played rock music; in the other classical music. The rock-music plants grew farther and farther *away* from the loudspeaker, until they were lying flat and retarded in growth; those receiving Bach grew *toward* the speakers and flourished lush and green. Once a professor in Education, after we chatted together about the subject, lent me a file compiled by one of his doctoral students. It was full of clippings about rock musicians, their life-styles (drugs, violence, sex), and their self-proclaimed devotion to Satan, in many cases. I couldn't even read the entire file, it was so dark and truly sickening.

You may sometimes hear lectures or tapes which expound these lurid details, but I am not sure that they achieve the correct purpose, which is to stop people from listening to the music. I wonder if they merely fan the flames of interest in the rock subculture.

In an essay written in honor of Dr. Hugh Nibley, Avraham explained an interesting parallel with God's ancient and modern covenant people concerning music. Drawing on an apocryphal work from *The Lost Books of the Bible and the Forgotten Books of Eden*, titled "The Books of Adam and Eve" (New York: Meridian, 1974), he shows the pre-Flood people of God living on a high mountain plateau, while the children of Cain lived below in the plain. Spurred on by satanic inspiration, these followers of Cain began to play music that tempted the righteous people to gather and listen. The musicians, dressed in gorgeous clothes, played loudly and with intense rhythm and volume, and gathered together especially to attract the attention of the people of God. The text points out that the power of Satan made the music more attractive, and that it inflamed the listeners with wild lusts.

After about a year of listening to these bands, many of the righteous came down out of the mountain and involved themselves in the sinful lives of the Cainites, which included drunkenness, licentiousness, hatred, murder, and secret combinations. After defiling themselves, these people could not find their way back up the steep mountain—even when they wanted to ascend. Avraham draws the parallel with rock music today, which lowers the standards of a people committed to righteousness, making it extremely difficult to find our way back to a higher level. Certainly the life-style of rock musicians resembles that described by the Books of Adam and Eve. I think the parallel is valid as well as very interesting for our time.

In our home, we try to allow no pop music at all. Our radio dial remains at 89.1 KBYU-FM, or KUER-FM, University of Utah, both of which play classical music, though some of the modern pieces are too jarring to listen to. From a very early age, the children can recognize immediately inappropriate rock rhythms and compositions. The toddlers and little ones look at me with an expression of alarm; the older ones with an embarrassed smile. Unless you have listened to classical music, you might think our music consumption boring, but such a variety of music appeals to even the young children, who can identify composers, instruments, and pieces.

Every Thursday KBYU-FM provides an As You Like It day, when listeners call in with requests for their favorites. The student-disc jockeys sometimes have a hard time believing the little piping voices calling to request *Peter and the Wolf*, the *Peer Gynt* Suites, a Carl Orff piece, *The Grand Canyon Suite*, The *William Tell Overture*, or any other of their favorites which they often tape from the radio for listening to again and again.

When lecturing at the Church College of New Zealand, my husband explained some of our views about popular music. He had been a rock star when in his late teens, but intuitively felt that the music was harming him and others spiritually, and so he gave it up of his own accord. He told the students that this was one of the hardest things he had ever done in his life, because the music takes hold of you, becomes a part of you. Afterwards, they swarmed around to ask, "Are you saying that we should stop listening to rock music? What about soft rock? What about those religious songs set to rock music?" He could only answer, "What do you feel in the Spirit?" They replied, "I guess that we should choose for ourselves."

They did raise a difficult question, though, about what we call "gospel rock," or "gospel pop" music. We even hear it often in our churches, the rock rhythms and harmonies expressing religious ideas. Some say that it is better for the young people to hear than the worldly rock, but I am not so sure. I always conjure the image of a sinful woman dressed in Sunday clothes giving the Sunday-School class on morality. No matter what the dress, she cannot hide what she really is. In the same way, the musical content of rock music, quite apart from the words, is self-indulgent, sensual, oriented to pleasure and eroticism. That is why it appeals so. Can you testify of Christ with such vocabulary? These radio stations for the Christian life-style deceive us, and themselves, unless we opt for a life-style which tongue-in-cheek I reckon to be upper-telestial/lower-terrestrial in quality.

In discussing this matter with other families, both with and without homeschools, we have found basically three reactions. Some of them already share this opinion about popular music, and have tried to eliminate it from their lives, often with variable success when there are teenagers in the home. They keep trying, however, and I find it amazing how the young people steadily move toward their parents' point of view. The second category of people know it's wrong, they say, but what can they do about it? The music is all around; who can eliminate it? Better to try to control it, to avoid the very worst of it, they say, and struggle with their guilty feelings as they go.

The third reaction is hostile and angry. They insist that there is good to be found in rock music, and that we should not ban all of it. They point to all the people who have grown up listening to it, and turned out just fine. One can't bury his head in the sand, they claim; you have to be part of the world around you, not some head-shaking freak. To such people I just apologize if I have offended them, and try to change the subject.

Yet despite how bad I feel when someone grows hot at the subject, it is a critical one for the homeschooler, and we need to discuss it, explore it, test it, and bear our testimonies about it. In some homeschools where no musical taste is taught, I notice that the level of morality in the children drops if they listen to much rock music.

When our older children became teenagers, we have had to assess anew our feelings about rock music, to make sure that we still stood in the same place. Although we have maintained our standard here at home, we have had to soften a little about the music outside the home. We didn't want our children to judge others harshly because of the music they heard outside. Similarly, if there were a church or community dance that the children wanted to attend, we decided to allow them to attend with no strings attached, even though inappropriate music was certain to be played.

Occasionally one of the teenagers has brought home cassette tapes with music from their friends' collections. I had to approach this very sensitively, rather than alienate the youngster. As it turned out, the teenagers shared their tapes with me voluntarily one day when the time was right (and I had kept myself from prying till that time). Imagine my delight to find that every single one of the songs on the tape was appropriate and tasteful, in complete accordance with the family standard, although they were chosen from popular music. And I was also delighted that the children offered to share without feeling they would be in danger of inappropriate criticism. We were thus able to talk about good taste in music, since I could compliment their choices sincerely, and reinforce what we had taught all along in the family.

Of course, we don't listen to strictly classical music. We like folk music as well, and sing it frequently; here we develop our round singing and three-part harmony (we haven't been able to stretch ourselves to four-part yet). We like to listen to Mexican and Latin-American music, to traditional American Indian music, to Maori songs and hakas (chants), to Pacific-Island music. Some children's artists really appeal; recently we have gone on a Raffi bing. This singer directly speaks to the heart. We also like the old-style country and western music, though purists would think we go too far. Those old cowboy songs strike a melancholy-sweet chord in our boys, and they listen to them over and over. Similarly, we don't mind an occasional evening of the old-time big-band sound. These evenings nearly always turn into dance evenings as well, with both spontaneous creative movement and some instruction in the waltz and two-step for the older children. The babies dance alone, or more often bob along in Mother's arms.

One evening when a special concert featured a blend of Eastern and Western music, complete with sitar and voices chanting syllables, we all flopped on the floor for an unexpected hour, spellbound. What intense joy it brings when the whole room bursts into dance at *The Hall of the Mountain King*, or Aaron Copeland's *Rodeo*. Homeschooled children dance unabashed, even the older ones—at least so far, my eleven- and thirteen-year-olds dance spontaneously and beautifully. Sometimes we practice traditional folk dancing as well; but the children, having seen creative dance, modern dance, understand something of what they're doing, and in a family home evening may create moving shapes and body sculptures as part of the fun. And perhaps because of this they enter into native dances without embarrassment, as they did in Rarotonga, and as they do at Pow-Wows we sometimes attend.

When possible, we have enrolled Chava in a year-long creative dance program through BYU. We had hesitated about some of the local programs available, because they leaned toward the cheerleader, pop-music type of performance, glitzy and hip-swinging. Loving modern dance as we do, we felt completely alienated from that kind of dance, especially for innocent children. BYU's program, however, offered just what we love— plenty of hard work, a real exercise in creativity, and performance with peers. Chava attended once a week, and we shared transportation with a neighboring family. We sometimes were invited to watch classes or performances. It built Chava's self-esteem so much to know that we were keen to see her progress.

Like most families, we sing to our babies—nursery rhymes, folk songs, special songs we make up: "Who's the little girl that I love, love, love? Who's the little girl that I love? Chava is the girl that I love, love, love. Chava is the girl that I love."

And we sing a lot, especially at our evening devotionals. We sing all the Israeli folk songs that we can remember, songs from other countries, rounds, and most especially the hymns. I want the children to know from memory the best hymns, and so we learn them verse by verse. It does me good to hear seven verses of "How Firm a Foundation" in those treble voices, and to see little three-year-old lips trill "We'll sing and we'll shout."

Perhaps because we sing so much, none of our children has any problem carrying a tune, and I often muse that most children—and adults—could probably sing well if they sang often, from early childhood. At devotional time, the children take turns conducting the songs, learning correct hand movements for 3/4 and 4/4 time.

Some mothers think we're mad, but we have a box of rhythm instruments for anyone to choose to play. We also have a big snare drum.

The littlest ones experiment with a color-coded xylophone, pounding tunelessly away, but often slightly older children take off with "Three Blind Mice," and "Twinkle, Twinkle."

Sometimes I sit on the floor, and we trade around the xylophone and rhythm instruments, singing and pounding out various songs. We learn the patterns for the various time signatures, swaying as we chant, "one, two three, one two three." Very often we make up more verses to familiar songs. From the library we bring home books with folk and nursery songs and dances, singing and dancing our way through them: "Nobody knows I can jump so high; nobody knows I can stand so still." Even the wobbliest toddler recognizes the musical staff, warbling and pointing when she sees it!

One year when we were visiting a hot-springs, one of our children began tootling away on a piece of garden hose, so we decided we were ready for a trumpet. We found one, second-hand, and one of Avraham's students kindly supplied casual lessons for David, who did quite well in reading simple music and producing the required sounds. Of course all the other children took turns blasting away on it, amidst helpless hilarity. We also have kept a recorder or two in supply, though they eventually get bitten or lose their bottom end.

Recently, working with Richard Perry's *Reading by Ear*, we have made some satisfying progress in reading music for solos and duets with recorders. We bought a piano, and because I play, somewhat decided that I would teach the children, which was a total waste of time, with no progress whatever. In the meantime, Sammy began to ask if he might learn to play the violin, so we bought a second-hand, half-sized instrument and found a good Suzuki teacher for him. At age eight, he found the discipline very challenging, breaking out in a temper frequently, but he made good progress until we moved house and stopped for a while.

In a new location we were blessed to find an excellent piano teacher, who taught with the Suzuki method, also including a course of note-reading. Most of all she was loving, kind, patient, and very intuitive with the children. And I liked her personally as well! We went to piano lessons every week, morning sickness, new baby, heavy snow and all. Initially David took flight with the Suzuki lessons; once he understood the variations on the Alberti bass, he learned the beginning songs with ease and speed, and launched into the more difficult ones cheerfully and well, though he didn't make good progress with dynamics and expression—not interested, he said.

Sammy went along much more slowly, but he learned every piece meticulously, and would not try something until he had thought it through and mastered it completely. For a long, long time he would only play one hand at a time, and then two hands in unison, but the happy day finally arrived when he played "Lightly Row," which is with Alberti bass; it must have been close to a year after we commenced lessons. Lisa, our teacher, evidenced not a shred of impatience, but worked with him at his own pace.

Yoni at age five poked along with the little exercises provided him, but then one day burst into the variations on "Twinkle, Twinkle Little Star," to the amazement of everyone! He rapidly learned most of the pieces in the Suzuki Book One, and made up many interesting compositions of his own, including quite a nice arrangement of the Primary song, "Book of Mormon Stories." We even took him to BYU to play for Reid Nibley, that kind-hearted musical genius, who gave us copies of his book with an extension of the Suzuki technique. Then, as the pieces got more complex, and as note-reading closed in on him, Yoni stopped playing. Completely. We were very disappointed, but decided to wait until he blossomed again.

Meanwhile, David and Sammy kept making steady progress, Sammy tackling and master-minding in his own way each of the Suzuki pieces, and David working through Book Two, filling our house with Bach, Mozart, and other beautiful music.

Every few months Lisa would arrange for a recital for her piano students. Everyone participated, from the first plunkings of "Twinkle Star" right through to the advanced students. One of these took place, with grand piano and all, in a museum of art, a very elegant experience. We also participated in a Music Festival at BYU, judged by various music teachers, but I felt ambivalent about this; it lacked magic and charm, and seemed to place pressure on nervous beginners. Fortunately my children received high ratings, but it could devastate a young aspirant to receive a "Good," instead of "Excellent" or "Superior."

We stopped piano lessons when we travelled to the South Pacific, but whenever we could casually play the piano, our children plunked through their various tunes. David had figured out the music to certain Primary songs, such as "Shine On," and "Tell Me the Stories of Jesus," which quite amazed his friends, particularly the children in Rarotonga.

While attending school in New Zealand, Sammy and Yoni got recorder lessons, which continued some rudiments of note-reading, though they only played once every couple of weeks.

John Holt pointed out that even though young children astonish us with their facile playing, as do the young Japanese who excel in the Suzuki method, not many of them continue on to be musical adults. Sometimes it is better to wait until the children are older, with more muscle control and understanding of musical symbols. This proved to be true with Sammy. At eleven he worked patiently and well through the succession of Suzuki pieces, without frustration, practicing cheerfully every day.

The children seemed to pick up right where they left off after a year or more without music lessons. David skimmed through his former pieces, soon finishing the last of Suzuki Book Two, plunging easily into Book Three. Sammy, at eleven, more patient and skillful, took on new piece after piece, still working methodically and meticulously, but learning much faster and more happily. To our delight, Yoni, at nine, resumed playing his old Suzuki pieces, though he learned new ones only sporadically, much preferring to experiment on and on with chord sequences and different progressions. The younger children picked out a tune now and then, but at six and four, Chava and Avi were not ready for formal work.

Recently, we have begun Suzuki string lessons with a gifted, talented teacher whom we found in a nearby town. At first, we were all going to learn violin, as we had a half-size instrument from the time that Sammy took lessons when he was eight. Denise, our teacher, convinced us to expand a little, Chava studying violin, Avi, cello, and Yoni viola. She rented us a quarter-size violin for Chava, and converted our half-size instrument to a viola by changing the strings. We were fortunate to locate a used quarter-sized cello in good condition that we bought on time payments.

This differentiation in instruments eliminated conflict and competitiveness. It also supplied the opportunity to come up with duets and trios! Although at first we felt we could not afford them, Denise convinced us to purchase the Suzuki string tapes, books, and accompaniment books for all three instruments. Listening to the tapes opened a world to us, and Chava and Avi have progressed smoothly and well. But Yoni! He mastered the variations on Twinkle Star that all Suzuki students begin with, and then plunged right ahead and immediately learned the next several songs, all from listening from the tapes, in one go.

Together we devised the Twinkle Star duet--violin and viola--which included Chava. Denise, delighted, supplied the cello part, which Avi could soon pick up. She combined the traditional Japanese approach, formal and disciplined, with a happy, tolerant, and joyful feeling. It has continued to work wonderfully well with our children. Over the years we have enjoyed recitals, group lessons, and, with some financial planning, a glorious annual week in Logan, Utah, at the Intermountain Suzuki Institute. Although it is expensive, this musical experience has proven to be so uplifting and so lasting (the good effects last for six months after) that it is worth the sacrifice.

Later, when Sarah turned about three and a half, we found a good, inexpensive, used one-sixteenth size violin, and she began lessons as well. All of the children have progressed satisfactorily as time goes on, and during the summer, Denise has added a children's orchestra, which gives wonderful experience in note reading and group playing.

During this time, we didn't continue with piano lessons, but I decided, after having observed our former teacher for a couple of years, that I could teach the Suzuki piano, even though I am not a polished performer myself. Sure enough, David and Sammy continued progressing well with their piano. David played a Beethoven sonatina in church during the winter he was thirteen, and Sammy blossomed into a comfortable mastery during the same year. At eleven, he learned new songs with more ease than when he was younger. I would play through the new pieces, working slowly through the parts, and the boys would catch right on and learn it themselves.

In addition, they listened to the Suzuki piano tapes, at the appropriate levels, that we purchased. Whenever we met a problem I couldn't answer, I'd call our former teacher (who had stopped teaching in favor of spending more time with her family) and she would graciously supply the answer, sometimes inviting us over to air a piece that would soon be performed.

What do we really look for when we give our children music lessons? Our piano teacher, Lisa, once asked me that question. I wanted the children to be able to read music and to play beautiful pieces well. She laughed, saying that some mothers want their children to be able to play the hymns or to complete this or that course as an end in itself. Of course we want our children to be able to play Church music, so that they can accompany when needed, but we can also look to music as a mutual discipline of the physical and the spiritual. Most of all, if we parents truly relish the musical sounds in our homes, the children will likely feel our joy and play more cheerfully. "It's just that I love it," one mother of strictly Suzuki-taught string players, twelve and under, exclaimed. Her children, homeschooled until age eight and then only attending school half-days thereafter, practice their music three hours a day! They play so beautifully that tears come to the eyes.

I lack that sort of commitment, but I love it too—I love to hear the music pouring out of my children, and often I'll shout from the kitchen: "No, that's B-flat!"—to the amusement of all.

Even if they are immersed in the finest music from babyhood, our young people might dip into less-desirable music in their teen years. Yet I feel convinced that the good breeding in their bones will always lead them back toward the finest, especially if we parents maintain our high standard of musical taste and don't lapse into less-worthy music. The quality of music in our homes makes a strong statement about our commitment to our journey toward Zion.

TOYS AND TOOLS

I think we might be surprised if we analyzed our true feelings about toys. Most of us buy toys to please our children, to give them gifts on holidays. Some of us feel that we need to educate our children through the use of toys, a highly developed extension of that idea being the Montessori plan. What are toys for, anyway?

Since the serious work of childhood is what we term play, we supply toys because toys are to play with. Many mothers also recognize and tolerate the fact that children like to play with almost any item around the house that they can put their hands on. A few really good mothers encourage their children to use genuine household items in their play, but most of us are afraid that the children will break our things.

We have gone through a genesis in our feelings about toys. When our first son was born, I was determined, á la *Teach Your Baby*, that his life would be filled with Educational Experiences so that he could develop his True Potential. Very seriously and solemnly I constructed a variety of mobiles to hang over his crib, some to flutter, some to clang, some to touch. I took him outside with some of these mobiles so he could experience them there. I read to him, sang to him, exercised him, and we bought him a goodly amount of toys. I also made him toys, using the Montessori materials as models, as well as putting kitchen utensils and books in his toybox, which we placed in whatever room we were in.

Fortunately, I also picked him up whenever he fussed, held him much, and took him wherever I went, rarely leaving him with a babysitter. Because I was doing an M. A. program at the same time, I would leave him with my husband when I attended or taught classes, but not with strangers and not for long.

I continued this same pattern with toys with my second and third children, putting much thought and effort into what toys were needed for their sound intellectual development. I didn't worry to the extent that one friend did, who, having become convinced of the Montessori method, set out to provide every one of the prescribed materials, feeling that her children be cheated out of some irreplaceable experience should she omit anything.

However, through the many books I had read, I believed that a child could not learn shapes unless you gave him a shape-sorter and taught him the words to go with it; he could not learn colors unless you proceeded through the series, "This is red. Point to red. What is this?" He could not learn relative sizes without the nesting/stacking blocks, he could not understand gradations of color without the color tablets, and, the most foolish of all, he could not articulate texture without experiencing the rough and smooth boards!

I cannot even remember what stimulated the experiment I undertook when we went to Alaska, to take no toys at all, only books, writing and painting materials, and some tools.

The children did follow my intuitions for those three months, creating their own play materials out of the sticks and stones, water and earth that were at hand. Little Chava, then 18 months, seemed to need something more, so we bought at a second-hand store a nice teddy-bear, which someone named Baby Jims, and who became everyone's beloved.

The children during that trip, and for the first time, were free to handle almost limitlessly the elements—fire, water, earth. Whenever we made a campfire, sometimes several fires in a day, any child was permitted to kindle it. We learned the various shapes of fires, teepee, Indian star, log cabin, and what they were good for. They children thrust sticks into the fires and pranced around with torches. They were free to do some primitive cooking, their favorite being mud potatoes. (You coat raw, cleaned potatoes with a thick jacket of mud. Put them in the coals and turn once after a half-hour. An hour should cook them. Crack them open and they should emerge, cooked and clean, out of a hardened, clay-like coat.) Through all the fire experiments (at this time the ages were eight, six, and four, with Chava being eighteen months and not into fire), no one got burned—except Mother, the cook!

Living by streams, ponds, rivers, and in rain with all the puddles, they also had plenty of water experience. We are a little more cautious about deep water, and watch quite carefully. But there was no limit on making little pools, dams, channels, etc. I became very casual about children getting wet, an attitude I carry around still; at the beach in New Zealand we would all go for a walk in our regular clothes, knowing that we would get quite wet (the weather being too cool for swimsuits), and just enjoying getting wet and returning home for a shower and change.

Similarly, I allow plenty of mud and dirt play without getting fussy about dirty clothes. A Maori friend once said, "If you let your children play in the earth, you will have happy children, healthy children."

The attraction of earth/sand play transcends childhood; my husband has always built a big sand-box wherever we have lived. The children drag the garden-hose to it, and make tunnels, caves, channels, and so on. Visiting children never resist it; even nearly grown teenage boys have found themselves digging out caverns and directing streams! At the New Zealand beach, even if the children wanted to lie in the sand and roll in it, getting it in their hair and clothes, I never remonstrated them—it would wash out.

In Alaska, with so many logs and sticks around, the children constantly used the hatchet and ax, as well as their personal pocketknives—again, few wounds, as I remember, and only minor. With other children camping nearby, they chopped down many saplings and notched them to make their own log hut. Most often, though, they just hacked at wood with no clear purpose in mind; though David here began his sculpting career, developing a gift for making small and charming wooden items by enhancing sticks' natural forms into bears, seals, dolphins, and so on.

Returning from Alaska, the children didn't dive back into the toy-shelf, as we would have expected, but continued using tools with great interest. At this point, we really got into woodworking tools for the kids. At first I let them hammer nails into wood, but soon they were interested in sawing. We had some difficulty in finding a proper saw for them. Definitely, a toy child's saw or child-sized saw is useless. Awkward and ineffective, it makes the children think that they cannot cut because of their own lack of skill. But an adult cross-cut saw also impossibly hinders the children's woodworking; it is too hard to push through the wood (even I have trouble doing it). After some experimenting, the children chose a hand coping saw. You can cut fairly straight with it, and of course cut curved as well. Its sharp blades cut fast through most wood, and when they break they cost little enough not to cause parental frenzy.

As time went on, we steadily bought more hand tools for the children's woodworking. Surprisingly, a file and rasp proved very popular. The children shaped sculptures with it rather than whittling with a pocket-knife, and the little ones loved to rub it against a piece of wood just to watch the pieces fly off and the wood change shape. The brace and bit take more strength than the younger ones possess, yet they love to make the big, clean holes, and so often enlist my help. We bought, some years later, a hand drill, easy enough to operate, with a set of bits. Before that purchase, the children drilled with an electric drill. Even Yoni at mid-six used it safely.

By far the most important tool purchase turned out to be the 4½-inch vise that we bolted to the large workbench Avraham made for the family. This workbench, by the way, is made of solid and strong wood, the front open to hold the tool box and larger tools. On the left side of the bench, the vise waited, in nearly constant use by all the children. Even Avi, at eighteen months, would open it, put in a piece of wood, close it, and file away.   With a vise, you can saw easily; you can file delicately and accurately; you can hammer surely.

We acquired a variety of hammers, all of which were used at various times, even the heavy ones. Usually the children hold the hammer near the head, not the most effective place. Occasionally I suggest a better hold, but without much effect. We bought a nice selection of nails, nuts and bolts, screws, hooks and eyes (wonderful for trains), hinges, and so on, often replacing the common ones and buying something interesting and new once in a while.

The year the three oldest were ten, eight, and six we bought an electric scroll saw from Sears. This lightweight saw bolts to the workbench, too. A serious craftsman would find it too light, but for children it's ideal. The small blade cuts nicely but proved to be quite safe (we never had anyone cut himself, even visitors, though the saw is in near-constant use, it seems). It also boasts a sanding wheel that quickly pares away layers of wood, allowing Yoni to make nice little curving animals. Avi, at four, used it to create various weapons—swords, bows and arrows—as well as homemade fishing gear. Although the children never abandoned the coping saw, this electric addition freed them up to make many different things as you saw in the chapter on "Crafts."

All of the children are free to use the wood tools but only David has really used the metal-working tools. With tin snips and wire cutters he provided metal adjuncts to his wooden creations as often as needed, using the soldering iron we bought for him. He also made wire puzzles with beads on them, a sort of 3-dimensional maze.

We obtain wood chiefly from the scrap piles at a nearby lumberyard. You can get surprisingly large pieces there, free. Occasionally we will buy a special piece, especially ⅛-inch hardboard, always in demand for puzzles, animals, and gameboards. Both David and Sammy have invented interesting games, such as marble hockey and board games with varying sets of rules. We provided a supply of dowels in graduated sizes, usually employed as smokestacks on boats, but often used to facilitate moving parts in some toy.

Everybody freely uses whatever tools he or she wants. I feel it's important to encourage girls in using wood tools, if only because I grew up in awe of them and only learned in my adult years to overcome my opinion that I could not work wood. I will occasionally warn about the sharpness of a tool, explain how to use one, or give a hand with a difficult one. When Yoni might undertake a sawing job that wore him out (though he perfectly conceptualized what he was going to make), I would turn a hand to sawing some of it for him. Only Avraham's large electric saw was strictly forbidden to all children. At first only David was permitted to use the electric drill, but when we saw that all the boys could handle it well we gave them permission, and now that Chava is older, she can, too.

I did interfere in the matter of sandpaper and paint or varnish, however. Sammy enjoys finishing his creations nicely, but David doesn't like to bother. I often push him to sand and varnish or paint something, with him resisting all the way! However, when he was attending school in New Zealand and made a bobbing kiwi pencil holder for his teacher, he initiated the nice finish on his own! Sandpaper sits available at all times, and though we store the enamel paint and varnish and brushes away from the little ones, the children may use them without permission whenever they want.

I must say that every child so far starts woodworking in the same way: making boats. They cut wood (or find it) the size they want, nail one piece on the other, add a mast of a long nail, or perhaps a dowel plugged into a drilled hole, and set out for the water-filled sandbox. David made a fleet of varying boats, launches, tugs, yachts, when he began his woodworking at age eight. This boat-building never pales; the children just graduate to more complex models, sailing boats with pieces of sheet and lines of thread to make the complex set of sails, or perhaps paddle-boats, powered by rubber bands. David once made a model of the Nautilus, á la Jules Verne, that he actually contrived to sink and emerge, using lead weights and air pressure.

I encourage wooden gifts, because people find them charming and they last so long. Sammy crafted a painted space rocket for our honorary grandparents, highly cultured people who graciously accepted the present, though I'm not sure where they keep it!

We have bought a fine set of wood-carving tools, very sharp and therefore potentially dangerous. David uses them with permission; but if he leaves them out where they can drop and be dulled, or where a child can hurt himself on them, he loses his privilege. This happens most of the time.

In addition to woodworking tools, we make other tools freely available to the children. From babyhood they are allowed to use kitchen utensils to cook or just to play with. I cringe to recall how many eggbeaters have been bent, rubber spatulas bitten, wooden spoons split, kitchen knives dulled. Generally, I have let anybody cook who wants to follow a recipe and clean up after himself, though they can't cook sweets before a meal. Only Yoni seems to be very interested in cookery, though for a long time he couldn't read and had to be helped through a recipe. He began young; at four, I recall, he single-handedly made peach cobbler, proudly serving it to the family. As the children have grown older, however, I can trust them to make and serve a complete dinner, if it is impossible for me to be home.

All of the children know how to make bread, but they are not much interested to; they do beg, however, to sculpt creatures out of bread dough, decorating them with raisins, and feasting on them afterward. As for kitchen gear, some might criticize me for allowing very young children the use of sharp knives. I figure that children can understand the dangers of knives; I can always say, "Be careful with that one, it's sharp." They like to chop vegetables for me at about eighteen months, and continue that interest for some time. Avi, at three, maintained a certain fascination for knives. In Rarotonga, where along with everyone else we used a huge bush knife for outdoor work and for opening coconuts, Avi claimed the weapon and went around, thrusting it into the ground and shouting, "How does that feel?"

As with the woodworking tools, only rarely does someone get cut. The worst damage results to the utensils, such as to a steak knife that lost all its serration one summer as David and Sammy carved sandstone animals with it when we camped in Southern Utah. (I'm overdoing this damage idea, though; most of the time the children are careful with my tools.)

The same freedom applies to sewing gear. Sharp sewing scissors can be used by anyone who can climb up to the shelf and apply them to fabric. Similar scissors, not reserved for fabric, store right along with myriad pencils, sharpeners, erasers, markers, chalk, crayons, and paper of all kinds, free for anybody to use. I am continually reorganizing methods for storing these messy things, because everybody tends to dump them all back together again heedlessly. Finally we have obtained plastic containers for each category, and woe to the offender who dumps the markers in with the pens! The only person forbidden the use of the sharp scissors is the baby at the moment, who can use them only to poke herself and not to cut.

We own some specialized tools, useable only with permission: a set of linoleum cutters and printing paint, with small linoleum blocks mounted on wood. When I allow a carving and printing session, the children truly enjoy the work and make some beautiful prints. The glass cutting equipment is stored where anybody can use it. Full-scale glass cutting waits on mother's permission, however, mainly because applying the copper foil and soldering the pieces together requires my undivided attention and assistance. We rarely use the lead method, because lead poisoning can result and because it is more expensive.

When we are making stained-glass ornaments, even the young children love to run the glass cutter across glass and break it with pliers. Chava at four experimented with great skill, never cutting herself, while Yoni at six constructed some admirable sun catchers, though he would often choose a pattern too taxing for his staying power. We buy glass scraps by the pound, only occasionally buying a piece of some specially-needed color or texture.

Anybody can fingerpaint, watercolor, posterpaint anytime, though the posterpaint mess sometimes deters big splashy pictures; because anyone who makes a mess has to clean it up himself (I do help the little ones). We buy large school paintbrushes and little watercolor brushes and sizes and textures in between. Sometimes we get those little pats of color common to childhood, sometimes squeeze poster colors, sometimes acrylics (by permission only), and I keep a supply of those large powdered posterpaints sold to schools. Recently I bought a set of paint containers with a sloping lid, hole in the middle, to mix posterpaint that won't spill should it drop. I also mix dishwashing liquid into the posterpaints; it washes out more easily. These relieve some of the burden of posterpainting, which the children do on large pieces of empty newsprint torn off a large roll that I pick up, free, from a local printer—it's called a roll-end.

We let the children sew with the sewing machines—provided they put them away properly after a sewing session so that baby fingers won't change the tension setting, a sure cause for fireworks from me! They can use needles and thread for handsewing books or dollclothes or costumes for puppets or freehand embroidery whenever they like. They may also use sewing patterns and fabric when they want, but they usually ask me before cutting into a big piece of nice fabric.

We are always in process of looking for and buying tools, for we feel that they are a permanent investment for the family. For example, when we were in Rarotonga we bought a small clip-on vise and a rotary hand drill, since we lacked both of these anyway, and so the children could pursue their woodwork there.   Like books, tools have grown to be a necessity for keeping ourselves amused.

Some may question the expense of tools and crafts materials, thinking that if the children went to school they wouldn't have to put so much money into these things.   Tools really are not that expensive if you stick to hand tools and compare the cost to other expenses.   When you compare the money spent for dinner for two and a movie out, you have nearly purchased the most expensive of all our tools, the big bench vise. Most tools cost much less.   If you must make a choice between the two, I feel that the investment in tools is worth more than entertainment.

When you homeschool, you face the need to fill the family's days with worthwhile activities.   Particularly if you choose to avoid commercial entertainment as we and many other families have done, after the day's hour or two of lessons, the children need to have things to choose from that will productively fill their day.   That is the grand lesson of homeschool, how to use your days wisely.   It may sound crazy but I get bothered to see the children sprawled over chairs and beds reading books a lot of the time, however good they might be!   Just by bringing the tools and materials into the home, with perhaps a series of woodworking and crafts books from the library, you build an interest and skill that can last a lifetime.   When children feel capable of shaping wood, fabric, glass into designs they have imagined, they feel capable of doing almost anything.   How often I hear observers comment on how confident my children are.   This is partially because we have always conversed together, but also I think it is because we trust them with tools; and they can create.

I don't preclude toys, however, but my attitude towards them has changed from when we began.   I think we should avoid thinking that we owe our children toys to make them happy, that they require them for a sufficient education, or that the toys replace real-life experiences.   Instead, I have come to feel that toys do for little children what good books do for adults: provide a positive and wholesome way to amuse ourselves, to educate ourselves in some ways—perhaps in some valuable ways—but never to replace our real lives.   Rather, these things only validate our experiences and extend them.   We ought to buy toys by the same standards we buy books for ourselves or our children, in good taste, of lasting worth, amusing, but always instructive as well.

Fine in theory but not always achieved!   Of course we cannot condemn dolls, but they should be in good taste, simple, soft and baby-like, certainly not full-breasted and mascaraed. I will not purchase this type of doll, although somehow neighbor children seem to donate one or more to our little girls. As soon as a leg or head comes off, I quietly throw the thing away. I am uncomfortable with the unspoken messages of this type of toy. What are we teaching our little girls when we supply them high-fashion dolls with all their accessories?

We own our measure of plastic toys—notably Leggos of various kinds—but I lean toward wooden toys if possible. They feel warmer and more interesting to touch, they age better (plastic turns into junk in short order; we have had three plastic sets of stacking rings and finally one wooden set), and they are more honest somehow. They certainly teach children that to get more toys, you can set to work and make some, while plastic teaches that to get more toys, you have to go buy some. In the same way I like soft toys of natural materials rather than synthetics, which might pill or turn sleazy; though we have some dear stuffed animals, such as our kangaroo with her little joey in pouch, made from synthetic materials.

If you can find them and afford them, you might enjoy playthings made of special materials, such as metals. I recall a silver perfume bottle-holder, hinged and highly decorated, always scented faintly with my aunt's perfume. Arthur King still owns a pewter christening mug, treasured over his life. What textural memories go with a special tea set or one of those mechanical metal reproductions of early American toys, those savings banks that feed the coin into the dog's mouth or through the clown's hoop. Of course you can make together corn-husk dolls, apple-head dolls, those skill games where you try to put the ring through the stick, bears that climb up the string, rolling hoops, and so on. These homemade toys can break just as store-bought ones do, but fixing them or making new ones enters us into a wholesome and sturdy tradition.

If asked to list some toys I like for my children, I might include the following things. First of all we love blocks. My mother bought us a large set of hardwood blocks, including some big cylinders, lovely bridges, and long building planks. A friend made us a set of pine blocks, including some hardboard roofs and many smaller pieces. I bought cheaply a set of geometric shapes, including unusual ones like truncated cones; we have some reject wood turnings, originally intended for furniture. I love to add to blocks what we call wooden-toys-by-the-pound—small wooden people, animals, cars, buildings that we ordered from Constructive Playthings. The children add Matchbox cars to their block constructions, and I like these miniature cars, provided you can avoid ones that are too flashy and vulgar looking. Sometimes they build block mazes to roll marbles through, ending in a rollway at the bottom.

We have also purchased quite a collection of Leggos—against our purist standards, however, because they are plastic and they are expensive. We have standard building sets, castle sets, space sets. We have decided not to buy any more Leggos, though they fascinate all ages; what we have already will have to do.

Less used but still pulled out on occasion are Lincoln Logs, an Erector set (the battery motor remains a constant favorite), and Tinker Toys (a frequent choice of the babies but a distinctly unpleasant set to pick up off the floor!). We have collected a fair amount of what you'd call educational toys—stacking rings; nesting blocks; lacing, tying, and buckling frames; shape insets; shape sorters; puzzles (wooden or rubber ones only will last; those cardboard frame puzzles self-destruct within a fortnight). Everyone treasures our tub full of "littles"—plastic figures of farm and zoo animals and various other creatures, including some cowboys and Indians and miniature soldiers.

I have never located a store-bought baby doll who, after two months of mothering in our home, didn't look as though she had been through a war or at least an electric shock treatment—with that synthetic hair. I have bought bald baby dolls but soon they too begin to look tired and battered. Probably the nicest doll gift came when I was expecting Avi. Our honorary grandmother wrapped up a baby and its cradle, to be opened when the baby brother arrived. The anticipation fit both Chava and me nicely.

I like the cotton dolls stuffed with wool fleece, with fuzzy mohair coiffures; these age much more beautifully than the commercial dolls. Although all the children like dolls and they all have used them, our little girls demonstrate their innate kinship with babies by fastening onto some little doll at a very young age and holding on doggedly and delightedly. Little Sarah, at just over a year old, squealed with a peculiar zest when she claimed a doll, carrying it around everywhere. To me it is another testimony that despite our differences, girls and boys are definitely born female and male.

We have a large collection of stuffed animals, some given, some purchased, many homemade. Except for the special ones, carefully chosen by loving relatives or charmingly crafted by our children, I don't care for too many stuffed animals, so often vulgar and loud and silly. Furthermore, what is a child to do with a shelf-full of stuffed animals? Better to tactfully retire the commoners to the shelves of a second-hand shop, so the well-chosen ones don't get drowned in the mess.

We do have a selection of shoddy plastic toys which no one is ready to give up yet. Some of them, such as the clock-puzzle on which you fit different-shaped number pieces, are in decent taste. Yet their slick plastic appearance makes you feel they won't last long (surprisingly, though, we rarely lose the pieces to these toys; one, called Keys to Learning, where you turn a key to push shapes out of their niches, lasted about ten years and through several moves!).

Like many modern mothers, I dislike guns. I don't buy toy guns (except, on the rare occasion, a summertime squirt gun) and prefer that no one give us guns as gifts. But my children, like most modern children, do like guns. Even if I don't buy them, they get them somehow; neighbors donate their used one, and the children craft their own. In fact, my older boys have sculpted some very good-looking guns, curving old-fashioned ones, which (if I were interested enough) have names. I let the children use these guns in their play—rather, I tolerate it—with one proviso: we don't point a gun at anyone. If a child persists in pointing guns at others, I remove the gun temporarily. This way, when someone happens to take the children shooting, they have proper practice in their bones. Besides that, I just find it offensive having a toy or any other gun pointed at me!

Sometimes people are shocked when they see our children using face cards at home. There seems to be a feeling that face cards are wicked, stemming I think from early religious feelings against people wasting their time and resources gambling with playing cards. Certainly I would feel wicked if I spent my adult time playing cards, because there are so many other things I should be doing. But the children can learn a great deal from cards: number recognition, math, color (for the little ones), patterns (also for them), memory skills, and graciousness and honesty and good temper! We first used playing cards in Rarotonga, where a neighbor boy introduced us to Last Card, a rather simple competitive game. We had to deal with cheating and temper, but overall I feel that this first dip into card-playing was somewhat positive. The smallest children really got into Last Card and quickly began to recognize colors, numbers, and suits.

After that first bout with cards, the children stopped playing pretty much, only renewing their interest when visitors would come and ask to play. David and Sammy did devise several card games of their own make, involving computation of number values based on suit and card, requiring mental math. Sometimes these got so complicated that everyone threw down his suit!

As long as children have plenty of other activities available, I doubt that face cards can lead to much trouble. Even when the children tried to unravel the mysteries of Poker, I held my peace (they haven't attempted gambling). And I smile my secret delight when I see them helping each other with their hand, showing which card would be most advantageous to play. As long as they keep cooperating, I don't worry about the wickedness of card playing.

We bought our first wagon, a classic Radio Flyer, bright red, when David was about two. That one rusted, and we bought another, which rusted. Finally we invested in one of those wooden wagons with removable red sides. Even if we abuse it—as we seem to do, letting it sit outside in the weather sometimes—Avraham repaints it and it comes out as good as new. In addition to the usual wagon games, we use it to haul wood or yard rubbish, to entertain baby when mother is busy elsewhere, and to sit in, using the wagon handle as a guide, for rollicking rides downhill (it looks much more dangerous than it is, and we haven't had any injuries).

We have bought a bicycle for everyone, from the tiny tot's four-wheeled wooden push-cycle to good-quality bikes for the bigger boys. When we were in Rarotonga, we used ten-speeds for us adults and a bicycle trailer for the three little ones. Apart from the hard work it took to haul those children around, I much prefer bicycle transportation to car. You can see and hear and feel everything as you go by. You breathe good air and get good exercise. You greet people and can easily stop and chat for a moment. When you're riding in a car, you feel one step removed from the world just outside; the children playing or stream running become just a part of the scene, not a part of you. (We still use a car, of course, but I love biking.) We have spent a little more and purchased good quality bicycles, and they are lasting much longer than cheaper ones; we can hand them down a couple of times.

We also bought a toy shopping cart, much loved and broken fairly soon. We have used a toy stroller, a hand-me-down, already much used when we got it. Avi at three immediately attached himself to it, taking it whenever we went on walks, however long, hauling it up and down steep hills, collecting rocks and shells in it, delivering laundry to each of the children. It is one of the few toys that has not worn out its interest over time.

Another such toy must be the rocking horse, or more properly, jumping horse. We have gone through a few of these too, usually repairing the springs several times, and finally discarding it when the saddle develops holes. Along with the mini-tramp, this horse provides the bouncing that children seem to need. I gave over my mini-tramp to the children long ago, though I still use it occasionally. Even when it broke, we had it welded back into shape. High-tension children might jump on it for as much as a half-hour at a time, singing or chanting to themselves. Sammy did this; the tramp almost seemed a necessity to him. When we bought our large trampoline, it provided for that need for all ages.

Of the board games we have bought, very few retain their original covers nor all of their pieces, a pretty miserable state of affairs to confess! The children like board games, of course, their favorites being checkers, chess, snakes and ladders, Yahtzee, Monopoly, and Battleship. When the two older boys were just beginning to read fluently, we used Uncle Wiggly, which supplies many cards with verses written in fairly easy language to help along their reading.

However, from about age five, David has loved making his own board games, the other children following as they have grown up. A friendly neighbor gave David a collection of classic board games from all over the world, to color and use, one of the few books we have retained over the years without destroying. Sketched on cardboard, paper, or wood, the children's homemade board games sport various configurations and rules, sometimes using dice, spinners, or wooden devices for taking turns. They cost nothing, so when the children grow tired of them and cast them aside, no parent frets over money wasted. If pieces are lost or broken, the children make new ones. I don't pay much attention to the details of these passing games, though when they are current the children devote themselves to them. The homemade chess pieces delight me, however—diminutive and nicely-colored; and I have taken a turn at homemade nickel hockey, complete with hand-carved tiny hockey sticks.

As the children grow older, we invest more in sports equipment, a ping-pong table, and so on. We continue to go through our quota of baby dolls—the homemade ones lasting much better than the storebought ones. We won't stop sinking a good deal of our pin money into books. I expect that I will occasionally get washed away by enthusiasm and purchase some educational toy or other that seems at the moment indispensable to my homeschool.

I hope that I have learned some sense about toys, and I hope that other homeschoolers will temper their toy purchases with good sense and good taste. By using restraint and good taste we can use even toys to teach our children principles of Zion. Beyond this, letting our children experience real life by contact with us and by using real tools and materials—this exceeds the limits of toys.

Prove it to yourself. The next time you buy your child a toy, see if he doesn't follow this pattern. He will be overcome with delight and perhaps a measure of greed when he first receives it. He will play with it avidly for one day to maybe a week. He'll taper off, perhaps using it every couple of days for a while. Then he'll pretty much forget about it, either forever or for a long time.

TECHNOLOGY

Television

"I don't agree with this idea of eliminating TV," one educator declared. "There are lots of good things on TV. The children will miss so much. And what about something significant, like the landing of the the Challenger spacecraft? Are we going to force our children into sneaking off to the neighbors to see something like that?"

Sometimes, while visiting relatives or neighbors, I observe my children before the TV, absorbed in a nature show perhaps, and feel a twinge of regret that they cannot experience these images and ideas in our home, for we have never had a television. But then, on come the commercials, the cartoons, the situation comedies, and I inevitably turn away, disgusted.

Gratefully, we are not alone in eliminating television from our lives. Wherever we go, we find people who have delivered themselves from the clutches of the blue-eyed god that monopolizes so much of people's time. Even in committed Christian homes, four to seven hours a day slip away in front of the tube. Once we visited a home, exemplary in many ways, the family intelligent and fun to be with. We enjoyed dinner together, and then everyone went into the living room to watch TV. Conversation stopped, hands were still and idle. During that time, we saw a murder, infidelity, and greed; we listened to music we would not have permitted at home, and we saw male and female role models—silly, sensual, exaggerated—that we could not possibly agree with. What a waste of brain power, I thought as we sat there! And there are many people who feel the same way and have decided not to try to control the television, because most people cannot (indeed, I have rarely met anyone who really did control it; most people who say they don't watch much TV are shocked when they add up how much they do watch!), so they got rid of it entirely.

Three powerful books, intelligently researched and convincingly written, explore the issues about television: *The Show and Tell Machine*, by Rose K. Goldsen; *The Plug-in-Drug*, by Marie Winn; *Four Arguments for the Elimination of Television*, by Jerry Mander. Here, I will only mention some of their ideas, ones that seem important to me; but I

184

recommend that everyone read the books and think through the arguments. People can feel very emotional about television, but I have never heard anyone who has read these books answer their contentions clearly and intelligently. Most people who insist on television speak angrily or emotionally without really examining the issues.

Television blinds us into inactivity by its very nature. Unlike work, unlike reading, unlike almost every traditional human endeavor, television demands that we remain in one place while it unfolds in a linear fashion, gluing us to the spot. In order to secure us there, the programs present fast action, short sequences, exaggerated or coarse emotions, loud music, and various technical feats.

In addition, television creates in the viewer a strange, trancelike inactivity that Marie Winn compares to drug addiction—hence the title of her well-argued book. Some observers have called it "zombie viewing" (Winn, 16). Glued to the screen hour after hour, we often see it; I have experienced it myself, not only as a child "addict," but even recently, as an adult dissenter to the medium, yet caught in its web when visiting relatives. At the time, I was in the middle of Solzhenitsyn's *Cancer Ward* and various projects, and I knew I was wasting valuable time; and still somehow I could not tear myself away. Because the action is so extreme and so quickly changed, it creates fierce tension inside us, instigating an impulse for action, then negating it, over and over, so that when at last we come away from the television, we feel tense, frustrated, even sick. There is good reason to keep hyperactive children away from the television set!

And of course when we—and in particular, when children—are watching television, we are not doing other things and cannot be ourselves: talking together, playing, reading, making music, doing crafts, cooking, exercising, even daydreaming or sleeping. What a waste of human potential, all the people in so many homes fixed to the tube, night after night! Marie Winn explains at length the damage this does to developing children, who normally would spend their days in activities that build their growing minds and muscles. We become so accustomed to filling in our spare time with prefab programs that we now feel lost and helpless if no television is available.

One of David's friends spent the weekend with us recently. He had a hard time adjusting to our nonmedia lifestyle; his mother, he reported, was videotaping all his favorite programs for him, so he could watch what he missed while he was away! Possibly the major benefit of our style of homeschooling is that children learn to profitably spend their days and hours, without adult compulsion and without long hours of inactivity in front of the TV.

Ask yourself: what did people do in the days before television, videos, computers? Were they less intelligent? Less educated? (And lest we parrot a smug yes, literacy rates have not risen since the technological revolution. Even among nonindustrialized peoples, who do not share the written tradition, their native skills and knowledge overwhelm ours in many key areas of life. Visiting one African nation, a biologist remarked that never in his lifetime could he duplicate their knowledge of their native botany: plant names, habits, habitats, uses by the thousands.)

This leads us to a very sensitive argument about television. "What about the evening news?" lament media advocates. "We need to know what goes on in the world." Mander and Goldsen both explore at length the inaccuracy of this assumption. Because of the nature of the medium, in no way could we understand the complexities of conditions as they are in the world. To explain a neighborhood conflict, Mander illustrates, you might have to talk for an hour or two; how, then, in thirty or sixty seconds—or even in five minutes—can the media teach us the truth about a coup, an earthquake, an accident?

Residents of troubled places or countries report that the media grossly overemphasizes the violence and conflict actually present. Sometimes people stage incidents for the media, just so they can get on film. Once we passed by a Peace Walk along a New Zealand country road. The media, zooming in on participants and interviewing passers-by, created a far different image than the actuality—just a straggle of hikers tramping along. More ghastly is the story of the photographer who bribed soldiers to shoot twenty prisoners so that he might capture the incident on film.

As Mander argues at length, only the coarser emotions and realities communicate well on television; subtleties, nuances, delicacy, and the aura or feeling of things are often obliterated by the medium. To me, that is the worst cheat of the evening news and documentaries—watching, we think we are learning something; but we are only ingesting selected images of the thing (from someone else's bias, inevitably), and don't feel the thing. We really don't learn much about it. We ingest it into our own emotional and cultural reality—how can we do otherwise?

Watching a program of modern dance recently, I was dismayed to find that we felt nothing at all, except perhaps admiration at the technical expertise of the dance companies. The most important aspects of performance, the feelings of excitement, rapport, drama, catharsis, are muddled or destroyed when put into television.

Even documentaries distort the realities they purport to explain. Viewers who are involved in filming of the program *Sixty Minutes*, which is supposed to explore some relevant issue in depth, complain of distortions, misrepresentations, untruths. The reporter has to select those aspects of a story that will make good television. He has to maintain his hold on his audience.   And, of course, he is reporting from his sponsors'—as well as his own—bias. While we retain the images of the thing, we usually miss the important realities.

For homeschoolers, this can be disastrous. When we rely on such programs to help us learn something about the world, we instead imbibe distortions and falsehood. Not long ago, some friends, perhaps a little annoyed with our anti-media stand, invited our family over for an evening together, and asked us to watch with them an educational video they had purchased in preference to the questionable ones that comprise the market. The lesson was about germs. Germs invade the body, the movie told us, and that is what makes us sick (even that we found slightly askew, for we feel that a healthy body will not fall ill when invaded by germs). We viewed an animated sequence of our body's immune system, soldiers rushing around through small tubes, zapping the offensive germs.

We then watched bacteria decomposing matter in a compost pile, and an organic farmer spraying his broccoli with friendly bacteria to kill invading pests—both excellent ideas, of course, but without the smell, feel, or time-sense of farming; the whole sequence only lasted a couple of minutes. A short laboratory sequence featured the show's host, a friendly black, with the laboratory technician, a friendly white. She scraped the inside of his mouth so that the germ population could be cultured in a petri dish. Of course there was no time for the twenty-four-hour incubation, so an already-prepared culture was displayed. A shot through the microscope in the lab showed the shapes of the different bacteria. Yet throughout this laboratory sequence, a stilted, artificially cheerful manner prevailed, infested with the usual self-consciousness that seems to be characteristic of television acting.   The final sequence showed the host reclining by a swamp, commenting that germs are everywhere, that we and they are part of an integrated, inter-dependent world. Very good! you might say. Yet I left this viewing feeling disgruntled.

Trying to analyze my feelings, I decided that I was put off by the brief treatment of a complex subject, which still gave the feeling that it was teaching authoritatively; by the glib presentation characteristic of television;

by items we didn't agree with, smoothly presented alongside good material, without a chance to hash over the discrepancies (after the program, the children burst out of the house to play); and by the general unreality of the television world itself.

And yet this program stood head and shoulders above the usual kind of drivel that most of us absorb in our daily television watching.

Some universities televise the beginning lectures of standard courses to relieve faculty overload. Many students I have talked to report that the program is far duller than the actual lecture itself—dull to begin with, they quip. You miss the presence of the lecturer, the energy in the hall, the spirit or intelligence that emanates from the teacher as he talks. I am not saying that you cannot learn anything from so-called educational television, but I am saying that the nature of the medium excludes many important things, many essential things, and that after the watching, rarely indeed do you feel compelled to go to a book for more information as you often do after reading a good book and skimming its bibliography.

Jerry Mander opens his study with a description of an actual cruise through the Dalmation Straits, dazzlingly beautiful—but he felt nothing. His technological life-style, including the absorption of the unreal television world, had inured him to the power of the natural world. I have experienced the same thing myself. As a television baby, I felt little on family trips to the mountains or beaches. "Look at the scenery" meant nothing, because my emotional reality, a television reality, dulled my perceptions of the natural world. Television alienates us from our most important tutor, the real world around us.

Instead of this world, television bequeaths us a world view we would certainly reject if we were to live in it directly, without time or tools to measure the morality presented. Mander, Goldsen, and Winn all treat this subject well. In television, you can always tell the good guys from the bad guys, and the good guys nearly always win. Very often, as one of Goldsen's chapters is entitled, "The State is the Good Guy"—the cops beating the lower-class robbers. So much violence appears on television that it ceases to shock or concern us. We seem to hunger for it. We get so used to televised images of violence that we cannot feel the full impact of the horrors in the real world.

I feel absolutely convinced that viewing violence begets violent behavior. One young man, having viewed a television sequence where a mugger banged a victim on the head with a baseball bat (the victim obligingly keeling over in the road), tried the same technique on an old man he wished to rob. But instead of falling down, the man cried out in pain, in agony holding his head. And in addition, children's cartoons are now riddled with violence.

For the first time, we hear of child violence, the young criminals often appallingly insensitive to the sufferings of their victims. A social worker once told me that prisoners confided to him that they can watch television and glean new ideas for criminal techniques to use once they get out!

Only in recent years have videos entered into the once-traditional culture of Rarotonga (no TV programs arrive there). Nowadays even the poorest hovel seems to have a video machine, and the uncensored stream of rubbish that flows on day and night is shocking. For the first time in the island's history, violent crimes and sexual crimes are beginning to take place and are on the increase. Without measurement by a scientific study, it seems obvious enough that the decadent images on the videos have brought the people to this kind of crime.

When Chava, at five, was hospitalized in Rarotonga with rheumatic fever, we were astonished to observe many island children, running up and down the halls and sitting in their beds, pretending to shoot each other with machine guns and other weapons; it seemed so incongruous with their traditional, warm-hearted culture. The video machine played all day and into the night in those otherwise crude hospital wards.

Equally serious and shocking is the presentation of sexual themes. As Goldsen so carefully demonstrates, television portrays a sick view of the family, capitalizing on the dramatic interest in adultery, homosexuality, divorce, abortion, unwanted or teenage pregnancy, multiple marriages, bigamous marriages, miserable children—and very often, couples with no children at all. Occasionally you will see a stable intact family, such as on "The Cosby Show," but it is an exception; even there, the mother leaves the home to work—acceptable in our society but at variance with the ideal of Gospel families.

So many shows exploit our society's addiction to aberrant sexual material: homosexuality, prostitution, incest, child abuse, all figure as dominant themes. A generation ago, traditional people committed to a moral life would shun the mention of these practices, much less sit for hours at a time watching programs about them. But now images flow into their brains, often watching together as families. Many programs combine sex with violence, and though we may not allow these programs for everyday watching, sometimes they appear as we switch channels or visit other families; and the images remain in our heads forever.

One mother told of her teenage daughter who babysat at a neighbor's home. While she was changing the baby's diaper, the children switched the dial to such a sequence, where a murderer violated his victim before killing her. The girl leaped up and switched the channel, but, having seen the thing, had nightmares for weeks afterward. While president of BYU, Dallin Oaks thoroughly explained the dangers of allowing such pornographic images to enter the mind; once there, they don't leave. Have you had the experience, as I have, of lying in bed prior to sleep, watching as images of cartoons or other programs you once saw proceeded before your eyes?

But to me, even worse than these explicit and vulgar scenes are the subtle, implied messages about sexuality that flood the screen: sly references, little jokes, glances exchanged, casual conversations about what should be a sacred topic—all these break down our respect for it and teach us to be casual about it too. Mander mentions the "television kiss," which he tried to duplicate when growing up and found disappointing. Can we really expect our children to feel reverence for their sexuality when they absorb such images about it?

Visiting one Mormon home—an exemplary family in many ways—on a Sabbath, we faced the problem of constant turning on of the television. Although the parents agreed in theory that television was not Sabbath fare, they felt they should compromise for the sake of their oldest boy at home, who was such a help to them in many ways, and who strongly wished to watch TV. It was sadly amusing to see Avraham, devotedly anti-Sabbath-television, contriving various ways to lure all the children away from the set—even inviting them to dessert before we were really ready!

Nevertheless, the children kept switching the thing on, and our little ones watched too. Unfortunately, one sequence, a dramatized rock dance, showed scenes which "weren't overtly lewd, but very much implied it," as David explained. They gave Yoni nightmares. This family was very firm in forbidding other Sabbath activities, such as jumping on the trampoline or roaming the beach, which ironically we felt were quite suitable if done in the right spirit.

Watching television, we absorb precise images about what is beautiful, and we compare ourselves, even if unconsciously, to those images, usually feeling inadequate or unbeautiful if we are not slimmed, coiffured, made-up and dressed like the gorgeous creatures on the screen (I have noticed that British programs, very common in New Zealand, more often portray homey, normal-looking characters as well). These images compel us to buy products, also advertised, to make ourselves better resemble the youthful, polished characters we see. But few of us really look like that.

I happened to visit a home of a middle-aged couple, newly-remarried. The walls were covered with magazine photos of these beautified media people, male and female, young, very sexual; near the fireplace stood a poor painting of a nude (eighteen-month-old Sarah toddled up to me to comment on the exposed "nurses," our family word for breasts). Instead of happily enjoying each other for what they were, this couple created impossible ideal images for themselves, constantly reminding them of their own inability to measure up to the pictures on the walls—and on the screen.

We feel compelled to purchase many things, including personal products, by the television. Advertisers hawk nearly everything imaginable—and also some products heretofore unmentionable, such as contraceptive devices or deodorants. Masters of the methodology of the media, these advertisers may offend, disgust, anger us, but they don't lose our attention; and that is what they want. Most ads promise or imply a happier life if we buy many of the products, and since we moderns feel chronically unhappy (because, I feel, we find ourselves separated from the elemental, satisfying aspects of life) we are willing victims. Resentful of the influence of commercials, I have bull-headedly refused to buy anything I have seen advertised on television!

Television critics always point to the appetites and tastes for products that we develop when watching the ads; certainly the worst offenders are toys and junk foods foisted onto children.

But another development of tastes is at work: the relentless formation of cultural standards. Goldsen analyzes the devastating assault that television music makes on the nation's musical taste—moving it into loud, bouncy, trivial music, "thirty-two bars in four-four time, a limited range of instruments, and a chord structure that smacks either of the ballad or the blues" (Goldsen, 85). Because of the media's electronic tricks, she contends, music reduces to mere noise on the TV; she contends that classical music doesn't stand a chance compared to this onslaught, noting that during 1970, the year commemorating the two-hundreth anniversary of Beethoven's death, almost no stations recognized the event. ABC produced one show, featuring bits of melodies played alongside rock music sequences, between jokes and gag-lines—"This is network television's customary approach to any kind of serious music: if it appears at all, it's played for laughs" (Goldsen, 86).

So when children switch on the television, they inexorably form a lifetime's tastes. How ridiculous to try to interest what I call "television babies" in what we insist is good music, when we have nursed and weaned them on cheap music. When an objectionable sequence of music flits by, no parent, no matter how conscientious, will turn to his child and say, "That wasn't good music; we don't listen to that type of music."

When I was a little child, we didn't watch much television; but by the time I was eight or ten, and in the years afterward, we watched nearly constantly, as many children do today. I remember feeling a sense of foreignness when I would hear classical music—or even big-band music, which seemed archaic! Only in my teens did I consciously cultivate a taste for serious music. When I decided to eliminate rock music completely, I found myself with two conflicting reactions: one, a distaste and revulsion for the coarseness of the stuff; and the other, a sentimental nostalgia for those pop tunes that shaped my adolescence.

Goldsen demonstrates that many children's shows, especially the animated ones, either feature rock groups or include them in the show's format, regardless of whether they fit into the plot. She also notes that soft or "bubblegum" rock, as she terms it, predisposes young listeners to accept harder rock; and she exposes some of the effects of punk or "shock" rock, as she calls it. She documents the fact that the television networks are paid by record producers to showcase their music in order to increase sales. So it seems clear that television music is designed to develop the kind of taste that will sell rock music to the masses.

Television teaches us what is funny, too; we can be sure of it, because the laughing sound tracks leave no uncertainty. Most of the humor centers on "one kind . . .drop-your-pants, pie-in-the-face, the big boff, and the one-liner" (Goldsen, 68). If we laugh at something else, we feel strange or alone, for no laugh track reinforces our amusement. We become desensitized as we chortle with the canned laughter at sexual innuendos, which comprise such a large part of the situation comedies. Rarely do we laugh at the gentle irony, or with bittersweetness; it is usually coarse or obvious humor that is laughed at on the tube. Even though we parents would seriously object to the vulgar comedy if our children were to produce it, we tacitly encourage it by letting the children watch and laugh. It not only dulls the moral sense; it blunts the intellect, because humor should spring from tricks we play on our minds—word tricks, image tricks.

What about educational TV—what about "Sesame Street?" parents may ask. Winn proves that the youngsters who watched the program year after year did not excel in school. Certainly, they can recognize letters from having seen them on the show, but Goldsen reminds us that "children throughout the land know the Jolly Green Giant and associate him with the Niblets he symbolizes for LeSueur industries" (Goldsen, 244) as well as other commercials' contents. But instead of proceeding from the letters into literacy, the children only receive a lesson in TV tactics: fast-paced, quick-cut sequences filled with snatches of music (rarely a complete composition, as most of the sequences only last a few seconds).

What children do get is a complete course in television literacy: all the tricks and techniques of the medium. Goldsen describes this in detail in her chapter "Literacy without Books," which every homeschooler arguing for "Sesame Street" should feel obliged to read. The result of this sort of programming causes "a decrease in imaginative play and an increase in aimless running around, noninvolvement in play materials, low frustration tolerance, poor persistence, and confusion about reality and fantasy" (Winn, 40). Does that sound like some little one you know?

Winn quotes various studies, pointing out that little actual learning takes places from television viewing and posits a very challenging reason why. Explaining that a newborn's brain is not divided into specific functions, she shows that as a child grows, the left-brain and right-brain functions differentiate. The right brain works in a verbal, feeling, image-making and -receiving mode, while the left brain processes the verbal, rational, problem-solving, mathematical, and so forth. When a child watches television a great deal during his formative years, the right brain receives excessive stimulation, while the left brain, which should be forming its language capacities, is being grossly neglected.

And as Piaget, Montessori, and other child-development authorities have emphasized, certain processes of growth take place at critical periods in a child, and if these learning processes are denied the child, he will never learn those particular things as well as he might have. If you are raising children yourself, you have observed these periods: at one time, a little one becomes completely absorbed in the minutiae around him: bugs, pebbles, leaves, seeds. Soon this period passes. At another point, he becomes impassioned with forming letters and trying to make words. If you nurture this one, it will mature into reading and writing; but if you suppress it, perhaps it will never blossom as it should.

Children in these sensitive, critical period perform tasks over and over, practicing relentlessly; if you tried to force them to do such work, you could never succeed. Winn suggests that children who spend their language-forming periods watching, not talking, may never regain the fluency and articulateness that they could have had.

Another moral issue attaches to this right-brain, left-brain problem. Mander cites research on children watching television. Having noticed that people viewing television seem almost asleep, in a trance-like state, researchers wanted to find out exactly what happens when we watch television. They found that human beings habituate themselves to "repetitive light stimuli (flickering light, dot patterns, limited eye movement . . .) The brain has essentially decided that there is nothing of interest going on—at least nothing that anything can be done about—and virtually quits processing the information that goes in" (Mander, 206). The left brain, which makes decisions and judgments about what the mind receives, subsides, and the right brain just receives the images from the television.

For an experiment, children were asked to choose their favorite television programs while their brain wave activity was monitored. Researchers assumed that there would be some activity in both brain hemispheres, since the kids would be emotionally involved in their favorite programs. Instead, "they just sat back. They stayed almost all the time in alpha (right-brain function). This meant that while they were watching they were not reacting, not orienting, not focusing, just spaced-out" (Mander, 210).

One of the researchers Mander quotes also commented, "The horror of television is that the information goes in, but we don't react to it. It goes right into our memory pool and perhaps we react to it later but we don't know what we are reacting to. When you watch television you are training yourself not to react and so later on, you're doing things without knowing why you're doing them or where they came from" (Mander, 211).

These findings should shake us all, particularly since for many Christians, including Latter--day Saints, a central doctrine is the principle of free agency. What does it mean to us when we ourselves, and when our children, engage in a protracted activity that short-circuits our conscious ability to choose, to act? Of course, we can still continue to think while we watch television, but this brain shift neverthless seems to characterize the bulk of TV watching.

"Well, what about General Conference?" continues the argument. "We keep a TV in the house so we can watch the Church's General

Conference." Here I have mixed feelings. We watched in our small New Zealand branch a videotape of some of the Conference sessions, since none of the live broadcasts reach that far. Sitting together in the chapel, we truly enjoyed watching the facial expressions, hearing the choirs and watching them sing, observing the organ swelling. After that, I felt a little twinge again that we miss all of that, listening to Conference on the radio as we do when we are in the States.

But even so, analyzing my real feelings on the matter, I decided that we still could not bring television into our lives, despite this one loss. Sometimes we can watch Conference sessions on other people's machines. Certainly we read the talks, though I know we lose much of the vocal inflection that illuminates the discourses. Not owning a television doesn't eliminate the experience completely—there are plenty of people who do, and who always invite us over for sessions. Often kind friends offer to bring us a set, so we can watch Conference! But most of the time we have gratefully declined, sitting together as a family around the radio. Although I feel unresolved on this one point, our inner feeling has been to stand by our decision not to admit the TV into our home.

Some deeper issues underlie our firmness about television. Mander explains at length what happens to us when we watch television. Our bodies and minds assume the posture of inactivity. Our eyes focus on a very small area, focused on infinity, as it were. And into our eyes flows a very limited spectrum of light: red, blue and green wavelengths. Mander discusses the research of Dr. John Ott, the time-lapse photographer who worked for Walt Disney and who later began to research on light in a research institute. His books, *Health and Light and Light, Radiation, and You* are scientific, and if you seriously want to look into the issues, they are very worthwhile.

Basically, humans receive light in their eyes in a corresponding way as they take food into their bodies. Until the last two hundred years, man only received natural light, but more recently we live much of our lives in artificial lighting, which, researchers are revealing, is damaging to our health—particularly fluorescent light, the way television images are produced (though in a fluorescent light, gas particles are excited to make light, while with television, particles in the screen are excited to produce the light). Researchers have proven that "malillumination," the prolonged reception of limited light spectra rather than the full spectra of natural light, adversely affects the endocrine system, including sexuality.

TV light is also suspected to lead to lowered vitality, less resistance to disease, aggressive behavior, hyperactivity, perhaps cancer and heart disease. The relationship of light spectra and trace minerals in the diet has already been established: if certain wavelengths of light are not available, certain nutrients are not absorbed. Most of the research focuses on light taken into the eyes, which Mander describes thus: "It is not quite accurate to say that when we watch television we are looking at light; it is more accurate to say that light is projected into us. We are *receiving* light through our eyes into our bodies, far enough in to affect our endocrine system. . . .. When you are watching television, you are experiencing something like lines of energy passing from cathode gun to phosphor through your eyes into your body. You are as connected to the television set as your arm would be to the electrical current in the wall . . .if you had stuck a knife into the socket. . .There is a concentrated passage of energy from machine to you, and none in the reverse. In this sense, the machine is literally dominant, and you are passive" (Mander, 171).

Along with others, I am very sensitive to artificial illumination, especially of fluorescents, but also every kind of electric light. They make me feel irritable, nauseated, and addled. When I walk or stand close under an electric bulb, I feel dizzy and out of reality. Watching television (and around a VDT of some kinds of computers) makes me feel the same way—restless, nauseated, unable to think clearly. Perhaps some people are unusually sensitive to it. Yet Mander and Winn cite many examples, anecdotal though they may be, where people feel the same thing. I am personally convinced that sitting and watching television is bad for the body.

Mander also explains at length that watching television changes the way we perceive the world and ourselves in it. Because human beings make mental images, anything that places images in the brain has the power to alter us indelibly. Mander suggests that we *become* the images we repeatedly ingest, and I agree. That is why Church leaders repeatedly warn us away from pornography. That is why, at least in part, they urge us to read the scriptures, for these are replete in images, visual, aural, tactile; they have power to move us, to change us. As we fill our memories with television images of the kind we have discussed, we ourselves become like those images.

You have probably met people, young and old, who watch so much that they have become "television people"; they live in a mental world of TV. When confronted with situations like the ones they have viewed, they react as they see people on television. They have become unable to function in reality. For example, Winn quotes an emergency room nurse who "reports that parents just seem to sit there these days when they come in with a sick or seriously injured child, though talking to the child would distract and comfort him. They don't seem to know how to talk to their own children at any length" (Winn, 147). She reprinted a cartoon from *The New Yorker* showing a man changing a flat tire during a rainstorm; his two children watched from the car window. "Don't you understand?" the father was saying, "This is *life*, this is what is happening. We *can't* switch to another channel." Constantly immersing ourselves into the very artificial world of television, real-life sometimes eludes us, and sometimes we cannot behave properly or even perceive properly what is really happening.

What about the families who insist that they control the television in their homes? For the most part, these families watch far more television than they realize. When they actually keep track of the hours in front of the tube, they are amazed. Also, the television presents a constant source of temptation and a source of contention: "Can't we watch this or that? Just one more show? Why not today?" and so on. Even families who closet their TVs to be pulled out for special occasions experience this, and once the machine is out, they have a hard time putting it away again.

The only real answer lies in getting rid of the medium completely. I am not alone in this: Wendell Berry suggests a ritual in which the whole family watches as the father takes the television out into the driveway and drops it (Winn quotes just such a sequence from John Cheever's *Bullet Park*). As I have shown, the content of the programs does not present the worst problem; it is the actual watching itself that is to blame. People do live quite happily without television. Everywhere I go, a few people say something like a lady I met, a Jehovah's Witness: "When I was baptized, I realized I couldn't have both things, spirituality and the TV. So I got rid of my television."

True, the first weeks without TV can be painful, like withdrawal from a drug, as Winn suggests. But once you are freed from it, you will find yourself progressively happier and busier and clearer in your mind. I know that this runs contrary to the opinions of many people, dear friends included, so I say it gently but surely: you will have a much superior homeschool (and a much happier home) if you get rid of your television and videos.

You can't really differentiate between the TV and videos—they both use the same technology and affect our brains in the same way. Some argue rightly that you might get a higher quality of viewing with videos, having the chance to select. But fine videos are a mere sprinkle in the usual video offering, and rare is the family that confines itself to the best. Occasionally, we watch a video at the library, or at someone's home; a kind friend allowed us to view "My Fair Lady" after we had listened to the sound track and read the play. When we can, we go to a movie instead of watching the video because of the superior quality and because the experience is more complete (Mander points out that in a theater, you can at least move your head and your eyes, while watching television renders you nigh static). We have seriously considered purchasing a VCR and monitor for playing videos without television reception but haven't been able to make the conceptual leap into even that medium, so far. Going to a play is infinitely better; putting on the play, better yet (two large homeschool families with a wide age range in their children wrote, costumes, staged, and produced a delightful drama, all child-initiated. A far cry from TV!).

A brief note of caution, however: in eliminating television, we must not fall into the trap of thinking negatively about those who do watch. Better to sit hypnotized in front of the tube daily, yet retain a compassionate, loving feeling about others, than to virtuously abstain and critically look down on others. The same applies to the music we listen to: more important even than taste is love. Homeschoolers can deceive themselves with a false sense of superiority, failing to bump shoulders with people different than ourselves.

Computers

Some time ago we visited the home of a friend who had invented some brilliant computer programs for teaching reading and for geography; the latter featured a space satellite hovering over various continents, the game consisting of identifying more and more specific places as you neared land. I wanted to see how it worked; my children played as our friend guided them, and I stood by and watched. Soon I started feeling queasy and muddled; thinking I must be coming down with the flu, I said nothing about it. Recently, some friends kindly inputted a large part of the manuscript of this book on their home computer. I offered to do my part by entering some of the editorial corrections. Learning the basic procedures presented no problems, but as the time went on, I began to feel more and more ill, and when I came home, Avraham commented, "You look pale and out of focus."

Of course, some people might be more sensitive than others to computer light, but though little research has been done on the matter, early findings seem to corroborate my empirical experience. Because a large proportion of office computer users are women, when cluster groups of such workers using certain VDT's began showing unusual concentrations of miscarriages and birth defects in surviving babies, researchers suspected unhealthy radiation from the machines. Unfortunately, no laws and no standard practices require routine checks on radiation emitted from these terminals, and the concentration of radiation can vary widely.

Dr.John Ott, mentioned above, performed some experiments with computer light. He placed bean plants in front of the leaded-screened VDT; the plants showed signs of sickness immediately, the leaves yellowing, the stems drooping. Considering that the plants might have been placed too close (though computer users sit that close), he positioned three leaded screens between the VDT and the plants. These plants showed the same symptoms, recovering their health only when placed in a normal greenhouse. Evidently computer radiation is more powerful than usual emanations to present such bad effects even through this shielding.

Dr. Ott placed a microscope with normal blood on a computer screen. Very soon the blood showed severe clumping, called *rouleaux*. He hypothesized that computer radiation causes this clumping in live users; he collected blood from a computer buff who had sat at the machine for about eight hours. Sure enough, his blood evidenced the same severe *rouleaux*. He recovered normal blood consistency after a day outdoors in natural light.

Doctors suggest that some glaucoma might result from computer light and some are concerned about the effects of x-rays, particularly on growing children. These are the immediate, short-term effects of computer radiation; no one knows the long-term results of continued exposure.

In addition to health considerations, I feel uneasy about using computers for learning. Teachers in computer-based schools have told me that while their students can work out math and grammar problems on the machines, when they are presented with the same problems on paper, they cannot do them; they cannot transfer their skills.

Even computer buffs admit they are fascinated with what the machine can do. This worries me; I keep feeling that we should care about what people can do. In a light-hearted essay in *BYU Today*, Marcia Stornetta, writing about a computer purchased to write a thesis, chronicled her experience: "Soon our lives processed around little Mac. Conversations with friends changed. We compared our computers' memories and print qualities as parents do toilet training and school grades. We demonstrated our newest software more readily than parents display baby albums. Software packages decorated our coffee table. Computer-illiterate friends stopped dropping by. And when hackers happened by, we dragged them in to see her perform. No one escaped our home without hearing how we'd taught her to do Beethoven's Fifth via disk.

"Suddenly not only our quality time, but our quantity time was spend on her. Dining alone one night while my husband babbled BASIC gobbedly-gook with her, I noted our new little, user-friendly addition had deleted our budget, our social life and our time. Undoubtedly, I concluded, her wiles would next win my husband away from me. Worse yet, no matter what software we gave her, she would write no thesis for me.

"Now my envy is not easily put by . . . So I marched upstairs, unglued my husband from her keyboard and unplugged her. Then straight to the nearest drugstore we drove, bypassing business computer stores, educational computer stores, computer outlet stores, discount software stores and even a used computer store. But not once did I blink. Nor did we linger among the rows of computer magazines once inside the drugstore. But a beeline we made for the desk supplies. And with no hesitation I grabbed a yellow, five-cent, no. $2\frac{1}{2}$ pencil. Triumphantly, I slammed down my dollar bill at the checkout while my husband, still stupefied with hacker's gaze, stared.

"I bought that pencil. Simple enough. That pencil, a sharpener, and an eraser. They don't write my thesis either, but they sure beat carrying around a computer" (*BYU Today* (June 1987), 56).

At the same time, friends explain to me how useful computers can be in editing, in genealogy, in accounting. I can't argue with them. But I feel sure that children learning at home—or at school for that matter—will do better without the machines; and I am not certain that they belong in homes generally. (As John Holt points out, nothing done in homes [as opposed to businesses] economically justifies buying a computer.) Although Holt, that long-time author and educator who became the staunch and successful advocate of homeschools everywhere, expressed concerns somwhat different than mine, his thoughts were so intriguing that I obtained permission to reprint his short article on this subject:

The Ideas behind Computers

Truly successful inventions are likely to have ideas behind them; that is, they meet human needs which are not merely physical or economic, but psychological and emotional.

The automobile is a good example. It has profoundly changed the face of the world and the patterns of human life. From where did it get its magic power? Mostly from a dream, a wish, which human beings have cherished and pursued since ancient times, but found only in myths, like Pegasus the flying horse or magic carpets—the dream of going wherever they want, and many times faster than their feet or even a horse could ever carry them.

A middle-aged Danish woman, who had just bought the first car she had ever owned or driven, once expressed this dream as we drove through Copenhagen, still mostly untroubled by severe traffic jams. In a voice of true rapture she said, "I feel so free!"

That was ten years ago. Whether she still feels so free, I do not know. Living in Boston, where I can walk to most of the places I go and take public transport to most others, I feel more free because I have not owned a car in ten years or so and do not expect ever again to own one. In recent years I have said this to many people; almost without exception they have said to me, "Oh, you're lucky! I wish I didn't have to own a car." Recent figures claim that for most Americans the cost of owning a car is now over $4000 a year. Clearly an invention, a tool, which most people feel they have no choice but to own and which costs them many thousand dollars a year is not a liberating but an enslaving tool. It has added much more to our burdens and problems than to our pleasures. Most things that we really love to do, we could do without cars; the things we have to use them to do are mostly things we feel we can't get out of doing.

The computer is clearly another successful invention. Whether it will prove to be as enduring as the automobile, or be a liberating or an enslaving tool, it is too early to tell, but successful it certainly is. What are the ideas behind its success, what psychic needs does it fill! Two seem very clear. The first is the Cartesian idea of which I wrote in my review of A SAND COUNTY ALMANAC in *Growing without Schooling* #32, namely that all of reality, everything that exists, is a machine, of which every part can be expressed as a number. The early educational psychologist Thorndike stated this flatly: "Everything that exists can be measured"—an idea which has corrupted and crippled education to this day. Or, as we might put it, anything we can't count, doesn't count.

Computers powerfully reinforce the modern myth that anything and everything important can and can only be expressed in numbers. People have of course believed this for many years before anything like the modern computer was invented. But computers make it much easier to believe and much harder to oppose.

The other idea embodied in the computer is the idea that information can somehow be a substitute for judgment, wisdom, courage, faith, and luck—that if you just have enough pure facts at your disposal you can know exactly what will happen, and make happen what you want to happen. This need for absolute certainty and absolute control, while understandable enough in a rapidly changing and dangerous world, is a weakness and sickness. Like the wish for unlimited mobility, it is also long enshrined in myth. The ability to know the future is one of the things which human beings have always craved and for which many have been willing to sell their souls to the devil. Since on the whole we do not believe the truths that come down to us in stories, but only what moves pointers on dials, we still persist in the folly of thinking that we can get the best of that bargain.

One reason I am more fearful than hopeful about the future of computers is that I find it hard to see how much good can come of an invention which so strongly depends on and reinforces two such bad ideas. The first idea, that everything that exists can be measured and that whatever we can't count doesn't count, is from a scientific point of view absurd; from any conceivable religious point of view, it can only be called blasphemous, and it is astonishing that so few religious thinkers point this out. The second idea, that information can replace judgment, that if we have enough facts we can't go wrong, is equally silly, and is contradicted by every day's news. Within the last quarter Pan American Airlines announced what the financial columns said was the largest quarterly loss ever reported by an American corporation. Yet we may be sure that Pan Am had as many and as good computers, and as much raw information, as its rivals. Where it failed was in not knowing which of its information was important, or in making wise use of it. This is something that in the nature of things computers cannot do.

Not believing in faith or judgment, we don't believe in souls, still less the Devil. But if the busy makers and sellers of computers could convince us, as they are doing their best to, that with their machines we can really know and control the future, we might be willing to make any changes in our laws, customs, morals, ideas of right and wrong, that computers might seem to demand, not least of them the right to privacy, to reveal no more of ourselves to the world than we wish to reveal.

Let me be a bit more specific about these dangers. I have said that an important freedom for me is the right not to own a car—or for that matter, a television set. So far the government has not tried to deny me these choices. But there are already strong signs that it may soon try to deny me the choice of not owning a computer or spending time learning how to run it. A very slippery, tricky, and sinister little phrase is beginning to make its way, I should say force its way, into our language—"computer literacy." It has appeared in practically every statement about education that I have seen in the past six months. A recent *Christian Science Monitor* story reports "Both [California State Superintendent of Education] Monig's proposal and one put forward by Democratic State Sen. Gary Hart . . .would require . . .one year of computer training for a high school diploma." My friend Ed Pino from Colorado told me just yesterday that already sixteen colleges require their entering freshmen to buy a computer, and 120 make some kind of computer training a requirement for admission.

What is it that these educators want to compel students to know? Probably a modest amount of computer vocabulary—names of computer hardware, etc.—most of which I have learned from a little casual browsing in computer magazines—and the ability to do some simple programming in BASIC. But BASIC is even now hardly ever used for any serious business or scientific purposes, and within a decade it will probably be useless. For many years the ability to type well has been a very valuable skill–I count it one of the most useful things I have ever learned. Even now it is a great deal more useful for most life purposes than the ability to do simple programming. But no schools, though they might have been wise to do so, have ever made typing a graduation requirement, or colleges made it an entrance requirement, or demanded that all their students own a typewriter. No doubt the makers of typewriters are kicking themselves for not having ever thought of the phrase "typewriter literacy." But the typewriters never pretended to be more than a handy tool to write things with, instead of some magical way of knowing and controlling the future.

Who is going to be allowed to decide what people shall be compelled to know about computers. Who will write the textbooks for all those "computer literacy" courses? In all probability, the same people who are making and selling the computers. Will the students be taught to be skeptical about computers and cautious about buying them? I doubt it very much. Will they learn, as in my casual browsing I have learned, that most computer hardware is incompatible with most other hardware, and that most of the people who sell this hardware either don't know that or won't tell you? Or that the first word processing program put out by IBM for use with their personal computer was so bad that they soon had to withdraw it? Or that nothing done in homes (as opposed to businesses) economically justifies buying a computer? Or that when you buy a new model computer you will probably have to wait two or three years for the necessary programs to go with it? Or that businesses should not spend more than about one percent of their annual gross income on a computer? Or that at all price levels computers have been and are plagued by serious problems of reliability, and that most of the people who sell them do not know how to or will not service them? All this seems extremely unlikely. What is much more likely is that the schools, which have long been teaching Science-Worship, will now begin to teach Computer-Worship.

There's an old Arab saying that if you let the camel's nose into your tent you will soon have the entire camel. We have allowed into our tent—our society, our laws, our schools—the nose of a very large, determined, clever, unscrupulous, and in the long run possibly dangerous camel. Unless we are very careful, we may soon find ourselves obliged by law to buy whatever the computer industry wants to sell us. I still think there is a chance that computers may become in Ivan Illich's phrase, "convivial tools," which, like bicycles, typewriters, and cassette tape recorders (to name only three of the many), serve and empower their users, instead of, like autos and TV, burden and diminish them. But it will have to be up to us, not the computer industry, to make sure this happens. (*Growing without Schooling* 32:22–23)

To test your inner reaction to the machine, you might try to do what a dear friend did. At first she explained that her children, some of them homeschoolers, do *creative* activities with their computer-drawings—writing stories (even a novel), making up original games. Then she decided to tune into her real feelings as she worked with the computer, and found out that she reacted pretty much as I did; she began to limit her time with the computer, and urged her husband to do the same, and encouraged her children toward other creative activities, which they gladly did—they are an exceptional family.

Despite all these arguments against computers, I have had to agree with friends who insist on computers' efficacy in editing, accounting, and genealogy. As convinced as I was about my opinion on computers, when complications arose in preparing the manuscript for this book, a friend kindly offered to *give* me a Macintosh™ to bail me out. I accepted.

I found what a powerful writing/editorial tool it was, and somehow the light from its screen didn't bother me like other light has. Still, the children want to spend hours before the screen; I don't complain if they are writing or doing schoolwork or scouts, but drawing programs and, lately a game disk they have been given, make me impose strict limits. Despite these reservations, I have had to swallow some of my words against computers!

You will be able to guess my feelings about video games, or "spacies," as they are called in New Zealand. As with computers, these games somehow seem to gobble us up; playing, we feel drawn more and more into them. One homeschool mother, commenting on President Reagan's approval of these games because they resemble operating military aircraft, felt upset that children should be spending themselves in activities that encouraged power, control, killing. A valid concern, but perhaps more elemental is again the problem of people fascinated with the antics of machines, immersing their human minds into the limiting and at the same time mesmerizing routines of video games.

Marie Winn comments, too, that these video games very much limit the kinds of play children normally enjoy. One computer enthusiast explained to us that these games develop the mind toward the abstractions needed for higher mathematics. Granting that this is true (and I am not convinced that it is), I would think that the price is too high to pay. Traditional ways of stretching the abstract reasoning powers still work.

Although I have emphasized television and computers in this discussion of technology, we do well to examine all of the technological gadgets that clutter our lives: ever-more complex digital watches, transistor radios in all their shapes, mechanical dolls that coo in various phrases and jerk their arms up and down, toy guns and lasers that rattle and glow, and even cassette players and stereos. Do we litter our lives with too many or with poor quality *things*?

Voluntary simplicity applies here as well. What is wrong with all this stuff? Fundamentally, it fills our lives—and our minds—with items in poor taste, usually made of plastic, which ages quickly and badly, and which lowers our activities to their level. They break soon and easily; they force us to look at them as they clutter our shelves; and, especially in the case of the toys, they demean us in the same ways that the biblical gods demeaned those people, forcing us to internalize their images every day.

Why not govern our lives by the principle "rather less than more?" In other ages, people lived successfully and intelligently without these high-tech gadgets. Indeed, along with others, I question the Darwinian notion that we are at the apex of civilization, as most of us seem to accept. If it were so, we would be more gentle, more refined, more understanding, more charitable. Instead, our technology coarsens us, subtly and grossly at the same time. It must explain at least in part the violent crimes that beset us everywhere; the shocking rate of abortion; the sex crimes; the theft, large and small; the drug abuse and alcohol abuse; the universal preoccupation with getting money, spending money; the shattering of families, everywhere.

We have been ripped away from the traditional way of life that people have lived for most of our planet's history. I am not saying that all technology is bad—thank heaven for the washing machine!—but lately I have been pondering the fact that two hundred years ago, and most of the time prior, about 90 percent of the population worked the land, 5 percent pursuing other work. Now in industrialized nations the tables are nearly turned to the opposite. What are we missing? Why was Adam told to work the ground "by the sweat of [his] face?" I feel that there is a great healing in the work we do outdoors, in the natural light, in the soil, in the wind, in the heat of the sun. I occurs to me that there might be a reason for crops taking their season to grow, requiring vigilance and care from us. We must go out, exercise our bodies, take in the sun, and even the rain. Perhaps there are deeper reasons than self-sufficiency that cause the prophets to urge us to make gardens.

As I was studying about the negative effects of artificial light, at breakfast we happened to discuss a scripture, *Doctrine and Covenants* 88:6–13. The phrases, "that [Jesus] might be in all and through all things, the light of truth; which truth shineth"; and then—after mentioning the lights of the sun, moon, stars, and the earth—"and the light which shineth, which giveth you light, is through him who enlighteneth your eyes, which is the same light that quickeneth your understandings; which light proceedeth forth from the presence of God to fill the immensity of space—The light which is in all things, which giveth life to all things."

"Does this mean that the sun's light is the same as spiritual light?" I asked Avraham. He thought that there was probably not a literal correspondence, but that both kinds of light were likely related to each other and that both came from the same Source. This line of thought brought home forcibly the notions of good light and bad light: the one enhances us, improves our health, blesses us—the other depletes, limits, and in some ways, harms us. All of which bade me to take my typewriter outside into the sea breezes and afternoon sunlight!

I have often toyed with the thought of writing a funny article titled, "Was there life before videos?" There are some kids who have never imagined a pleasant evening at home—or with friends—without videos. Many adults feel very threatened at the thought of losing their television/video watching. Perhaps we are so immersed in our high-tech culture that we have lost our ability to see ourselves living in any other way.

But homeschool presupposes another way. We are trying to develop our children into superior adults, not copies of the troubled people all around us. Rethinking the effects of the technology in our homes seems a vital part of this process.

One homeschooling mother travels a lot with her husband and two sons. Sitting by an IBM regional executive one day, she discussed home computers with him. He adamantly expressed his opinion that computers have no proper uses in the home, though they can be appropriate in business settings; children should be spending their time with more creative, growing experiences. He certainly would not allow any of his children near the computer games that have spawned out of the software business!

During another conversation with a Houston child psychiatrist, she learned that many children are developing difficult psychological problems because of computers. These children use the machines enough to develop a fondness, a relationship with them, and so have a difficult time relating to the human beings in their lives. Further, they have a hard time understanding the realities of situations around them, of thinking logically about real-life problems. The particular mind-set that computer games and programs create make it hard for these youngsters to live in the real world. Of course, most often those who are immersed in the technology cannot see this. Unless we stand away from it for a while, it tends to cloud our thinking.

We experienced some of the effects of computers (and television too) when we lived for several weeks with friends who allowed their use freely. I found that the children became more and more attached to using the machines the more they were allowed their use. Though they seemed pretty willing to let each other take turns, they wanted to spend more and more hours at the computer, even inventing excuses to go downstairs so they could tinker with it. In addition, with both the computer and television in the house, the children now expressed that there was nothing to do when they weren't permitted access to the machines. Interestingly, I have noticed that children who are thoroughly enculturated into school where they are told what to do throughout the entire day, often feel there is "nothing to do" unless they can plug into a television program, go to a friend's house (to watch TV!), or pursue some activity under an adult's supervision.

OUTINGS

Most of our homeschool outings fall into two categories: things we have to do, such as errands and shopping, and things we want to do for the school experience, like trips to the museum. Of course we often mix the two.

When we first started homeschool, I felt that we had to contrive many different field trips to enrich the children's lives. Right away I ran into a frustrating problem that only grew as the children did: the older children's tolerance for running around and seeing things far outstretched the younger ones'. By the time we made it to the end of touring the newspaper company, I would be wrestling with a squawking, squirming year-old, grimly vowing never to venture out again. Part of the problem of course is timing. I try to begin trips early before the little ones wear out. If we arrive at the natural history museum at 11:15, someone small is going to grumble by noon. Furthermore, I have tried to relax about fulfilling some high duty to show the children the entire world in a formal field trip.

Instead, during the normal course of our errands, we view and experience plenty of the real world. When we pick up feed for the chickens, we can walk around the mill, examine the big machinery (with permission), watch the bags fill up, smell the good grain smells, observe the different kinds of feed and seeds, and watch the office workers tot up our purchases.

The older children can help carry out the sacks and load them into the car. Visiting the bakery for some whole-wheat loaves (although we usually make our own), we slip into the back room to watch the big racks of pans emerge from the ovens, crusty and fragrant, to see the doughnuts come tempting out of the fryer, and to marvel at the amount of sugar going into various confections.

Sometimes we stop at the printers to get copies made or to pick up some offcuts or roll ends of paper. The workers take us out back to watch the big web press and offset and the sophisticated photographic equipment, all running off advertisements and newspapers. We stop by the room where workers sit together in a circle, assembling booklets and chatting. We haul off a big box of different kinds of papers from wedding announcements, advertising leaflets, book covers.

At the butcher's shop we gawk at the huge sides of beef aging in the cooler, feeling a little queasy at the sight! We watch the workers routinely slice through the hunks of flesh, watching the hamburger being ground up or the steak being tenderized. Afterwards we talk about the fact that every time we eat meat, some creature has had to give its life for it; and we recall that when we raise and slaughter fifty odd chickens for the freezer, everybody helps, even David, the vegetarian! We feel a sense of poignancy and regret at the life-taking process, though our carnivores don't give up their occasional meat meal.

Sometimes we just visit friends, enjoying the company and different selection of toys of another family. Especially we enjoy stopping at homeschool families, where the two mothers chatter at a furious pace while the children play with toys and show each other their latest projects. Stopping at someone else's home helps all of us; it gives the children time to play with others for an extended time, especially someone like themselves, and gives us all a refreshing view into others' hearts, reminding us that we are all so much alike, minimizing our problems as we view them in another family as well.

Often Avraham will take the children with him to the university as he has to photocopy part of a manuscript, pick up books, or run other errands. Without formal instruction the children absorb the routine of the world of offices and classrooms.

On our trips, we like to stop at the hardware store to replenish our supply of nails, screws, hinges and hooks, paint and sandpaper, and wood scraps. Everybody loves the hardware store because of the fascinating little things you can buy cheaply. We rarely leave without a few dowels to be made into ships' masts or into axles. Sometimes we get permission to carry away a series of paint sample chips to fashion into a Montessori color shading game. At the art supply store, we gaze greedily at the many supplies that we cannot usually afford, coming away with pads of paper, water colors or acrylics, paintbrushes or varnish. Occasionally we make a big purchase like the set of sharp carving tools David wangled one year. We might visit the stained-glass shop for some scrap glass, or a glass cutter or some copper foil. We moon around the crafts stores, avoiding the tasteless decorations if we can, but buying balloons, pompoms, felt, paint, or occasional indulgences like clockworks, piggy-bank music box kits, origami papers, balsa wood.

We like to visit bookstores, but the new books always dismay us with their prices. At used bookshops everybody collects a few volumes that his heart craves, and then I make the final selection. Once a soft-hearted used bookseller donated a miniature Bible which you had to read with a magnifying glass, and the children gallantly shared it among themselves until someone lost it and everyone forgot about it. Most of our book purchases come from the used shops, though Avraham often picks up a random volume or two from the university bookstore, often books for the younger children in the picturebook format. We like stationery shops too, for pads of paper, stamp pads, brass fasteners, paper clips, stickers, glue . . . As you can see, many of our field trips center around buying materials for the homeschool.

Sometimes we take off on genuine educational trips, of course. We often visit the art museum, the natural history museum, various pioneer museums, the educational toy lending library, and of course the public library, which seems to run from year to year on the fines we pay in overdue books (we check out forty or fifty books, which collect impressive fines after a week or two overdue). Quite often we invite other homeschool children or neighbor children along with us, and we buy a package of crackers or a treat on the way home. We especially love the science displays and the dinosaur museum at BYU.

We have visited radio stations and movie studios, art workshops, and rehearsals for concerts in music and dance (it's very interesting to watch these rehearsals, and if you come into a dress rehearsal, it's much easier than trying to arrive at bedtime for the beginning of a concert). Because I love modern dance, we sometimes go to evening concerts, though once in a while, you can catch a matinee. Concerts are problematic, of course. As soon as you all file in (if you attend as a homeschool—which means mother and children), the two-year-old has to go to the bathroom or the baby starts to cry. Ideally one can leave the younger children to play at a friend's home and take their older children with you to the concert. And then, if the concert disappoints you for some reason, you throw up your hands at the endless intricacies of arriving there on time with the correct age of children, only to wish you hadn't come!

When people realize that you are visiting as a homeschool, they often go far out of their way to show you things you might have missed as part of a bigger institution. One day we ambled into the local firestation and asked if we might have a look at the fire engines. Not only did we examine the entire station and learn about each function, but the kind officer unloaded paramedic kits and ladders and, of course, turned on the siren for us. After a mid-day concert, the musicians patiently demonstrated their instruments, allowing the children to experiment a bit themselves. The lady in the back room of the five-and-dime took us up and down the aisles, revealing the seasonal items that were stashed there until Christmas or Easter time. And let us look at the shoplifting detection system! The tire salesman allowed the boys to turn on the automated wrench that removes the lug nuts in a twinkling, and let them put a repaired tire back on themselves.

As we have mentioned elsewhere, our favorite trip takes us outdoors, without a specified purpose. We love to visit the pond near our home, where a natural spring spills down a concrete system into the pond. The children never tire of racing leaf boats or stick rafts through the pools and the pipes. We love to explore the edge of the pond, watch the ducks, catch frogs, examine the bugs, collect the bulrushes, puff open the cattails. When we go home, we unload insect specimens, different stones, and sometimes shells and fossils we have found.

When you venture open-ended into nature, you end up finding many things to study, to expand into further lessons. Living by the beach during our year in the South Pacific always brought us new images: an albatross, beached, exhausted, after a big storm (he died shortly after we found him); a live sand dollar, which we kept in sand and salt water and watched swirl his way into safety as we repeatedly brought him up again; shells of different kinds which we categorized and made into charts; strange sea creatures, full of tentacles with shells, cemented into rotting logs that washed up from some deep during a storm. In Rarotonga we never tired of the coral.

Camping or visiting in the forests and canyon lands of Southern Utah always brings home unusual rocks of different colors. Arriving from our New Zealand trip, we spent a few days in the Bryce Canyon area, and I was delighted to see the younger children pick and sample rose hips, the flower buds of marshmallow plants, and fallen apples of different kinds in the orchards. Quite apart from the fruitful scientific studies that blossom from outdoor trips, we return home relaxed and at peace, which doesn't usually happen with a town field trip.

Probably our worst failures are trips where we feel artificial and silly, like the time we visited the glassblower with our rather young home-schoolers. He, a scientific fellow, felt he had nothing to say to such little ones, but we assured him that he could explain in his usual way and that they would follow. He tried, but none of us felt natural and composed, and we came away only a bit assuaged by the delicate glass swan he blew for us.

We also fail when bad timing or tension bring the little ones to exhaustion and bad behavior. Even so, the older children have learned to tolerate some tension with the little children, though I wonder if it will make someone hope never to have children when they get older! So often David or Yoni will take the baby in big arms, circling her around the grocery store or music shop as I complete our purchases.

As the children have grown older, they have often gone on outings on their own. Everyone attends his weekly scout meeting; and sometimes children are invited to spend the night at someone's home or play all day. At first, I discouraged overnights, because invariably everyone stays up late, watches too much television, eats junk food, and arrives home grouchy, tired, and dissatisfied. Yet these visits can be so valuable, helping our often homebound children to live in another family's reality, feel the love those parents have for their children, observe the different routines and disciplines, and make comparisons for themselves. I like for the older children to experience these things, and we can just try to go to bed earlier the next night.

As the older children enter adolescence, they visit places without me, perhaps helping neighbors with their yard or shopwork, perhaps going shopping, or to sports events with other families, perhaps just going to someone's home to see a program or play games. Sometimes I have had to push the kids into these experiences when they become too lodged in the homeschool routine, but the effort is worth it. Each day one winter, when the three oldest boys were thirteen, eleven, and nine, I required them to spend at least an hour out of doors, biking, walking, playing sports, visiting—anything to remove them from the daily routine and create outings and adventures of their own. In the summer months, however, they spend most of their daylight hours outdoors without a word from me. And especially after they have spent some time attending school, with their social circles much expanded, they spend many hours with their friends easily and naturally, both at their homes and at ours.

Outings provide this important function for the homeschool. So often we entrench ourselves into our own four walls; and while I do not advocate expensive or frivolous trips, I know that walks in the neighborhood, in the hills, to the pond, and shopping trips, visits to the dentist, the health-food store, or repair shop, give us a broadening break from what can sometimes develop into too much routine.

TRAVEL

Seven children, two years apart, the eldest thirteen—not a very relaxing prospect for a vacation.

For the first eight years of our marriage, laden with babies and toddlers, we did not travel or camp with our family. We thought it would be too stressful and too expensive. Our first grand trip, however, proved us wrong, and we have travelled often ever since.

Especially when homeschoolers live in isolated country areas, they need to travel to other places to experience what life is like there. Actually, all of us need to do this, otherwise we become "stuck in place" (a term I use, coupled with "stuck in time," to express conditions of our mortal existence, but that doesn't apply in the eternal worlds; I sense that these ways of being "stuck" are an inherent frustration to us, because our spirit knows that we have been and someday will be otherwise). We become less and less aware of ways of being and thinking outside our little place. Insulated from other realities—which themselves are just as viable as our own, and are often more so—we oversimplify the world and can even grow smug about ourselves.

Reading helps, of course. In fact, reading makes us feel certain things we might not or should not experience ourselves. Still, a book about the ocean, even an excellent book, cannot let us smell the sea, feel the breeze, hear the breakers, see a pelican swoop for a fish (let us not even mention those ridiculous video tapes that present a "relaxing" ocean "experience"). Most of all, a book cannot supply the full sense of being there, the aura or vibration of the place.

By travelling, I do not mean taking tours. Tours usually operate on the idea that we want to see as much as possible in as short a time as possible. We should not think that the more places we visit, the better off we are. Accumulating place-names can hardly change our hearts. Some people tell me they have experienced real growth on tours such as those in the Holy Land. But I feel that this is the exception. Touring can supply us with many images, but mostly it makes us tired and prevents us from seeing the realities around us.

When we lived in Rarotonga in the Cook Islands, local people there would show us their tourist-faces, either an exaggerated grin or a blank mask. Only when we chatted, explaining that we were living there, renting a house, that our children were learning to dance, that they had attended the Maori school (we sent them for three weeks before the Christmas summer holidays—it being the Southern Hemisphere), their faces assumed their natural and beautiful expressions, and they were most interested in whether we liked it there, what we were doing there, and so on.

Granted that we have missed a great many sights in our travel experiences; we have only stopped at convenient or truly significant historical spots on our trips. But we have gained something else—a real sense of the places we have visited.

As I said, our first trip destroyed all our misconceptions about the hardships of travelling with children. I was expecting baby number five, and our children were aged 18 months, 4, 6 and 8. A neighbor designed and manufactured machinery for placer mining, which removes gold flakes from the soil. He was planning a mining trip to Alaska and wondered if we might like to go along, accompanying him, his parents, another family with children, and a young couple newly married (a few single miners later joined the expedition). Our imaginations caught fire, not so much with the promises of golden treasures, but with the romantic excitement of seeing Alaska and participating in real gold-mining.

We fortunately had a bit of extra money at the time, and so we plunged into writing lists of what we might need for such a vast undertaking (as it turned out, we planned and took far too much, a great learning experience for later trips, and a mistake that other families, we have noticed, repeat all the time). We purchased a large cotton canvas tent, which has been our friendly home in many camping trips since. In addition to the usual sleeping bags, Coleman lanterns and stove, etc., we thought of a toilet seat to make our own outhouse, a shower head to attach to a black-painted barrel for a solar shower, plenty of grains and beans and nuts and dried fruit, and a huge, glorious slab of carob bar. We even bought a $50 washing machine, to be run on the camp generator, which was lashed onto the mining machinery.

All the talk and planning involved the children, as did the many trips for purchasing, and the packing. It turned out we thought of just about everything we needed, except one thing—rain gear. It rained frequently, and, especially just at the end of our stay, for three weeks solid. Little Chava, my toddler, would scoot out of the tent, heading in her sneakers for the first available puddle. I would remove her sneakers, replacing them with the other pair, and dry the first by the campfire, scorching them on occasion.

This scene, I remember, kept repeating itself.

We also bought some new, strong Levis to wear with our second-hand flannel shirts (far too hot for the 90-degree Alaska summer). We ended up buying short-sleeved T-shirts and shorts at a thrift store in Fairbanks. We later decided never to purchase new clothing for an extended camping trip.

We also decided to take along a mother's helper; at five months along in my pregnancy, I was unusually large, and I had had no experience in cooking on campfires, doing camp chores, etc. The young woman we took, one of Avraham's former students, was very willing to help, but she was going through some kind of emotional turmoil, the extent of which I had not known. She would become very upset inside, and being the emotional barometer that I am, it would throw me completely off balance. She would rarely be able to admit something was wrong. It also became uncomfortable to tell her to do things around the camp, because she resented being commanded, though she could not express this easily either (if I did not tell her, she would often neglect to do things I felt were important—I know now that these can be typical problems with a mother's helper situation). After a few weeks, we had to dip into savings to send her home.

The grand day arrived for leaving, packed to the gills. We hauled a trailer behind with most of the equipment; we put the mattresses on the back floor of our van, covering them with the sleeping bags—a big bed for an expectant mother and small travellers. Covering five hundred miles a day, we would stop at campsites in towns and on the road. (I tried to locate good campsites from one of those camping information books which lists all the available campsites along the way, but not always did I choose good ones.) Usually we drove into an area and located a suitable spot.

I remember our first stop—in Great Falls, Montana. We found a nice (pay) campground where we wanted to stop, on a Saturday night—to spend the Sabbath (my husband and I have always avoided travelling on Sunday as one of the ways to keep the Sabbath day holy). Unfortunately, that night and day were terribly windy, so that we couldn't light a fire, put up a tent, etc. We all huddled in our van to sleep, ate crackers, cheese, and fruit during the day, and roamed around the fields or rested, not even going to Church that day. I remember being very tired and grimy. Later my mother's helper told me that she had camped with her aunt and uncle, but that they would never have stayed in such a windy place; they would have travelled again—Sabbath notwithstanding—until they found a more suitable campsite.

We passed through the endless wheat fields of Alberta and into British Columbia, where we camped in a most beautiful campsite, rolling and green, with swans on the lake and lectures on nature at night. Avraham had not wanted to spend the time cooking, as he felt camp cooking would take too long and be too messy. But we were hungry for some real food, so I made soup, toast, vegetables—after travelling on finger food, it tasted marvelous. From then on I insisted on cooking breakfast and supper while the family handled the tent and made or broke camp.

For the first time the children had free access to fire. They kindled the campfire, kept it going, put sticks in to carry about as torches, poked the coals around. Our children could be trusted with fire! No one got burned. Just as children are fascinated with earth and water and air, so they love fire; that's why they like to play with matches. I recommend camping if only for this reason—the chance to play safely with fire. Let them know the rules (no sword-play with the flaming torches!) and let them go; put them in charge of kindling the fires.

Interestingly, we rarely sat around the campfire singing songs or toasting marshmallows. To us, the fire cooked the food and warmed us up. We did our singing in the tent before bed or at other times. And I learned to love cooking over a fire. To this day I would rather do the family cooking outside, over a fire (in the shade) than even an electric or gas stove. There is something about the wind, the trees, the smoke, the fire itself that makes me happy cooking there instead of indoors.

Soon we hit the worst section of road—the Al-Can Highway; those bumper stickers, "I survived the Al-Can Highway," are no joke. Because it was the beginning of summer, the roads were all cracked up and saturated with melting snows from the severe winter. Highway crews and equipment stopped us at intervals, sometimes for half to three-quarters of an hour at a time. We would sing, talk, read, get out and walk around. We saw one giant Caterpillar tractor mired in the muck, buried several feet deep, the driver vainly trying to rock it loose.

However, we survived the road, eventually arriving in Whitehorse, Yukon Territory. From there, we decided to go on to Dawson City, in the Klondike area—a somewhat longer route to Fairbanks but one where we could learn something, we thought. We camped across the Yukon River, reaching the beautiful campsite by the ferry-boat that left hourly. I convinced Avraham that after a week's hard travel, we deserved a short rest, so we stayed there the whole weekend.

We ferried over to town on Saturday to buy food, and we hoped to have a swim and a shower. But the swimming pool was closed, the lifeguard not having arrived for some reason; so we went to a pay shower, and, at a dollar a person, had a wash. When you travel, camping, showering can become a problem, especially if it irks you to pay so much for it. I remember, on our return trip, someone wanted to charge us $3 per person for showers, even for the little children! The answer, of course, is to take a cold bath (in swimsuits) in rivers or lakes. It has taken me a long time to learn to enjoy it. We swam in the Yukon River and shampooed our hair, but I still wanted a hot shower. (Only in the Cook Islands, when Cyclone Sally demolished the solar water heater mounted on the roof and deprived us of hot water, did I really get used to cold water.)

Dawson City was an old Klondike mining town, so we visited derelict mining outfits and ruined boats and a renovated river ferry. We had a Sunday devotional in camp and spent the time playing and relaxing.

We travelled to Fairbanks after the weekend. We were so excited to arrive! We found a campsite just outside the city, a pay site with showers and a coin laundry. There we settled in to wait for the mining outfit to follow—soon, we hoped. But they had to deal with delay upon delay, so that week after week they didn't arrive.

What did we do? We unwound, we rested, we recuperated; we drove around Fairbanks, locating raw milk, good eggs, and smoked salmon from a farm near a river; we went to Church, got a library card. That excellent library had the most liberal lending system! You would just write on your application the location of your camp, "Mile 62, such-and-such highway," and they'd issue the card. They supplied many wonderful story hours and crafts activities, and had a superior book collection. I read most of George Eliot there, including the difficult but rewarding *Daniel Deronda*. We checked out books on the flora and fauna and history of the area.

I thus recommend getting a library card wherever you go, even if you only stay a month or so. In Rarotonga, the library checked out books to tourists, for a fee (locals didn't have to pay). In this way you can read much related to the area without having to purchase the books.

Some libraries offer extraordinary services. When we lived in Toronto, working on the completion of my husband's doctoral degree (we had three children then, but I don't count it as travel; it was more like a family move), the local libary lent films—full-length Disneys, shorts of all kinds, full-length literature movies. This, of course, was long before the days of videos. For the small effort of sitting through a free, half-hour training session on projector use, we could rent a projector from the library and check out any number of films overnight, to see at home. What fun we had! Of the many films we took home, I cannot count how many times we watched Disney's Grand Canyon Suite; and, most especially, the Mickey Mouse short, Band Concert, a hilarious rendition of The William Tell Overture. If ever I assemble a film library, they will be the first purchases I make.

I supplied a constant stream of children's books for learning and pleasure in Alaska. Before we left for there, I had given my children the Stanford Achievement Test, and both of the older boys, ages eight and six, were reading at about a third-grade level. When we returned from our trip three months later, I gave the tests again, and this time they tested at post-high school level in reading! This happened without a single lesson from me, just a constant supply of books.

There's another factor, too, though it might seem a little zany. I believe now that just being out of doors, in the light, the air, enjoying the beauties and natural energy of the earth, the intellect grows and expands in an unexplained way. My husband and I ourselves felt a clearing of the mind, a quiet focus of the spirit, as we left Provo for this long, extended camp. We all relaxed. And I feel these influences caused a great intellectual growth for the children, as evidenced by the testing when we returned home.

We moved camp from the Fairbanks location to a public camp about 40 miles from town. What memories I carry from the Chataneeka campground. It was a wild-rose season, and the whole area was filled with the tender, fragrant blossoms, as well as many other wildflowers. A soft, sandy beach bordered our campsite and the snow-fed waters of the river. Wild raspberries surrounded the camp, just coming into season. On the other side of the camp were a lovely little pond and some wild currant bushes. We took buckets and bowls and picked wild currants one day, fighting off the hordes of mosquitos (Alaska's "national bird," they say) with various natural and store bought applications—all ineffective, till a seasoned camper guided us to military "mosquito dope." This would last for a week if you didn't wash, and it burned the skin off your face.

We simmered the currants with sugar over the campfire, poured the mixture through a clean nylon stocking that I had brought to house a cake of soap, and poured the sparkling jelly into a jar on the picnic table. We ate it on our wholewheat pancakes, which were cooked on the griddle over the fire. I recall that Sammy, our star complainer, was the champion berry-picker that day, sticking with it and never complaining at all.

Watching the river, and bathing daily in the icy water, going into Fairbanks once a week for supplies and a visit to the library, seeing the fish and various creatures that visited camp, chatting with other campers, sleeping, cooking, eating, hiking, reading . . . we found it took about three full weeks to overcome our tensions and tiredness and begin to live harmoniously.

The mining company, however, did not arrive till toward the end of July, when the midnight sun was beginning to give way and the 90-degree days beginning to cool. We then moved out into the primitive, to the mining site. Avraham dug our toilet and set up the outhouse, piped in water with a couple of connected garden hoses (from the most cold and pure, delicious stream I have ever seen), dug a fire pit and set up my primitive stove, built a homemade picnic table, built a prefabricated outdoor shower, and set up a kitchen. We learned to know our fellow miners, and enjoyed the fellowship after being alone for so long. The mining operation, however—starting so late in the season and, as it turned out, in an ore-poor location—was a sheer loss.

But the trip to us was 100% profit, though we didn't even earn our expenses! We learned how little we actually need, to be happy, away from advertising and shopping centers. Living timelessly, like nonindustrialized people, outdoors, we felt more healthy and content than we had ever before in our lives. For an entire month, our appetites soared ravenously, till our bodies adjusted to the healthy lifestyle. When we levelled off, we felt like new people, untouched by the stresses of our society.

We went to town to Church, and for shopping once in a while—nearly eighty miles each way. The children played furiously with the boys of the other family, making log cabins, wading in creek and pond, scooting down banks. We all picked blueberries endlessly and ate them in various recipes, often twice a day (growing wild in the highly mineralized soil, they were incredibly delicious). We feasted on Alaska salmon cooked over the smokey fire. The children read an hour or two every day, drew or painted when they thought of it. They listened and watched as the mining failure unfolded (as does 90% of Alaskan gold mining), sitting on the huge machines occasionally and sometimes being allowed to operate them. They endured the misery of nearly three weeks of rain, it stopping only twice, once when I badly needed to dry some laundry, and the second time on the day we broke camp and moved. Thus they learned the power of prayer in everyday affairs!

Now you can read about this kind of adventure, or discuss it with others. But living it put the learning into our bones, and it has remained part of us. When we returned to civilization, visiting Yellowstone on the way back (and even that seemed very civilized after our Alaska camp), we could tangibly see the tension that attends life in the city. And, within a couple of weeks, we were full of that tension ourselves. I remember driving in Provo a couple of days after arriving home and feeling that I could not tolerate the crowded, tight feeling I had. Yet, I recognized this feeling now only after not having had it, standing away from it for a time.

I had my baby (Avi) that following November, a big nine and a half pound boy—over two pounds heavier than any of my other babies. But I was so taken by the travelling and camping experience that I talked us into an extended trip the following year also. We had to move house that year, leaving Provo and going south about 20 miles into a removed, country home near Spanish Fork. That should have been adventure enough; but away we went, this time responding to the advice of a friend, whose visits to the primitive Indians, the Seris, in Mexico on the Sea of Cortez, had taken him to a pretty spot, Bahia Kino—Kino Bay. In preparation for the Mexico trip, we had hired a tutor, Maria, to visit us twice weekly for Spanish lessons for the children. She taught by singing, games, stories, and brought much fun into our home.

This time when we packed we took much less; but we did pack our grains, our grinder, some bottled juices, etc. Our trip was much shorter (six weeks) but involved more culture shock; the two border towns, each called Nogales, were two different worlds! It was just a couple of hours from the border to Bahia Kino, a small, nontourist, typical Mexican village. We rented a campsite, just a place to put up the tents, with a covered veranda-type enclosure for table and shelves. We camped virtually on the beach, which, not being on the open ocean, but on the long inlet of the Sea of Cortez, had rather small breakers splashing up.

Our children made friends right away with the families living around; but to our surprise, they never used any of their Spanish. "We can communicate without words," they said, and so they did. I found, however, that my Spanish (learned in college and buried unused for over ten years) emerged complete and ready for use, both grammar and vocabulary! We were all very surprised by this, and, combined with our possessing a beautiful little baby (Avi), it opened every door and heart we met in Mexico.

We bought our tortillas in a tortilleria, a factory-shop, a furnace affair in the burning heat of Mexico. A long machine took the pre-mixed dough, shaped it into tortillas, and baked it, the room rising to the temperature of the oven. The tortillas were sold then and there, so the children observed the whole process. We bought our groceries from village shops, adapting to the Mexican way of eating. Everything of course ran in Spanish.

Most interesting of all, Mexican visitors from everywhere came and went; and since we were outdoors, many came up to visit and chat, improving my Spanish daily. We were living at the site of a marina, where fishermen took in loads of fish every day. We would ask to buy fish, but they would only give them to us, so we gave them jars of juice or little bags of dried fruit, delicacies they rarely found in Mexico. The children played in the sea all the time, finding and identifying—with our guidebooks—the various shells, watching the seabirds, most especially the pelicans and their queer ways. We lived directly opposite Pelican Island out in the bay, so covered with pelican manure that you could see it from miles away.

We enjoyed warm friendships, with camping Americans (one couple, grandparents, took us over in kindness, offering us pitchers of punch and other friendly gifts and lots of love) and with the Mexicans. With one family in particular we became close friends, Francisco and Gloria and their four children. Gloria liked to cook outside, and we learned how to construct a useful little outside stove from a 50-gallon barrel with a hard steel top. She taught me how to make tortillas and beans.

During this time we hit on the plan to send our children to the local school so as to learn Spanish. Bucho, the owner of the campsite and marina, who was prominent in local government, encouraged us and made arrangements with the school principal. All three boys, nine, seven, and five, were assigned to the first grade, where all ages, right up through teenagers, were put if they didn't know how to read and write.

After a few days, they climbed out of the window when no teacher appeared, and hoofed it home. It was too dirty, they said; they couldn't understand anything; and they had to sit still all day and do nothing. So ended their very first brush with school!

We left Bahia Kino when the weather got hot, our camp there having lasted one month; during that time my husband worked on a project rather than just relaxing and enjoying himself. This, in addition to the fact that the bathrooms and showers were a hundred yards from our tent, and the daily flow of visitors, and the oppressive heat, and the need to carry around a heavy six-month-old baby, made our Mexico trip less relaxing than the Alaska one. But we learned much and, after a couple of weeks' stay at a beautiful campsite in Southern Utah—Calf Creek—we moved into our little country home and started life there.

We didn't travel the year after that because by then we had acquired milking goats and laying hens, and they demanded that we stay around. Also, my husband's research projects at the time needed his constant attention; no matter how I cajoled, we didn't camp that summer, or the summer after. But Avraham finished his projects, and had obtained a grant from the university to continue work on his second book on Isaiah. So we devised the trip we had long dreamed about, a foray to the southern hemisphere. Avraham's family were in New Zealand, where he was raised, and we wanted to visit some of the Pacific Islands as well. It was an expensive proposition, and the grant money wasn't intended for tickets to faraway places! So we got busy, myself writing a book for an herb company and he working with the Hebrew translation of a scriptural text for a translating institution. By selling our car, we soon assembled the money for our return fare to New Zealand, with a stopover in Tahiti and an extended stay in Rarotonga in the Cook Islands.

As we prepared for this trip, we tried to locate material about the Cook Islands, but most books and encyclopedias only contained short paragraphs about the group. We stumbled on a volume called *Islands of the Pacific*, a National Geographic publication. Its long article about the Cooks gave us plenty to dream about, especially the pictures. We read it aloud to the nonreaders, while all the readers went through it several times.

This time we could not overpack; our luggage was limited to 44 pounds per person; since we planned to take a bicycle per person (including a bike trailer to haul the little ones), this seemed extremely minimal. Avraham and the boys weighed the bikes, subtracting the difference. Most of us could take about twelve pounds or so! My husband contrived a way out; he packed much of our year's things in carry-ons, which we hauled about with us, including an additional pillow per person. We scraped by with this arrangement, though the airlines now enforce the minimum pretty strictly.

We spent the last few weeks in Utah finishing up writing projects, myself polishing and indexing a volume on herbs, Avraham completing his translation work. The children helped by doing much of the housework and tending the baby. We packed nearly all we owned in storage, another opportunity for decision-making (David had sculpted a large wooden manta ray which he had hoped to carry with him on the plane).

We left one morning for California, traveling easily to Las Vegas by evening. Though we usually rent a motel room outside of the city, this time we drove right down the Strip. The overwhelmingly gaudy casinos and sinful activities around us upset the children, but we thought it was a good experience for them to see it, to feel it. Sammy said, "Are we going to sleep in one of those places where they're gambling? I'll sleep in the van rather than go into one of those places!"

We found an inexpensive place to spend the night, feeling rather choked by the goings on around us and the ubiquitous cigarette smoke.

The next day's drive to California was marred somewhat when we called the French Embassy and found that our visas, necessary to enter Tahiti (where we had a day-and-a-half layover), had not been sent. We rang up my mother and asked her to drive into L.A. to pick them up, a difficult chore for her. This resulted in much family conversation about passports, visas, permanent residency, and other such matters.

My mother, as usual, treated us to Disneyland, which venture I looked forward to for the children's sake. Imagine our disappointment when the whole experience, instead of being fun and magical, seemed sort of hollow and unreal to us (which, in fact, it should: Disneyland is after all just a gigantic and super amusement park, and amusement in itself fails to feed the spirit).

The day finally arrived, our friends driving us to L.A. International Airport: standing in long lines to check our much baggage, walking the children and the heavy carry-ons to what seemed to be the farthest reaches of the airport, entering the big plane of which we had spoken so much (through an entryway that didn't let us see the plane at all!), taking our seats, taking off. The older children, unused to much indulgence, lapped up the dinner served to them, the choice of juices and soft drinks, the games and books, the taped stories and music; fortunately they fell asleep before the movie came on, which was crude and violent.

Avraham struggled with the little ones, who couldn't settle down very well. I tended the baby, who was provided a bassinette and eventually fell asleep. We all fell asleep just before we were awakened with orange juice and sandwiches, to climb off the plane, laden with babies (and those carry-ons!) at two in the morning. There, in Tahiti, hostesses placed fragrant flowers behind every ear and a ukelele-strumming trio was singing valiantly—at two in the morning! After interminable lines, we retrieved our bicycles and luggage and put them into storage; and there waiting for us were members of the Tahiti Temple presidency, who drove us to their flat and put us down for the night, cuddling and singing to the children. We didn't expect this gracious early-morning greeting!

We stayed the day and evening and part of the next day in a hotel, (which was pleasant, but extraordinarily expensive). . All this time we learned about dollars-and -francs, shops that closed from 11 a.m. to 2 p.m., buying in French, riding *le truc* (the bus), eating mangoes and papayas, and all such unfamiliar experiences of travelers. We also enjoyed our first taste of the ocean, not being used to the sight and sound of reefs and lagoons.

Our flight took off around lunchtime, our ever-present carry-ons saving us from a heavy airport tariff ("Okay, everybody, grab your carry-on!" "Why don't you just check them?" asks the Air New Zealand attendant, who has processed our bikes and boxes, "It's just a two-hour flight to Rarotonga." "Only 20 kilos per person," says the Tahitian customs official; but by then half of the luggage had entered the plane, and he wasn't going to recall it.) Somehow, praying all the while, we squeaked through.

Landing in Rarotonga was a bit anti-climactic after this build-up. It was raining, and soon the children and I were packed into a taxi to find Rena Jonassen, with whom Avraham had corresponded and who was therefore expecting us, we hoped (it turned out he had given Avraham's letter to a missionary, so he wasn't expecting us that day after all). The taxi driver had just returned to Rarotonga after ten years' absence in New Zealand and didn't really know the place. He kept stopping by the side of the road and asking in Maori, "Do you know where is the place of Rena?" He seemed to be asking the most unlikely people; no one knew. Finally I glimpsed a Mormon chapel with a car parked there. Against his better judgment, it seemed, he followed my suggestion to stop there and get advice, and we soon found ourselves at Rena's place at last. He greeted us with the traditional island kiss, and commented, "No one can get lost in Rarotonga." "He can!" I said, pointing to the driver, so we all had to laugh.

We stayed for a month in a vacant missionary flat adjacent to the Mormon chapel in Avarua, the main town on the island. It was crowded for us, and the flat had only a gas burner and intermittent hot water. We were so near the airport that the daily planes and jets brought the children scooting out the door at the spectacle of the huge airliners seeming to hang in the air directly over us. Despite these problems, including a solid week of rain, sick babies, and adjustment to the new diet, water, and weather, living in that flat proved to be quite a blessing.

People came to visit us constantly, though I admit with embarrassment that their Maori names eluded me for a long time. There, we could be present at all the church functions—missionary farewells (at which everybody gathered to have a typical Maori feast and give long speeches of thanks); Sunday meetings, including firesides, but most especially Primary (with a handful of children and our own, who nearly doubled the attendance), Relief Society (often the president, the teacher, and me), and Sacrament Meeting; branch and district conferences, often conducted almost wholly in Maori.

The highlight of our stay there was a program prepared for a returning Utah couple who had contributed money to the district Primary. Each of the four village branches had prepared some "items," which is meant to refer to dances or songs. Our branch featured a band of drums and guitars, the drums ranging from a bass to a high-pitched one, drumming being a special skill featured in the Cook Islands. Twice a week during our month there the branch members would gather to practice for this event, afterwards sitting around and singing songs just for fun. This took place in the recreation hall, a large, barn-like building with open spaces all around the top, situated directly opposite our little flat.

Sitting among those island people, dressed as they were in any old thing (usually because they couldn't afford something better), playing guitars and drums and singing island harmonies into the night was a pure delight. Our children were invited to perform in the program, and so they practiced along with the island children, doing the boys' hula and dancing the action songs. On the evening of the performance they were dressed up along with the others in *eis* (Maori for leis), on head and torso, and woven waistbands and flowing coconut-fiber skirts.

David and Yoni had learned the dances fairly well, but Sammy had entered late, and we hooted in delight at his sideward glances during the dance. Yoni in particular had accurately picked up the stance and style of the dancing; so when each child-couple did a solo, everyone shouted and clapped for him and his tiny partner. Yoni, his hair now bleached white, and she, a classic black-haired Polynesian beauty, made a sight together. Somewhere a photographer snapped this, and the picture was printed in the local paper.

Children were always visiting the church yard after school; and during church meetings parents brought their little children along to play outside, so our little ones had plenty of friends to play with. The missionaries also dropped by occasionally, as some lived in a flat on the same property. People in Rarotonga treated us very differently when they knew we were staying for months, not just visiting for days. The Polynesian people are so different from what I expected from Americans; as a rule they are not materialistic; they are open and honest, and they have a very pure and unpolluted spirit about them. Even a teenage boy walking down the street looks you straight in the eyes and smiles an open, beautiful Polynesian smile—quite a contrast to his counterpart in the U.S., and quite a surprise to me!

Partly to facilitate our receiving temporary residency permission, and partly to encourage our children to experience the island culture, we sent the oldest four, including Chava at five, to Maori school. After a couple of days Chava stopped going, because kindergarten seemed to consist mainly of sitting on the floor and talking Maori. Yoni, seven years old, only went intermittently. The older boys, eleven and nine, didn't mind school; but they didn't like it much, because of sitting still and being bored, and also because the teachers cuffed the students freely and used verbal abuse to humiliate them. Although our boys didn't receive this, they felt sick to their stomachs from the daily tension. All in all, I am glad they felt this second-hand, without enduring the oppression themselves; they thus understood the reality of it. Fortunately we moved, and the school holidays began.

Because transporting or buying a car was so expensive in the South Pacific, we had brought our bicycles for transportation, including a bike trailer to haul the babies; and a seat on the bar of Avraham's bike to take one of the smaller children. The island, we had read, was only 20 miles in circumference, so anything we needed would be within biking distance. However, hopping on my bike and hauling behind me 100 lbs. of children, and our groceries on top of that, was quite a shock for me. But soon I started getting into shape. The children rode just everywhere, for in Rarotonga people present no dangers—no kidnappings, no perversions. This in itself was a true culture shock for me, for even in our small Utah town you would hear tales of these things. Nevertheless, we found that even biking four miles to go shopping with the children, then returning, was too great for everyday practice.

We rented a vacant house on the church's welfare farm. This was located in Arorangi, about seven miles (which seemed a tremendous distance, biking) from Avarua. We were now out "in the country," about a mile from the beach.

The children and I daily biked to the beach, consisting of a lagoon created by a reef out several hundred yards that circled the island. These lagoons changed color with the weather, sometime bright blue, sometimes ultramarine or turquoise, sometimes gray. Avraham bought the children masks and snorkels, and though we arrived in Rarotonga with David as our only swimmer, soon Sammy and Yoni were paddling around, eventually able to swim without the snorkels at all. You could see bright fish and corals in these lagoons, and the water was silky and absolutely pure. The little ones didn't dig much in the sand, but spent most of their time sitting and splashing in the water, even the baby toddling right in.

From friends, and especially from our neighbors, we began to unravel the ways of island life. So many things, large and small, differed from America. If you give an islander a gift, he immediately gives you one in return. This is required etiquette, and it seems to me a lovely practice. For a get-together at church, everyone is expected to bring a nice dish, every time. Children, well-loved by all, are welcome at any and every function. Mothers breastfeed their babies (and children sometimes three years old and up) freely in public. If someone doesn't want to answer a question directly, he might look down and say nothing at all, so as not to have to be embarrassed or to offend.

We learned to enjoy a new world of island foods. Taro, the root staple, showed up daily on our table. Nourishing and rich in minerals, it's a remarkably satisfying food. (Unfortunately few of the children liked any of the several varieties.) We ate papaya (locally paw-paw, pronounced po-po) almost every day; again the children took a long time learning to like it. When pineapples were shipped in from some of the outlying islands, we ate them, ripe and mild. Most of all we enjoyed the various kinds of coconuts, free for the gathering. My favorite but least accessible (for a child had to climb for it) was the *nu*, the drinking coconut filled with delightful juice and a soft meat with a delicate flavor. You could pick up the regular mature coconut almost anywhere, but you had to husk it, forcing the outer fibers off on an iron tool. All the children liked this, rich and fresh. *Uto*, the sprouted coconut, contained a marshmallowy sweet flesh considered a true delicacy. Most islanders didn't eat the mature coconut directly, only grating it and squeezing out the cream for cooking; or whacking it open with a bush knife to feed to livestock, especially chickens. We actually became quite good at using the bush knife, an unexpected skill.

Of our children, Yoni in particular made himself at home in Rarotonga. While David and Sammy loved to go swimming, they spent their spare time reading library books (which we checked out bi-weekly; the Pacifica collection in Avarua was very good, and we learned so much about the Cook Islands and New Zealand and about Polynesia in general) or working on projects. Not Yoni! He hopped on his bike and made friends.

He hung about a nearby shop (unlike anything you'd see in America—just a tiny shed stocked with canned goods, various household items, and occasionally produce), chatting with all the family members. He made friends with neighborhood kids, picking the various fruits with them and eating them (the Cooks are a tree culture, with many foods unfamiliar to Europeans).

Families invited Yoni into their homes, sharing food, joking with him, taking him on short excursions—to a waterfall, or a papaya plantation. He turned dark brown and, except for his shock of platinum hair, he seemed to be on his way to becoming an Islander himself!   I was so grateful for this experience of Yoni's, because up until then he was rather left out of things, not able to read books like his brothers, not particularly interested in the younger children's games.

While we were there, Yoni turned eight, and he was baptized in the Blackrock Lagoon along with two island boys, Manu and Liahona, on his birthday. He invited many friends to attend. When our family went to a floorshow at a local restaurant, and people from the audience were brought up to participate, who should be called up by a beautiful young Island girl but our Yoni!

Probably the turning point in our Rarotonga experience was the hurricane that appeared on New Year's Day. During the day's festivities, which we shared with our neighors the Ngarupes, hurricane warnings were issued; but few people paid serious attention to them. The rain increased into a fierce tropical storm, with winds from 80 to 100 mph, coupled with spring tides and strong ocean swells that swept through many beach-side homes and businesses. Homes blew down or lost their roofs. Our house remained snug and safe, though the solar water heater crashed down and broke, and several tall trees were uprooted, with torn-off branches and leaves blown everywhere.

Our power was off for two weeks after that, with water going off intermittently during the month or two that followed. Since our stove was electric, we could not cook; nor could we keep perishables in our electric refrigerator, so we lived mainly on canned food and what fresh things we could find in the shops. We soon got unusually sick. David spent three days in the hospital with some kind of dehydrating flu; Sammy and Avraham endured for weeks a strange edema-like flu that constricted the breathing; Avi and Sarah got fevers; I had strep throat; Yoni had earaches; and Chava, worst of all, got a sore throat that developed into rheumatic fever symptoms, necessitating several days in the hospital, but fortunately not affecting her heart.

While illness doesn't often plague us, and we seldom if ever go to a doctor (we are so used to taking care of our own problems), this time it looked as if we typified a family in poor health. Several of us suffered relapses, and by now my husband, his work severely disrupted by these problems, decided to go on to New Zealand. His parents and brothers and sisters were there, and it offered a more temperate climate and an abundance of fresh food (most crops were destroyed or damaged in the hurricane).

Even though our Island experience was thus cut short, we learned so much and we were grateful for it. All our everyday experiences and our church experiences brought us close to the people there and gave us some real questions to grapple with. How much of our religious practice is conditioned by culture? How much American culture do we thoughtlessly impose on church members around the world? Is there a minimal living standard all church members should be encouraged and helped to reach (some of the homes we visited in my church work were shocking, just shacks, with holes in the walls)? Should the bad elements of Western ways, rock music and its attendant culture, suggestive videos, and so on, be evaluated for their negative effects? These questions center on my most important learning in Rarotonga.

Up until very recently, the Island culture had remained quite stable, but now every home has acquired its tape deck, video player, transistor radio. Unprecedented sights and sounds invade the minds of people who have traditionally been pure and moral. For the first time ever, violent and sex crimes have appeared and escalated on the island. Children for the first time fill their fantasies with guns, murders, and war. One day I realized that only through the media could such people sink to a level that might merit their inclusion in world-wide judgments prophesied for the last days. Without them, these people could not merit such punishments, for their pure culture would preserve them at a high level. So a rock dance in the Cook Islands means something quite different—and in my view, something much worse—than it might in America.

We recently read an article that suggested much the same thing in Africa and other third-world countries. People are able to buy the equipment that brings the decadent images and sounds into their homes. But without possessing the traditional means to measure these foreign influences, they are unable generally to discern between bad and good. Certainly the attractiveness of the media makes it nearly irresistible to them.

Pondering these ideas and discussing them with local people, we found that some felt that the influences were very negative and should be eliminated from our lives. But people generally felt that our opinion was extreme, that the music and video tapes were probably to the good, though you had to be selective about the videos. Rather than dispute the issue, I decided that perhaps in time the bad effects of these things might become so apparent that our observations would be unnecessary.

When we arrived in New Zealand, how refreshing were the good roads, the clean and trim environment, and most especially the abundant food! For the first time we enjoyed visiting with our large extended family—grandparents, uncles, aunts, and cousins in a great family reunion!

As soon as we got settled in a lovely, large home (quite elegant after Rarotonga accomodations, though we were comfortable there), we sent our four eldest children to school. Their experiences, detailed in **Introduction: An Autobiography**, initiated them into the culture more quickly than anything could. Soon, New Zealand expressions and pronunciations invaded our dinnertime.

In New Zealand, for the first time, we indulged in some tourist-type travel. We travelled around the county to visit relatives, who showed us places of interest; we also travelled on our own to the ancient kauri forests and the different beaches. In Auckland we visited museums and a Maori culture center. Yet doing these things within the context of our long stay gave them some real meaning.

On one trip we visited the Waitomo Caves, famous for their large population of glow-worms (like myriads of stars in unfamiliar constellations shining from the ceilings as our boat silently glided from one cavern to another). My strongest memory of the place was that the tour guide warned Avraham, in a friendly way, that if the baby cried, he would have to take her out, money cheerfully refunded; we struggled to amuse and pacify her so we wouldn't be thrown out! We happened to come in line with a tour-bus of Americans, who were so loud, aggressive, insensitive, and somehow crude in comparison to the local people that I shrank from my own identity as an American. This little cameo of experience was enough in itself to justify my argument for long-term, meaningful travel—seeing how little those Americans were actually feeling and knowing about the myriad of differences in life New Zealand style from their own North American existence.

Bound by jobs and homes and duties, many people have sighed and wished they could travel freely as we do. Of course, not everyone will enjoy the conditions to live in places as we have done; but families can still spend their vacations in this kind of travel-learning. One of my friends recalled how, growing up, she travelled through Europe with her family, shoestring-style (as we do), camping and cooking outdoors. Even when we cannot afford long trips, we still need to explore peoples and cultures near at hand that have so much to teach us.

Those who live near universities, for example, have access to students from many different countries (BYU, for example, asks families in the community to host foreign students who cannot go home during holidays). BYU also sponsors International Week and Lamanite Week, which include many activities that genuinely teach something about various cultures (during Lamanite Week, we try to attend the annual Intertribal Pow-wow, a long evening of traditional dance conducted as other pow-wows are across America). Indeed, the reservations that dot the whole of America and Canada provide a rich source of learning, if we will only make friends among members of the tribes and allow ourselves to be friends instead of casual spectators.

Truly, it sometimes takes time for members of other cultures to trust and love us; but if we are genuine, we can enjoy some lifelong friendships as well as some humbling lessons about other, perhaps in many ways superior ways of being. One woman in New Zealand, who married into a Maori family, had attended a week-long language-cultural immersion program at a Maori meetinghouse (marae). She told me, "At first I thought it was my right to learn about these people, but as the week progressed, I became very humble for the first time in my life, and I realized that it was a great privilege to be among these people and learn about them."

This made me recall an incident from the book, *Black Elk Speaks*: a group of Indians went to tour England, giving culture shows. They noticed, when Queen Victoria attended, that the population bowed down to her; but when she came near the Indians and felt their spirit and their nobility, she bowed herself down to them, whereupon the men cheered and the women cried ululations (much to the consternation of the loyal subjects in the audience)!

For a truly dramatic cultural experience, you can travel into Mexico. All you need are your birth certificates and the certificate of ownership of your car (and Mexican auto insurance!). Just a day or two's drive from home you enter into another language, another diet, and a completely different way of being. If you travel there with the intention to learn and love, you should have no problems with militants or other hostile and angry people.

As you see, it is not the distance we travel, or the places of interest we accumulate on our itineraries, but the opportunities to experience other people's ways of life, and to learn something of God's love for his children.

BABIES

You may have noticed that I refer often to Jean Liedloff's *The Continuum Concept*. Every family with babies should read this book. Liedloff took a trip to the deep South American jungles where she spent time with the Yequana Indians, a "stone-age" Indian tribe. After a period of readjusting her cultural values, she began to notice that the Indians lived so peacefully, without the conflicts and stresses we endure. As she watched the different age groups deal with each other calmly and happily, without anxiety or falseness, she asked herself what made them so different from ourselves.

Although there are many details that illuminate the good in that primitive society, Liedloff focuses on one especially, which speaks to us moderns—baby care. She grimly illustrates a typical model of dealing with babies in our society—feeding the infant, laying him in a beautifully decorated crib, and letting him scream his heart out there alone in his room, because with his dry diaper and full tummy he doesn't need anything; he must be getting spoiled to cry like that.

Liedloff contrasts baby care among the Yequana, who provide constant human contact from the moment of birth. During the first four months, the mother takes charge of the baby, feeding him when he needs it, carrying him constantly on her hip or in a sling, sleeping with him at night. Liedloff comments that babies seem to need human contact, motion, and a changing scene just as they need to be physically fed and comfortable. After the baby grows a little older, a child, preferably of the same sex, helps by toting the baby, bringing it to the mother when the baby needs to nurse; and when the mother is away, because that baby is elementally content, it can often wait for a time until the mother comes back again. Sometimes grandparents or other relatives help hold the baby. This continues until the baby indicates that it wants to roll and scoot and crawl, and, because it has been held during those first months when the need was intense, it leaves the mother easily and happily, returning only when hungry, tired, or hurt.

As the baby grows, the mother allows him to do whatever he *can* do, not trying to protect him from dangers in the environment, but trusting in his intelligence to understand self-protection; this contrasts strongly with

233

our phobic approach, as we warn, "You'll be hurt; you'll fall; you'll get burned; you'll cut yourself; watch out, watch out!" Little people one year old toddle around with sharp knives, have free access to fire, tumble around deep holes, and rarely does anyone get hurt. It astonished Liedloff that so very few accidents occurred where the children were so free. She wondered if our warnings could become self-fulfilling prophecies, that if we say it often enough, the children *will* burn themselves.

Later, as the children grow, they again do whatever they *can* do. Because all in the society share the same values, the same notions of appropriate behavior, the same ways of living well, the children grow up wanting to conform to the code of proper behavior. And no one has to tell them to behave; they just know. They work because that is what people do as they grow up. Yet there is no competition or coercion to work hard; everybody helps, participating in a relaxed, consistent way of life, enjoying each other's company as they perform daily tasks.

Having raised several of my babies in somewhat a continuum fashion, I am convinced that it can produce the good results that Liedloff describes. Looking at it logically, what do helpless babies need, what is intended for them? After being cradled in a warm womb for nine months, do their inherent needs suddenly change, so that they require lying in a static, unmoving crib? We try to supply a variety of crib toys so that they can amuse themselves, but these nonhuman, limited items soon lose their appeal.

We run into one big problem in our society as we try to mother our babies this way: rarely do we enjoy the company and help of the extended family to take the pressure off the mother. I don't believe that the mother should always be the one to hold the baby. Sometimes a child takes to the little one and wants to carry it around, but too often, in our nuclear families, Mother establishes a closed relationship with the baby, who comes to demand her attention too much. Hopefully, Father will also bond with the baby and take it for walks, drives in the car, etc.

Liedloff suggests that if we leave the baby with a sitter, we ask that she carry the baby instead of leaving it in the crib. If we are so fortunate as to have extended family living close, we should extend our continuum baby care if we can. Having the baby's needs met by people other than the mother short-circuits the possible parasitic relationship that can develop with the mother; and it also makes the mother feel that she can move freely, without always having the baby on her hip. But of course she is the primary caregiver, and from my experience, a baby mothered in this way bonds beautifully with the parents, so that everyone enjoys holding him or her. Certainly the father can take his turn mothering the baby in this way! I saw a picture of a Indian father slinging a sleeping baby as he went about his work. That infant looked to be eight or nine months old, big and beautiful!

Liedloff is not alone in suggesting that parents sleep with their infants. To most of us the idea of sleeping with a baby makes us fearful; we might roll over and smother it; it might grow too dependent on us. Certainly the time comes that the baby leaves the bed, but I feel that little babies derive important comfort and assurance and warmth by sleeping with their parents.

In *The Family Bed*, Tine Thevenin explores this in detail. Dr. Robert Mendolsohn, M.D. self-styled medical heretic, promoted the same practice. And, of course, primitive people all over the world do the same, and I have come to trust long-held customs practiced among nontechnological people. In Polynesian cultures babies sleep with their parents. A Maori woman with a new baby, attended in the hospital by a Samoan nurse, was delighted when the nurse brought the baby in for her to sleep with, warning her to remain quiet so that other, more conventional white nurses would not remove the child! My Maori friend commented that the Polynesian people understood the right way of doing things.

Fortunately, breastfeeding babies has become much more acceptable these days; though most of us still cannot nurse comfortably in public places, retiring to the ladies' room when the baby gets hungry. I feel frustrated about this; I say that nursing is not a bathroom function! In New Zealand, every town boasts one or more Plunket Rooms, provided with a comfortable place to nurse the baby when the mother goes out shopping—even with a hot water jug so the mother can make herself a cup of tea!

Primitive peoples teach us much in matters of breastfeeding too, allowing their infants to nurse when hungry, giving solid foods as the child leads, as he reaches for them, weaning gradually, often nursing the babies for what seems to us to be protracted periods of time. When we were in Rarotonga, I felt delighted to see the wife of one of the local church leaders pull her three-year-old onto her lap, pop out a breast, and nurse the child during church! And this was a mother of fourteen children! In our family we don't usually last that long. My little ones usually breastfeed till about two, when a new baby comes along and takes their place.

There is one danger in prolonged breastfeeding, however. Some experts insist that babies cannot get tooth decay from breastfeeding. They point out that the babies do not sleep with the nipple of the bottle dribbling milk on their teeth all night; the nursing process draws the mother's milk to the back of the mouth, where the swallowing reflex gets rid of it. However, three of my six breastfed children have gotten the nursing bottle syndrome. With Yoni, never having had a bottle, I was shocked to see his teeth brown and begin to decay. We decided not to have a complete restoration under anesthesia, feeling it would be too dangerous to him, so we visited understanding dentists who allowed us to hold him, by about age three, as they fixed the teeth.

Chava did take a bottle in addition to her nursing, however, drinking milk and juice in the day and also at night. Though I tried to stop this bottle drinking, since Avraham and I did not agree on the subject, we never succeeded. Again we chose not to have her put under anesthesia; but her dental work turned into nightmares as the decay continued, producing brown stumps in the front teeth that eventually, when she was about three, necessitated removing four of them. Then Sarah, long-time nurser, began to show that telltale brown around the front teeth. (Avi, in between, had stronger teeth, and though he nursed just as long as the others, he, like the two older children, has not had problems with tooth decay.)

Sarah's teeth showed the classic symptoms of nursing bottle syndrome, though she never drank a bottle. One dentist considered the problem a deficiency in enamel structure, thinking that mother's milk would not cause this kind of decay. But the dentist who worked on her mouth told me he thought that the prolonged nursing certainly did cause it. He said that wiping the child's mouth out with a damp washcloth would have solved the problem, though this doesn't work with night nursing. If you wipe out the baby's mouth, she wakes up, and you begin the whole process over again.

I think the only way to avoid this distressing problem is to make the baby sleep through the night when he or she is about a year old. If the baby wakes, you can give a drink or a bottle of water. In our family, sleeping with our babies, and trying to be sensitive to them, we have not done this very well. I often pull an older baby, crying in the crib, into bed with me for a nursing, to sleep with us all night; and I know that there are many families who do this. Yet the distress and trauma of dental work—not to mention the expense—showed us that this practice isn't right. We did choose to have Sarah's work done under anesthesia and everything went smoothly, though it was stressful to her and to us.

Liedloff illustrates how continuum babies differ so much from ours. They smile, they relax, they are contented. They can wait for a meal—once they are old enough—with good grace. Instead of being stiff and unpleasant to hold, always trying to wriggle out of our arms, they are soft and relaxed, a delight to hold. Once they begin to crawl and later to walk, they show a beautiful independence; having their needs met by their family when they were tiny, they do not try to wrest that warm mother feeling from their parents when they have passed the time.

With our first child, I could not wait until he crawled, until he cut his first tooth, until he said a word, walked, pieced together a sentence. As much as we loved him, we experienced him in the future, impatient for the next landmark. (This attitude prevails in our society; baby books blankly await the next important entry.)

As other children arrived, we began to experience them all in the present, savoring what they were at the time, without wishing for the next thing to occur. Somehow the new tooth, as exciting as it always is, began to mean less than the feelings we had of living together, loving each other. And inevitably, as we grew older ourselves, we hoped that the landmarks would come less and less quickly, so our babies would remain babies as long as they could.

Despite our social inclination to achieve, to get ahead, we should stop ourselves and experience our babies for what they are right now. I think it teaches them to be more peaceful within themselves when we can accept them as they are and love them for it. So what if your one-year-old doesn't walk yet, or if your two-year-old still wears diapers? In another six months, you'll be chasing a toddler and—most likely—no longer changing a child suddenly bigger and more mature than you expected.

Although Liedloff doesn't treat the matter of birth in her book, other people have written and thought a good deal about it. Certainly, hospitals have tried to adapt to the public's changing demands about birth. Instead of providing sterile atmospheres, children and relatives can attend if the parents choose; the mother can hold the baby and nurse it right after birth; and the mother can return home right away if she chooses. Michael Odent wrote of an ideal hospital in *Birth Reborn*, where women are allowed to give birth in ways they feel most comfortable with.

Many people, like ourselves, have felt that even with the many welcome improvements in hospital birth environments, the experience still falls short of what birth could be, what it might be intended to be. Having had our first baby in the hospital, and enjoying a very good experience, we chose to have our next (and then all of the next) at home, attended by a skilled midwife. As long as good prenatal care reveals no problems, and as long as the parents receive a definite witness of the Spirit that a home birth is right for this particular child, I have found home birth so superior to hospital birth that there is no comparison.

We usually invite a close friend to help us brew a drink, bring in needed items, rub pressure points on feet or hands, and help with the children. At the birth of Sarah, our friend commented, "With the births of my eight children, I stood up for what I wanted in the hospital and got what I needed. I always thought that they were good births—and they were. But they don't compare with this!" A special feeling or spirit surrounds a home birth. The mother stays relaxed; she walks around; she showers if she wants; she eats and drinks if she wants. In the hospital you feel that everyone else is in charge; and during the vulnerability of a birth this can be very disorienting and uncomfortable.

At home, the father and mother are in charge, especially because labor always makes the mother vulnerable; and the father builds love, trust, and strength into the marriage as he takes care of his laboring wife. A skilled and experienced midwife—one whom you feel completely comfortable and good about—knows how to monitor and guide the labor and to manage the birth (though many midwives like to have the husband participate in the actual birth, to "catch" the baby, as another important bonding experience in the marriage).

Certainly a home birth benefits the baby, provided that the midwife is skilled and experienced and the parents have educated themselves and know how to recognize incipient problems. We often forget the statistics—that over 95 percent of all births proceed normally. Of course we become frightened at those few dangerous ones, but many midwives are very skillful, and I am convinced that parents can know spiritually the right place for having their baby. As for me, if I did not receive a sure witness that a home birth was the correct thing, I would go to a hospital. Fortunately we have felt very good about it, and I am grateful to have my babies at home.

Dr. Robert Mendolsohn also endorses home birth, as do other medical doctors, medical midwives, many writers, and, of course, a growing multitude of parents who have experienced the joys of giving birth at home. After the baby is born, it rests quietly with the mother for a while, until the cord stops pulsing and the baby is breathing. Then the cord is cut and the baby bathed, weighed, and carefully examined. Warmly dressed in soft clothes, the baby cuddles with the new mother, nursing when it is ready, safe and secure. There is such a contrast in *feeling* to the hospital experience, as careful and considerate as the staff tries to be. At home, the entire family gathers around and an indescribable aura of quiet, love, and euphoria reigns.

Beyond the actual birth experience, I feel that having babies adds immeasurably to the richness of a homeschool. Our society frowns on having many babies, two children being the acceptable maximum. Even some members of the Church, knowing that we believe in having the children whom God sends us and not limiting their birth except in dangerous circumstances, still react a little negatively to mothers having large families. "What, are you pregnant *again*?" is a refrain we often hear. Being pregnant and bearing children is hard for me, I admit. Morning sickness throws me into despair for three months, and colic often does the same when the new baby appears. Yet the children love the babies, and they bring a love, a closeness, and certainly a nurturing experience into the family that I feel cannot be replaced.

In the Zion concept of families, we ought to welcome babies into our families with immense joy, not only for the happy promise of a new individual in the scheme of our families, but also for the pure experience of the baby itself. Hopefully we can tap into our extended families to help us bear the burden as well as share the joy.

I always let the children carry the baby and do for it what they can. Some children naturally excel at baby care; Yoni, for example, can quiet and amuse a little one better than many adults seem able to do. And the little girls in the family naturally take to mothering an infant, despite the claim of feminists that these dispositions are bred, not born into our children. Wouldn't it be pleasant to live in a society, like the Yequana, where people innately understood baby care? We saw it in Rarotonga. Even young people without infants at home knew how to hold, feed, and comfort babies; and people loved babies and little children in a natural, nurturing, unselfconscious way that contrasts so much with ours. How different from a society that discourages babies and, even worse, terminates pregnancies at the volition of the mother!

One Mormon church leader, J. Reuben Clark Jr., commented that our society could solve many of its problems if our children were born and raised properly. As ingrained as child-care methods can be, we should prayerfully evaluate the way we mother our babies. Quite apart from the good we can do for the children, it can also turn having babies into a better, more joyful, more welcome experience—and an important learning time for our homeschooled children.

Take toilet training, for example. When David was two years old, I read *Toilet Training in Less Than a Day*, which describes signs by which you can tell if a child is ready to be potty trained. A child should be able to walk steadily, to understand spoken instructions, to follow them, to show awareness of bowel movements and urination, and possess enough motor skills to take up and down some loose underpants. Certainly at two David possessed all these attributes, so I decided to train him using their method, which includes giving treats when the child performs correctly, and giving lots of drinks to encourage frequent urination—to speed the training. The parent is also to admire vocally each correct performance.

I think David understood what we were up to, and yet for some months after his training, he continued to wet his training pants, and even to run outdoors and make piles on the driveway, which frustrated me and made my husband angry. After a couple of months, he suddenly fell into line and became more predictable about toileting.

Contrast this training (which approach I adapted with each child, becoming less interested in rewards and more quiet and calm about the whole thing) with Sarah's training. She showed symptoms of readiness for training at fifteen or sixteen months; she informed me of impending productions consistently. But we were just getting ready to travel at that time, to return from the South Pacific, so I deferred thinking about training. We stayed in the home of friends for a while after our return; and though she seemed very ready indeed, I delayed thinking about training to avoid messing up carpets, and also because it was wintertime and I didn't want her to run around in underpants during the cold weather.

Finally, we moved into a comfortable home, but it was still winter (and I was coping with morning sickness), so we kept her in diapers, though she was very ready according to the book notions. We talked often about using the potty seat, and even went and bought one, a nice wooden potty with a bear painted on it. She used it a few times, and then asked to be put back in diapers!

Rather than resist her, I let her wear diapers as long as she wanted, perhaps three more weeks. Then we pulled out from storage our old potty, shaped like a little toilet. We set it up in the children's playroom (not carpeted). Sarah took an immediate shine to this version; she removed her diaper and requested panties. That same day she was completely trained, though only on rare occasions, such as when playing in the park, she might accidentally wet herself. She even trained herself into night dryness (I saw after a couple of weeks of diapering her at night that she didn't need it).

Perhaps coincidentally, David and Sarah were well-trained at about the same age, though we endured some months of unnecessary unhappiness in David's case because we decided, not him, that he was ready to train. We learned that readiness includes all the symptoms outlined in the books, plus one: an emotional, inner decision from the child himself to do the thing. Obviously, this can apply not only to these early-childhood experiences, but to learning at older ages as well. The homeschool environment tends to preserve the child's own agency, which I feel is a vital character trait for raising wholesome children.

WINDOWS

Animals

Funny how our methodical, precise scientist, Sammy, has also turned out to be the Chicken King and the Dog Affectionado, teaching himself all about the different varieties, manner of care, and development of each. Each time that we order baby chicks by mail, which arrive peeping and ravenous, he assigns himself to them, learning their quirks, personalities, and habits. At present he is the master of a particular, promising Buff Orpington rooster he hopes to show at the State Fair next month.

When we slaughtered the mixed run of Cornish-cross-Rock chickens we had raised for meat, Sammy felt bad because his Champion, the Buff Orpington rooster, had his harem reduced, altering his established kingdom. (I pointed out that chickens have short memories, and that Champ would soon content himself with the Buff hens and Leghorns that remained.) He has persuaded Champion to come peck alfalfa greens out of his hand—not a bad feat, considering it is a rooster, and occasionally he or Yoni will pick up a chicken and cuddle it.

For almost a year, Sammy craved ownership of a Golden Retriever, reading the want ads in the Shopper's Guide faithfully, debating how much cash of his own he would sink into such a beloved creature. Finally, one day we located a *free* female Golden Retriever not far from us, so we drove over to get her. Young and beautiful, she delighted Sammy from the first; he took over her care and dutifully cleaned up the heaps that she occasionally deposited on the lawn (it turned out she wasn't too keen a learner and took a while to remember to make her deposits out in the field).

Everyone loved Digger, despite the fact that she would ruffle up the garden soil, chase the children down the road when they went anywhere, or jump on anyone who ran too rambunctiously. The little ones could climb on her back for a horsie ride, and Digger would sit quietly and patiently as long as they played. However, when our neighbors started to let their two pet rabbits run around on the lawn, we had a hard time convincing Digger to leave the creatures alone. One day she chased one of the rabbits, Sammy running to the neighbor's for help. Soon after that, the rabbit disappeared.

242

Later, the other rabbit, a slow old fellow, showed wounds with decomposition and maggots in them that necessitated killing him.

The neighbors were concerned that Digger was doing away with their pets, and also worried because they had a beloved Siamese kitten coming up who might also be attacked by Digger. (Digger also had the unpleasant habit of burying bones in the garden and, true to her name, digging up the remains of chickens that Avraham had buried out in the field.) The neighbors felt it would be better if we got rid of her.

Dealing (not too well) with his initial anger and hurt, Sammy accustomed himself to the idea of giving up his longed-for pet. Finally he pulled himself together and agreed that we could give her to a young man who had wanted a hunting dog, though these arrangements proved a little frustrating to pull together. Right away he began scouring the want ads for *another* Golden Retriever, Avraham gently reminding him that we would probably wait to get another dog until we moved or bought a place of our own!

When we first had goats, the older boys were about ten and eight, and though they understood how to milk, they were not able to stay with the goats long enough to milk them completely dry in order to keep up the milk supply. So Avraham assumed that responsibility, taking him away from his research, which became critical when deadlines hovered. The second time we had a goat, Avraham began that old routine: milking, watering, feeding Bessie. He began to feel the pinch on his time. "Well," we agreed, "we have always planned to have these animals for the children's sake, not for you to do the work. Why don't you have them take over?"

David and I had tried milking Bessie several days when Avraham was away, with pitiful results; she kept trying to get out of the shed, and we had to spank her, cajole her, practically sit on her to get her milked—and; predictably, she stepped in the pail. But Avraham took David out and taught him how to control the goat, just the two of them together. From that day, David took over the milking, soon able to milk her out completely in a short interval and effectively taking charge (though he sometimes required reminding about giving the hay when needed).

Dreaming of ponies, horses, cows, and sheep, we all plan our someday-family farm and its animals, intending for the children to care for them as they do now for the chickens and goat.

One summer evening, after our devotional, the boys begged permission to run on the lawns around the house in the dusk, to work out their "wiggles" from the hot day. As they zoomed up and down the lawn playing tag, Avraham noticed out the window that Bessie the goat was running up and down in her goat pen, so he called out for the children to release her. For almost an hour, as the boys played tag, Bessie played too, running frantically around with them, kicking up her heels, bouncing along on all four feet, turning when they turned, stopping and waiting patiently next to the boys when they stopped together to talk. It was obvious that she felt she was one of the kids, especially as she is an "only goat," her only companions in the goat pen being the chickens (who often sit on her back or head when she sits down or stands to feed).

Report Days

During the summer months, after some of the children had gone to school, I decided to modify my school approach for a few weeks, until an order of new school materials arrived from Learning at Home. I wanted the children to relax and enjoy themselves, and, being together, to renew a good feeling about homeschool.

So I asked them to practice their piano each day, and gave them little research questions to answer and report to the family. Some of these originated with the child's interest at the time (for David: How are caves formed? How would you make a model cave?—at a time when he was already plotting such a structure); and some of them were geared to the level of the child (Avi's: Teach the family how to make a paper hat).

Predictably, Sammy responded most intensely to report making, producing nice charts and samples, answering such questions as, What are the different kinds of rocks? How are they formed? Show us a sample of each; or, Why is it hotter in summer than in winter?

Chava's demonstration of making paper dolls, David's lecture on glassmaking, Yoni's explanation of how a refrigerator works, including some gelatin made from frozen orange juice—all delighted us. But the best, most poignant example had to be Yoni's response to, How do plants make seeds?

He used the simple, two-page explanation in Childcraft for his information, reading it alone first (and not understanding it too well) and then reading it with me. I sent him outside to find an iris in bloom; Avi brought in a couple of wildflowers that actually showed the stamen and anthers much more clearly and simply but Yoni wanted to use the iris. First explaining all the terms he would use, stamen, pistil, anthers, pollen, pollen tube, and ovule, he demonstrated the obvious parts on the iris and explained how bees and other insects push the pollen onto the stamen, which causes the pollen to grow a tube right down to the ovule, connecting with the egg, making a new seed.

But since we couldn't see inside the flower, I suggested that he cut the flower in half so we could examine the ovule. What excitement to see the little eggs inside there, ready for fertilization! Of course no one could see the pollen tubes, though there was obviously plenty of pollen, as it kept Mother sneezing!

I told Yoni to look outside for an *old* iris with its swollen ovule. A moment later he came back with one, cutting it in half as well. Inside were some little, unfertilized seeds just like the ones he had seen in the bloom, but also some mature seeds that had obviously been fertilized. He kept exclaiming, "I can't believe how those little egg-seeds grew into these big ones!" All the children got excited about these iris seeds, going out and getting another fat ovule with even more mature seeds in it, which they took and planted in the flower garden.

And of course, close to giving birth to our seventh child, we took the opportunity to wonder at how small the egg and sperm cells are, and yet how miraculously they grow into a new baby.

Banking

Sammy decided that he would open a bank. Charging 2¢ bank fee a week, and providing 1¢ weekly interest, he proffered his services to all and any comers, including checks into the bargain. He would store all the money and distribute it on demand. Because Avraham insists that coins (and marbles) not be left around the house, to prevent babies from swallowing them, the children had been stowing their earnings with him; but occasionally both parties would forget what the sum was, or it might grow so big that we adults would have a hard time redeeming it!

So Sammy's bank supplied a need. Yoni was the only person with moveable cash in the house, so Sammy's accounting book chronicled Yoni's $1.54 first. Since the others had no money, they began to ask me for money. "To earn money," I replied, "you have to work for it." "What work can we do?" Yoni (eight) and Chava (five), and later Avi (three), asked.

So they set to work folding laundry and putting it away (20¢); taking Sarah for a walk in the stroller (20¢); vacuuming the living room (35¢); washing windows (25¢); and so on. They performed the task first, and I decided the amount of payment afterward. Yoni began to be excited, because he wanted to buy a torpedo pen (the kind that has ten colors in one fat pen) and soon only lacked 50¢ to make up the proper amount. Sammy, on the other hand, was busy adding up sums, which he would occasionally ask me to do, and which I sent him back to do on his own!

Last week we had discussed how banks make money, lending out people's money at a higher interest than they paid to their clients. At 1¢ per week increment, Sammy will not make much, but I love his idea of banking! What a nice way to get the children to perform extra chores!

A Morning at the Beach

One morning, while we were in New Zealand, Yoni didn't feel well enough to go to school. After cleaning house, we went for a walk on the beach, Yoni, Avi, and Sarah, and Beau, a three-year old neighbor.

It was high tide, the ripples of the waves approaching the gulley where we lived. A large truck had disgorged horses and sulkies, the thoroughbreds that practiced daily on the wide hard sand. We watched the stableboys hitch up the sulkies, a complicated procedure. What excitement as they galloped far off down the beach!

We walked a bit to a deposit of lignite located near a tall sandy cliff. This cliff and its adjacent boulders appeared just like rock, but when you scratched at them, they crumbled into sand. We talked about the lignite, standing on it as the waves washed around it and occasionally came up over our ankles. You could see ancient pieces of wood still in it, brown amongst the black half-coal. I stood on the projecting pieces of wood to give myself a foot massage! We discussed the difference between wood, lignite, coal and charcoal.

A few paces away, alongside the sand cliffs, we carved our names with our hands into the cliffs alongside those of others. I am usually against defacing natural surroundings with grafitti, but the wind and weather wear away these carved names before very long. It was good practice for the three-year-olds, feeling the grooves of the letters of their names. Yoni asked me about the unusual spelling of Beau's name (shouldn't it be Bo?)—a discussion of French spelling and spelling conventions in general. We tried drawing on the cliffs; sticks worked better for this, and we drew some lovely trees.

Then Yoni decided to carve out a seat for himself in the sand cliff, just like one on the other side of a protrusion in the cliff. Pieces of wood didn't carve too well, but tua-tua and toheroa shells worked perfectly. As we scraped along, we noticed layers in the sand. Sedimentation! The sand makes sedimentary rock after time, heat and pressure work on it. We had experienced sandstone in Utah. And when sandstone undergoes high heat, such as in a volcano, you get limestone and other metamorphic rocks. Buildings made of limestone sometimes still have little seashells in it, which you can see and sometimes feel.

Beau's band-aid came off, so we headed home to have his mother treat his dangling toenail. On the way, Yoni and Avi ran to the top of the dunes, leaping off into the sand below. Beau safely deposited, we sloshed our feet in the shallow stream leading up the gorge to our house and arrived home just over an hour after leaving.

How would you evaluate our curriculum? Spelling, penmanship, science, art, P.E., social studies, compassion. Most of all, we were relaxed and happy after our walk, and the children remembered the discussions we'd had, the sand still in their fingernails and the shapes of the letters in their muscles.

Going back again to that spot, we'll note how our drawings and names have worn down and perhaps entirely disappeared, discussing erosion, wind and water. Sometime, if I'm feeling ambitious, we'll ignite a hunk of fallen lignite for a little beach campfire, perhaps toasting something over it. We always dunk our feet in the waves, watching how high the tide comes in at full moon, as well as how very far it goes out.

Instead of feeling academic, frustrated, anxious, nervous, or otherwise schoolish as we sometimes do after science or spelling lessons, we felt contented and relaxed, had a good lunch, and went and took a nap.

A Holiday

Perhaps you, like me, felt uncomfortable growing up with some of our holidays. As much as we children greedily anticipated Christmas, for example, I remember the day with a feeling of eating too much, watching the grown-ups drinking too much, and experiencing a kind of letdown after all the presents were unwrapped. A sort of spiritual dreariness and emptiness pervade my memories of the holiday.

Not all holidays affect us that way, of course. I like the way we celebrate the Fourth of July, with picnics, fireworks, parades, lots of outdoor family activities. Even though the children might find Thanksgiving a little tedious—just a big meal with perhaps too many vegetables—conceptually you feel it to be a splendid kind of holiday. I also can't argue with Mother's and Father's Day, though to be truthful they can become pretty soupy and sentimental for my taste!

But other celebrations trouble me because they seem to be a time for getting something for yourself. So often the proper conceptual meaning behind the celebration gets lost in the materialism of it, as do the good memories that can come when families give service or experience spiritual meaning.

In fact, for the first few years of our marriage we didn't actually celebrate Christmas! But one year, our neighbors brought a tree, lights, decorations, food, and a Santa who distributed gifts on Christmas Eve (belying to our children, then four and two, that Santa Claus was a pleasant story and fun game but not a real person!). After that, we adapted a bit, celebrating Christmas as a fun holiday, a time to share, and a day to receive a couple of nice presents apiece. We spend the few weeks ahead of the day making presents and cards, and from crafts books creating homemade ornaments.

We have similarly adapted to Halloween (just visiting selected homes that offered wholesome treats), using the time to create homemade costumes with and for each other. For Easter we enjoy the scripture stories and a special meal, but avoid most of the other trappings. As for other holidays, we remember them but usually don't celebrate a great deal.

Nevertheless, we find ourselves wishing for some appropriate days for celebration, the tradition forms that enrich a society. I love the *idea* of holidays, holy days, special times we can anticipate, prepare for, look back on happily. When we feel this longing, I think we share it with many people who have lost the religious sense of cultural roots. Recently we bought from Hearthsong a couple of books that reflect this same feeling. *Festivals, Family and Food* by Carey and Large helps to create a spiritual and cultural base for appropriate celebrations. The book is British and loaded with more recipes for holiday foods than I might choose, but the sense of the book helps us feel the seasons, the specialness of each holiday, and gives lots of ways to decorate, feast, and celebrate. The *Children's Year* by Cooper, Fynes-Clinton, and Rowling approaches the seasonal celebrations with a crafts point of view, not so many recipes. This is also a British book, yet the projects translate easily into an American context.

This year, for example, we followed the directions for forcing a cherry branch into bloom, blowing and decorating eggs, and making an Easter tree as is common in many Eastern European countries. The whole process took a couple of weeks, and what joy we experienced as the branch bloomed and we filled it up with eggs decorated in the spirit, if not the skill, of the Ukranian egg decorators! Many of the projects, moreover, are not just holiday oriented, but are simply seasonal, as for example, using long-stemmed grasses to make animals, or weaving raffia into crowns which we decorate with summer blossoms. It has seemed to me that the results from any of these projects far exceeds the effort we have put into them.

The Jewish calendar has impressed me for these reasons, with appropriate spiritual celebrations geared to the seasons of the year. Unfortunately, just like our American celebrations, these Jewish holidays seem to have the most meaning when you enjoy them within a community. However, even without that support we have sampled a few of the holidays, lighting candles and making spinning dreidls for Hanukkah, eating outside, in a booth, for the Feast of Tabernacles. One particular holiday has worked well for us, the Passover. We chose this one because of the scripture that says that it will stand as a covenant between God and Israel forever.

Passover centers around a meal. We don't celebrate for a whole week like the Jews do, scouring the house for yeast and doing a whooping spring cleaning as well, and avoiding leavened bread for seven days. But we like to have a Passover evening. Our celebration in New Zealand was such a peaceful time. The full moon was just rising as we sat down for the meal, having lit candles at the elegant table. We prayed in our usual way before starting the meal, and then, like the Jews, sang songs and talked as we went through the ritual meal. We dipped parsley in salt water to symbolize the bitter lot of the Israelites and the salty tears they shed. We broke and shared the unleavened bread, hiding a third of a piece to be ransomed by the adults when the children snatched it. We drank grape juice—our variation on Passover wine—at the appropriate intervals while reciting the Exodus events.

A big plate contained some of the symbolic foods of the supper: a roasted egg represented a festival offering; a roasted lamb bone stood for the passover lamb; the bitter herbs (we used parsley and horseradish) symbolized the bitterness of the children of Israel; the salt water you dip the parsely into stood for the tears they shed; and a mixture of apples and nuts represented the mortar that the children of Israel used when they built with bricks. We ate roasted lamb and some other special dishes made specially for Passover, and we enjoyed having matzoh, a delicious cracker, unleavened.

But these were only the externals. What made this evening so special to me was the retelling of the Passover story after a child asked the question, long prescribed by tradition, "What makes this night different from all other nights?" and sang the Hebrew song corresponding to that question. Avraham retold the Passover story, and we relived it ourselves, putting our own selves into the story, feeling and understanding it all anew again.

And we talked about what it meant to leave Egypt, such a

comfortable, predictable place, and wander in a miserable, thirsty, sometimes hungry desert for so long. We wondered how we might handle it, and what the story could teach us about prophecies in the last days. Somehow, with all the physical props there at hand, in a beautiful holiday setting at a lovely table, the thing became alive for us, and we were filled with a peaceful, beautiful spirit that helped us to newly feel and understand the Passover story. I remember the children all going to bed quietly, the light of the full moon filling the windows.

It makes me wonder: When the society of Zion is instituted among us—as it was in Enoch's time—what kinds of holiday celebrations will we be enjoying? If our family's experience of Passover is an indication, holidays centering around the seasons and around the scriptures will be something to look forward to with real anticipation.

Cub Scout Whimmydiddles

On a visit to a museum, we saw, in the gift shop, a basket of whimmydiddles—wooden folk toys made of a long, notched rectangle of wood, with a top piece of dowel drilled and nailed on. You rub the notches with another piece of dowel, and the top piece magically spins—one way or the other—depending on how you rub it.

More than paintings and displays, whimmydiddles impressed Yoni, at age nine. As soon as we got home, he descended to the basement workbench to make himself one. His whimmydiddle operated just as well as the museum's, which had cost $2, so he felt satisfied and happy.

Come Christmas, Yoni made a whimmydiddle for one of his friends, who also couldn't understand the mystery of how the thing spun.

Yoni was supposed to work on his Bear Cub Scout award, he had only a month to do it. In three days, he completed most of the requirements, which we had done as a matter of course during our homeschool and family activities. But he was also to supply a den activity, and he chose whimmydiddles.

He cut and notched the wood, cut and drilled the dowels, cut the rubbing dowels, and provided sandpaper, nails, and hammers for the Cub Scouts. He also took with him a snack of peanuts and dried fruit, although he felt bad about this: he wanted a more conventional snack, one the boys were used to.

But when Yoni came back from Cubs, he was all aglow. "They kept saying, 'Thank you, Yoni! Thank you, Yoni!' They loved the snack and they loved the whimmydiddles. Sister Green kept trying to figure out how it turned one way and the other way!" I wish I had been there.

The triumph—of course—was that Yoni devised the activity entirely on his own, found and prepared the materials, assembled everything, and taught the children on his own.

Rocketry

For months David and Sammy had been thinking model rockets, reading the Estes catalogue and contriving ways to connive me into buying kits for them. I pointed out that the least expensive model, minimal supplies included, costs $15; and it goes up from there. We knew other boys whose families bought a steady stream of rocketry parts and supplies, but I was not prepared to do that; and they were not prepared to do it for themselves with their own money either.

A stop at the fabric shop netted us some light cardboard tubes. (We had gone there to buy nylon for David to replicate a fancy kite he had seen in a nature catalog, but that experiment failed dismally; the kite wouldn't fly.) David and Sammy began to craft model rockets for themselves out of the tubes and stiff cardboard, David a big, fancy affair with wide wings and ornate fins, Sammy a sleek, two-stage invention. They created parachutes for their homemade rockets.

David went into the crafts shop to buy rocket fuel: "What rocket kits or parts do you have already?" the shopkeeper asked. "Nothing yet," answered David. The man tried to convince David to buy a basic kit with extra parts—a real bargain at $29.95. David spent a long time looking at the kits and parts and in the end came away with a new Estes catalog and three cylinders of rocket fuel, costing $3.00. I could see from the man's face that he doubted anything could come of this!

Later the boys went to the hardware shop to buy parts and high-gloss paints with their own money. Using a honey can rigged up with a fencing wire launcher and clothespins that had metal bits attached to wires, David invented an igniter from a nine-volt battery, activated by a button switch he happened to have from his electricity experiments. David and Sammy painted their rockets a shiny black with red and yellow decorations, sleek and a little wicked looking. Collecting their gear, they invited the family and neighbors to watch the launching.

To tell the truth, I had my doubts about this venture, especially after the kite failure. We all gathered around the camping trailer out in the alfalfa field while the boys set up their gear.

David went first. The igniter setup worked perfectly, but because

David's rocket was so big and the fins so unpredictable, it only went about a hundred feet and then spun dramatically downward; the parachute ejected but was not able to perform against the downward velocity the rocket had created. Sammy fired second. His small, two-stager soared up about 800 feet, ejecting its parachute perfectly, coming down way out in the alfalfa field. The boys all shot out to retrieve it. They bubbled with plans about their next rocket inventions, David bending body and fins of his model to predict a better flight. They began to bargain about who would pay for more fuel, Sammy gently wheedling me, "It doesn't cost much, really, and it's such a nice family activity."

It almost goes without saying what I liked about this rocketry venture. Seeing something in a book and replicating it (of course with mistakes and refining) teaches children so much more than just purchasing expensive get-ups and experiencing the thrills without the work—another lesson in self-sufficiency and confidence, and a big boost in self-concept.

A Typical Day

In the year before this book went to press, I wrote down the doings of a typical day. One morning, the children kept busy while breakfast was cooking: David was reading *Stone Soup*, an excellent magazine with works by children; Sammy was observing the hungry anole, for whom he had neglected to buy some crickets to eat; Yoni, Chava, Avi, and Sarah were all drawing, having learned to include mountains and more than a line of green foreground in their pictures.

After breakfast, David cleaned up the kitchen, Sammy picked up and vacuumed the house, Yoni picked up toys from the linoleum, Chava tended baby Joseph, and Avi mopped the dining room and kitchen.

Then all the younger children danced with me to a tape of the Cambridge Buskers, who play familiar classical pieces on accordian and flute with a great deal of flair and gusto. I held the baby while we danced. The older children started on their schoolwork, David with American School materials and Sammy and Yoni doing their workbook and text assignments as usual. Yoni took a break to dance with the other children, devising a "sewing dance," with Sarah weaving in and out between the joined hands.

As everyone finished up their schoolwork, the older boys shoveled snow while lunch was put on the table. We sat at the table and joked a bit about making our own dictionary, "Accident: a hole made by an ax."

After lunch, David worked on a collection of drawings he was doing about medieval times; Yoni practiced drawing animals for a children's book he and Sammy envisioned writing; and the younger children played Legos, the two girls dressed up in fancy dresses and scarves and Avi in cowboy gear.

When baby Joseph went down for a nap, I cut the boys' hair—which badly needed doing. When he woke up, we piled into the car and went down to the public library to check out books.

Although some days go better and some go much worse, this portrait gives a pretty clear idea of how a typical day might run, each day, of course, developing with its own set of unique activities.

QUESTIONS HOMESCHOOLING PARENTS ASK

Next door to us in Rarotonga, Cook Islands, lived a couple with three young children, the oldest nearing school age. Imagine our surprise to learn that these people had decided some time ago not to send their children to the local schools, but to teach them at home! Almost everywhere we go, we meet people who have long been preparing for homeschool, and who invariably seek direction and guidance in doing it.

A large variety of homeschoolers appears at homeschooling conferences, from mothers, casual and relaxed, to high-powered business-women who command a disciplined regiment of learning children. You find political thinkers, those activated by the theoretical wrongs in public schooling, and on the other hand, parents who took their children out of school simply because the little ones were unhappy.

Yet they all share a common thread of concerns, especially the conviction that "the buck stops here," with themselves, that no one else carries the responsibility of raising, of educating, their children. And they often ask me the same kinds of questions. My point of view won't suit everyone, but here are my answers to some basic questions homeschooling parents ask.

We can't firmly decide whether or not to homeschool. Many parents initiate homeschool in the heat of anger, concern, and high emotion, as they observe their children suffer in some school situation. There's nothing wrong with that. But once the children are home, they undergo the "de-schooling" process, as they have to unlearn their negative responses to books, papers, assignments, adult direction, and a myriad of other, perhaps subtle, learning-related attitudes. When the parents, at home with a houseful of tense children who resist their every effort to teach them, try to form a routine that closely resembles school, they feel their task is impossible.

Well, it *is* impossible—to do it that way. What fails in the schoolroom won't work very well at home either. Some homeschool counselors advise a cooling-off period between taking children out of school and starting a structured routine. This might be a good time for a camping trip or an excursion to Grandfather and Grandmother. When you come home, fresh and new in your point of view, you could implement some of the ideas in this book, setting the stage for child-initiated rather than parent-forced learning.

Read to the children. Walk with them and observe interesting things in the neighborhood, in the orchards, in the hills. When the children ask questions, guide them to encyclopedias or books that contain the answers. When the child asks, "What causes wind?" you can find interesting books at the library at various levels. Perhaps you will make a model wind-sock or anemeter. You might write some poems and certainly draw some pictures. Older children can prepare a talk on the subject, a lecture to deliver to the family, with chalkboard illustrations and perhaps a nature-walk included. Pretty soon you will be enjoying serious learning without the hassles of forcing, and resisting.

Some people take their children out of school because they observe a working homeschool and feel they want to try it themselves. Again, that could be a good beginning, but most of these families last for about a year and then send their children back to school, not because the experience was bad—it is usually very positive—but because they don't have the strong commitment that helps us last through the tension, exhaustion, drain on resources, and so on. In one family that followed this pattern, I noticed a tremendous improvement in the children. They were happier, more relaxed, and somehow more child-like. But the mother said that she couldn't handle the demands on her—a legitimate complaint; and the children seemed somewhat bored when the parents found it difficult to supply materials and activities.

Unfortunately, some parents de-school their children because they have a bone to pick with society, extended family, or institutions. "I'm sick of society and everything it offers," might sum their views. Likely they have some buried hurt or resentment to work out; that is too bad for their children who imbibe these poisons from them. I have seen this happen in some families and feel it is truly a bad reason to teach your children at home. Because we are living in the last days, in "perilous times," we can expect to see many, many things around us that we dislike. We are obliged to think about these and reject them. But we should also be positive, sorting the good from the bad, seeking a haven of peace and safety in the midst of trouble and distresses—one way we can "stand in holy places," I feel.

I suppose the only lasting reason for establishing a homeschool might be knowing that there exists an ideal way of educating children.

Feeling that there is, groping toward it, unsure of ourselves, breaking ground day by day—all very challenging. But perhaps our pioneering efforts will bear fruit when other families come to us in need of direction and we, painstakingly, will have carved out a proper path. Certainly homeschool takes time, and it evolves as you and your children grow. We need this kind of deeper commitment if we are to keep our homeschools going year after year.

I can't homeschool and keep house too, many mothers say. In the chapter, **Keeping House**, our struggle with housekeeping appears together with some solutions we have found. The foundation for a workable household must be the move toward voluntary simplicity, eliminating unnecessary or improper items or behavior from our homes. It is difficult for some women to locate themselves at home or in one's neighborhood around the home. We always want to be flying to the grocery store, to the crafts shop, to this or that class. I always say that you can't keep house if you don't stay home.

When we lived in Alaska, and also in the South Pacific, we saw few or no advertisements and so we stopped wanting things. Advertising creates an unnatural desire to get more and more, which almost always requires going out. You may find it a release to trim away the burden of excess household gear, to enjoy simple, homemade foods, to create your own entertainments at home, and to cultivate stimulating relationships in your church and neighborhood.

My spouse opposes homeschool. If the husband adamantly opposes you, don't begin a homeschool until you sort out your differences. All the positive energy you possess will be needed to manage your new life with twenty-four hour kids around the place. You cannot handle husband-wife conflicts as well. However, if he shrugs and says, "It sounds crazy, but if you want to do it, go ahead," I would. Many husbands who begin this way grow enthusiastic over the changes they see in their children; pretty soon they help out, and sometimes even take over the schooling themselves!

But if the husband endorses homeschooling and wants to impose it on a hesitant wife, they shouldn't go ahead until the wife is convinced. In most homeschools the wife carries the lion's share of organizing, sorting out conflicts, supplying activities and materials, seeking solutions to problems. Even if the husband is motivated by the best possible feelings, he shouldn't ask an uncommitted wife to shoulder these responsibilities.

In both cases—convincing husband or wife—you can see walls of resistance fall down when you pray for help with the problem. Women have told me that by praying about their resisting husbands, within months they were homeschooling happily.

My neighbors (or family, or friends) are giving me a hard time about homeschooling. In our twelve years of homeschooling, only once has someone thrown a negative comment my way. This was a new neighbor, who, observing our children at home, growled, "Well, what have you got against the public schools?" Otherwise, most people have commented on how well-behaved and well-spoken our children are, on how much they know; most say, "I wish we could do it ourselves, if we only had the courage."

Yet many young parents say that someone in their life is giving them a hard time about their homeschool. Often these couples bring it on themselves by expressing the bad feelings they have accumulated about school. Without realizing it, homeschoolers can come across as belligerent and polarized, creating an angered challenge to any who disagree with them.

No one should choose to teach his children at home to spite someone, to prove the family's superiority, or to register a political comment about society. (It is true that homeschooling is a political statement, but that should be an effect of homeschooling, not a reason for doing it.) How often I have listened to parents lament the basic wrongness of our society; while there is nothing wrong with that, the spirit in which they do so is often unpleasantly critical. And frequently they express negative comments about what they think is wrong with the Church, offering their home practices as an improvement.

Having worked through these problems myself, I have painfully concluded that this hypercritical attitude extends from one's adolescence, when we all go through a time of finding fault with everyone and everything around us. Some of us just carry these immature habits into our adulthood. True, there are plenty of incorrect practices all around, but I feel that these problems arise from within our culture, our society. When members of the Church around us practice what we feel to be wrong, it doesn't mean that the Church is in trouble; it means that we members have problems. How important it is to avoid the heavy, negative, critical attitude that some people, home-schoolers and others too, fall into!

Instead, we can learn to be very positive, cheerful, and willing to emphasize our similarities with those around us, not our differences. As an example, I think back to a rural ward we lived in. Our interest in healthy foods, our ongoing homeschool, and even our means of making a living (as writers, teachers, editors, while the rest of the community was largely rural), set us apart from the everyday world of many of the members. Yet we truly loved the people there, and we felt a genuine love from them.

The same approach should cheerfully color our dealings with others when we discuss homeschool. Naturally, we bubble over with the good things that are happening as we teach our own children; I never hesitate to share my delight with those who want to listen. But we should avoid criticizing other methods of education: the public or private schools around us. Usually the *other* person brings up how bad he or she thinks the schools are, and I just smile and nod sympathetically!

If we take this positive, loving approach to people around us, they usually follow our lead and respond the same. If someone wants to dispute issues, I just look them in the eye and say, "I understand your point of view," and change the subject. Most extended families, if they disagree with their relatives' homeschool, have enough respect to restrain pressures. We met the father of a homeschooling couple who felt his grandchildren were growing up with a too-limited view of life, too little exposure to the world outside their immediate neighborhood. Yet he expressed himself quietly to us, indicating he didn't wish to interfere with his daughter's life.

If dignity characterizes our dealings with others, they nearly always respond with respect themselves.

What happens when you have a new baby? One homeschooling mother rang me up to discuss their recent decision. She had given birth to their fifth child, and her husband, noticing her fatigue and nervousness, felt she could not handle a new baby and homeschooling too; they sent the children to school. Although they were doing well there, the mother struggled with mixed feelings, saying that she really could have handled it after all.

Still, you can fall into trouble with a new baby. When we bear our first children, we feel physically strong, hopping out of bed and continuing our daily activities soon after the birth. All of us have heard the stories about the Chinese laborers who give birth while on the job, strap the baby on their shoulders, and continue on in the rice paddy. Aside from my real suspicions about those stories (maybe the mothers get exhausted and sick within two weeks just as we do when we overdo things), most of us cannot handle such a drain on our systems. The theory that life goes on as usual after a new baby is mistaken.

What to do with homeschooling children when the new baby arrives can be a cause for concern. When my fourth baby, Chava, was born, Avraham helped me the first few days, and I spent the first weeks sitting a lot with the children, reading to them, taking it easy but still doing more than I should have. I was fairly resilient then, too. When Avi (Avraham), number five, was born, a homeschooling teenager offered to stay with us until I was stronger, even a month, if we wanted. I was very grateful to her and her family, yet felt nervous, hearing the children in other parts of the house, wanting to call out instructions, worrying, feeling guilty about lying in bed when others were working, and just over-reacting to the presence of someone else in our home. After a week, she left, as I just wanted to get back to my own schedule. Without enough real rest, it took me longer to get over the strain of the birth.

When Sarah was born, the children stayed for nearly a week with another homeschooling family. That was a blessed, peaceful time in which to recuperate and communicate with my husband. However, the children arrived home with the flu, which Sarah and I both caught, too. After we recovered, we entered too soon into the routine of housework, schooling, shopping, library trips, etc. We all got sick again, and this time, weakened by the first illness and only five weeks old, Sarah developed pneumonia, which necessitated four days in the hospital and several long months afterward of therapies and massage to strengthen her.

From such stressful experiences I would therefore recommend that, when your new baby arrives, you cut your home schedule right down, just making sure you have morning scripture reading, your evening devotional, and perhaps some interesting new crafts materials available in the house. Let Father do the grocery shopping (taking the kids along so you can rest), and let him take the children for their weekly library visit. It would be a good time for visits to grandparents, for a relative to take the children to a movie, or for family home evening at someone else's home—without Mother.

During the daytime, you should rest, sit and read to the children, hold the baby, and take it easy. I feel that Mother and baby should be "on hold" for a month to six weeks, only slowly easing into the full routine. Call it a school vacation (if you're like us, you homeschool year-round, so four to six weeks off for a new baby will be quite legitimate). Besides, as we have so often observed, even if you are not *teaching*, the children will likely still be *learning*. You can be sure, if you have books and materials around, that they will find something to occupy themselves. Let them help with the cooking and cleaning, too, under Dad's guiding hand.

From this you can see that, though there may be many reasons for sending children to school, the new baby is not necessarily one of them!

How can you homeschool if you are living in a difficult situation? I remember Joyce Kinmont describing her homeschool in a small trailer—certainly not ideal. I think we all struggle with less-than-ideal circumstances—no workshop, nobody close by to play with, undesirable influences in the neighborhood, even dangerous neighborhoods. When we homeschool with frustrations, we want to throw up our hands and send the children to school; it is just too difficult!

We kept our children at home most of the time in Rarotonga. We had few tools or crafts items there, and of course the neighbor children were in school. Yet, as we adapted to new conditions, so many avenues of learning opened. It became one of the most educational of all our experiences. Using the library and spending as much time as we could outdoors, we avoided feeling desperate.

On returning to the United States after our year away, we stayed for some weeks with friends who opened their home to us. Their large home certainly provided enough room for us all, though we had to learn to handle the presence of those seducers, television and computer games (I had to open up, relax, and let the children experience some of each; it would have been offensive to forbid them).

In that situation, all of our homeschool gear remained packed, even most of the things we had used abroad. Just before I sent away for some prepared curricula—*Oak Meadows*, etc.—a neighboring schoolteacher invited me to her home, offering a selection of books—very good ones—learning programs, texts, paper, materials . . . I chose what we could use, and brought them home, setting up a temporary school. David unpacked what tools he had, and we replenished our stock of tape, glue, and hardware.

In that home I felt very sensitive to making undue noise and disorder so I spent more time than usual regulating the children, playing games with them, hushing them. The family we were staying with was incredibly tolerant, yet they were not used to the inundation of six homeschool children much out of focus from a lack of routine. We nonetheless moved toward internal order and ran a school, supplementing with Scouts, gymnastics, and playing indoors in the winter weather. I was grateful for our time in that home, but consider it one of the difficult, yet workable challenges of our homeschool, often longing for our workbench, toys, paints, and library.

My older kids won't do a thing I say. They fight me on everything, even the simplest things. Homeschooling friends who have large families with young children, and who have never sent their children to school, validate our experience: sometimes the first steps to maturity, to breaking away from Mother's apron-strings, come early in a homeschooled child's life, the teenage symptoms appearing even before the teens. Children who have learned to manage their time responsibly, who have worked hard in a household of little ones, tending, cleaning, cooking, managing crises, often begin to restlessly seek a larger world. A first step seems to be crossing Mother's path. But there are ways of easing such pressure.

Dr. Rex Wadham, recently deceased, outlined the Hero Journey as an essential pattern in our lives: the initiate leaves his home—a safe place, which he shares with those who love and honor him—and goes out into a challenging, dangerous, frightening, demanding world where no one knows him, and where he must work out his problems himself. Thrown on his own resources, he rises to the challenges and conquers them, growing into a new and better person because of it. He then returns home triumphant, strengthened and renewed, to a loving welcome. You recognize this pattern in many characters in literature, such as Odysseus, Joseph in Egypt, even Pinnochio; children's books are replete with the Hero Journey. Sometimes our young fledglings are yearning, without knowing it, for their first Hero Journey; and sometimes we are long in recognizing what the problem is.

We should welcome these first flutters of independence, as unpleasant as their symptoms may be! You may feel, as we did with David, that a short stint in school is the answer. One young mother said, "My children are in school this year. I feel it's important to have both, homeschool and public school. We do it alternate years." They lived in a small community where the local school offered no serious problems. If you live near an institution that is acceptable, some schooling might be an answer, at least for some of your children. The Holy Spirit will let you know if it's right for your child.

One single mother, having homeschooled her two boys from the beginning, strongly resisted even the notion of school, feeling, as so many do, a real antipathy to all that goes on in schools. But she didn't realize that her children had never experienced what she was opposing and that they longed for the challenge of the experience. Her thirteen-year-old finally asked to go to live with his father in another country, so that he might attend school without hurting his mother's feelings. He soared right to the top of his class, and loved the experience, being thoroughly ready for it.

If the school in your area doesn't seem suitable for sending your child full-time, you could approach the principal about part-time attendance. Many school districts in Utah have turned positive about this approach, especially when they have found out that they receive full compensation for a child who attends even part-time. By stating your desires professionally, dressing neatly (this shouldn't make such a difference, but it matters to school people), having a cheerful and positive attitude, and armed with accounts of precedents in nearby districts, you should be able to achieve what you want. By being out of the house a few hours, experiencing the rules and ritual of a peer group without being drowned in them, your youngsters or teenagers may come home with a fresh perspective, ready to enjoy his home routine. The older girls in one homeschool family swim on the high-school team and attend an art class, a drivers' ed class, or whatever subject they desire.

Years ago, when teaching high school in a small Utah town, I was approached by a student's mother. The girl, brilliant and very active, was often absent from school, although she kept up in her studies. Her mother let me know that she was working part-time in a local restaurant. I think this is a good idea, if there is suitable work available. Even if the job doesn't pay, as in an apprentice type of situation, your young person may grow from the supervision of someone other than Mother. I have noticed my children setting other adults on a pedestal—perhaps "having a crush" on them, as we used to say—a positive development when the adults' lives are worth emulating.

One young man found himself helper's employment in a small school for the handicapped near his home. Because he himself was deaf, he wished to train in that field. Two sisters worked as hospital volunteers. One young lady landed an aide's position in a preschool. This harks back to the old-time practice of children doing real work, productive work. Today we suspect child-labor-abuse if young people work; but adolescents want to do real work, and they can do it well. If they can work, still keeping up their studies at home, nobody feels cheated.

Community schools offer a variety of interesting courses, usually in the evenings. Sometimes a community college or even a local university will allow a motivated youngster to sign up for a class. Teachers may have to swallow some prejudices when a pint-sized pupil expects equal treatment with his older peers, but homeschooled children are very confident and usually overcome the initial reaction.

Sports programs, drama programs, dance classes, music lessons, Scouts—all offer a few hours out of the house a couple of times a week. You may feel one drawback if you live far from the town where these are held, as we did in one home in Utah. Expecting baby number six, I ran our three boys to soccer practices at various times and to soccer games at other, various times. To this day I get tired just thinking about it. Ideally, the children should be able to walk or bike to activities and the classes they choose.

If your child is resisting your efforts to advance his academic work, you could enroll him in a correspondence course. We were overwhelmed by the variety of courses available, from kindergarten through Ph.D.—at a cost, of course. Sometimes having another adult supervise a certain area of study can ease the pressure, and make the work exciting for your child.

Quite a few homeschoolers in our acquaintance have found ways to send their children to live with friends or relatives in faraway places, such as France or Mexico, for a short time—up to a year, in one case. The children learn the language and culture, and experience renewal through the Hero Journey. Especially if they stay with trusted relatives, a stint away from home can ease a building parent-child conflict.

The ideal answer to a child's need for more autonomy may be the family farm. Living in a safe community, in a rural environment, the children can work with the father, a strong, positive, male role model, several hours during the day. They could play with friends, roaming the hills and fields, in safety. And their hours in the home, learning with Mother, would be a pleasant balance to their outdoor activities.

The year that our seventh child, Joseph, was born, we came to a kind of homeschooling crisis. The older children felt their lives were too hemmed in, too static, boring. They felt cut off from the world outside, restless for a broader view. Because we were heading into winter, I couldn't take them out for an explore of the world with a little baby who was constantly coming up with a runny nose.

We asked our friends, who homeschool on a farm four hours from our home, if our boys might come for a visit, which they had often discussed with us. They though it would be a good time for that, as they needed help on the farm. So we drove the family down and dropped the three older boys off.

What a surprise the following week turned out to be! The younger children, released from the pressure the older ones had evidently been exerting without our understanding it, played intensely, did their schoolwork with relish, and created a beautiful harmonious balance together. We compared it to the times we enjoyed when all of the children were little, when we had a smaller family. At age seven, Chava in particular relaxed and seemed a different person, less explosive and temperamental, more willing to share with the younger ones.

When the older boys returned, Avraham and I had made a decision: they would travel to BYU three times a week, working near Avraham's office on the fifth floor of the library (right next to the Juvenile Collection). At noon they would run for an hour in the gym; at five they would swim for an hour. In addition, they would be able to sit in on music performances, movies, exhibits, talks and other interesting activities as these came up. The boys looked in the university newspaper to find anything that might be worthwhile attending. Sometimes I would bring the other children (and perhaps another homeschool family as well) to enjoy a concert, a museum, or cultural display together.

We also found a student tutor to work with the boys in composition. I felt they weren't producing consistently enough for me. A tutor would compel them to come up with more work, better work. Sure enough, when Laurie, a BYU junior in English, sat with them twice a week, they all began writing much more than before. In particular, Sammy began to evidence a real gift for fiction, especially science fiction. They all—including the tutor—enjoyed the time together.

Avraham took his editing and translation work with him and was there to answer any questions the boys had. In particular, Yoni blossomed academically during this BYU time; he buckled down to his work, enjoying the one-on-one with his dad. The older boys, just turning 12 and 14, were relieved to get out of the house, to escape the trials of being with little ones all day.

Nevertheless, they all stayed home Tuesdays and Thursdays, doing their schoolwork as usual, but also working on projects, performing their science experiments, visiting friends later in the day, and just relaxing and reading at home. I liked having them around and felt better about them because they were absent part of the time!

Not surprisingly, however, this BYU routine got tiresome after a semester, and all of the children voted to stop it. After a summer at home, we decided with the older two boys to try a half day at the local intermediate school, spending the other half of the day at home doing correspondence coursework. This worked quite well for a semester, as we shared the transportation with another homeschool family doing the same thing. At semester break, however, the mother of this family had a new baby, and could not share the transport anymore. In addition, I found myself struggling with morning sickness again. We thus visited the principal at the school to ask for permission for the boys to attend school half day and do their correspondence school in the library in the afternoons.

At first the principal did not like the idea. He felt that if he provided such a tailor-made program for a couple of kids, the rest of the school might feel entitled to the same thing. At that point I tried hard to listen to him from his own point of view, to be sympathetic, understanding. Soon, miraculously, he was saying that if the children were pursuing serious academic work, and if they could be trusted to behave properly without supervision, it could be an excellent approach. He wished all students might be that serious about learning! We found this arrangement to work very well with David and Sammy. Not only did they progress well in their high school correspondence course, but they all did top-notch work in their school classes, making the honor roll each term. In addition, they were able to experience the larger world at a time when they seemed to need it. Sammy, who had suffered much of his life from shyness and unsureness socially, blossomed out and began to enjoy many more social experiences with his peers, including spending time with them at our home and at other boys' as well. David entered essay contests, art contests, and other competitions, often finding himself a winner, which built confidence in himself in a larger context. Although I had had very strong reservations about the climate of the school, which were sometimes called a jungle or a zoo by other students and their parents, I was astonished to see that this climate had little negative effect on these older two boys. Evidently their long-time homeschool training had given them the tools to experience school with strong character and mostly positive effects.

In fact, David expressed the desire to attend school full-time during the following year, which would be the first year of high school. We stipulated that he graduate from his correspondence school before enrolling in public school full-time. He agreed to that, although he enrolled in tenth-grade curriculum which paralleled his peers, including course requirements for graduation from the local system! We envisioned that the children would graduate from correspondence school and then take AP courses to earn concurrent credit for college, but David wished to approach it this other way. Since his choices were solid, honors courses, we could not argue with such choices at age 15. Although he pursued a way that we had not envisioned, we felt that it was positive, and we allowed him to do it. We thought that he might likely look for earlier college attendance as he grew and matured during his high-school year.

These approaches may serve as a stopgap to finding a more peaceful, whole way of life on a family farm. Although not many of us are achieving a rural way of life right now, we can look forward to it as a future blessing. Such a life doesn't preclude cultural experiences like concerts and plays and good conversation, though admittedly most small towns at this time are short on these commodities. Joseph Smith's plan for Zion communities places families in large lots within a central town, furnished with theaters, concert halls, temples, and so on. Families work the outlying fields—a system to look forward to!

Some days I get so discouraged and tired of it all. After many years of homeschooling, I finally realized that this often simply means, "I'm tired." A good meal and a nap will bring me back to normal.

At first I thought I needed to get away from the home and children, and my husband would tend the little ones while I spent an afternoon or evening at the library or shopping mall. I would usually return from these excursions as weary and addled as I had left. Now we know that when I say, "I'm sick of being with the children," or "I'm tired of the frustrations of homeschool," I need rest—in bed. We have even hired babysitters to tend the children while I had a sleep, when no other help was available. Avraham has minded the family sometimes, and now the older children do. During my last pregnancy, another homeschooling family, understanding this need, graciously offered to take the whole crew while I slept and my husband worked, and I didn't wake up from an early nap until late in the afternoon, I blush to say. This doesn't happen often—but it is comforting to know that we generally do not tire of the people we love the best.

If we do get stale in the homeschool routine, we are free to alter or even suspend it for a while. We can drive or hike to the pond, to the foothills, to the park, to friends. We can go see a library movie (in Orem, Utah, the audio-visual services provide a large selection of video films, which now and again we would go and see). Sometimes a phone call to or from a homeschooling friend can change the color of a day.

Reading homeschooling books brings you back into a proper attitude. I always liked John Holt's *Teach Your Own*, but found his newsletter *Growing without Schooling* somewhat unnerving because of the myriad points of view it presents—a good technique, for what his organization is trying to do, but a little dizzying for a faltering mother. *Mothering Magazine* is well worth subscribing to, not so much for their occasional articles on homeschool, but for their advice on parenting generally, which always softens and centers me.

Finally, you might be surprised how your view improves after you pray about your feelings. So often I have felt the quieting influence of the Spirit when, smitten by the crisp autumn air and the neighbor children trooping off to school in their new clothes; or wrangled by children bent on teasing each other, I feel that maybe I am wrong after all, or that I can't stand it any longer. Prayer brings that sweet comfort which makes me believe that God cares about me and my homeschool, and that these unhappy feelings will soon pass.

Recently, I have talked with many long-time homeschooling families who have found themselves in almost all the same predicament, asking this question: *"I feel burned out and unsure of myself after homeschooling so many years."* I have chatted with homeschooling mothers who often describe a similar situation: they are physically and emotionally tired, often expecting babies or nursing them; they have long since outgrown the initial flush of excitement as they began home- schooling; the children bump around the house, bored and cantankerous.

Most of these mothers do not want to send their children into the public schools, and either cannot afford or locate an appropriate private school. But like stretched-out elastic, they cannot find the resilience to pump new life into their homeschool. Ofttimes they are struggling with redefining their relationships to their spouses as they move toward the middle years of marriage. New homeschoolers, of course, cannot imagine this burntout state of affairs and may categorically blame a mother for lacking commitment. But I have experienced this miserable burnout, and it can be a difficult problem indeed.

Sending three of our children to a rural grade school, as an answer to burnout, released me from the common homeschooling point of view that the outside environment threatens too much, that the society outside offers too many pollutions, that the children will be ruined by exposure to school. Of course, children can be irrevocably changed if they attend school at a time inappropriate for them or if they stay in too long, but I found that certain school experiences can be good for everyone, expecially if the children have not experienced the school environment before. In these instances, a change is as good as a rest, as the saying goes, and the children, tired of homeschool freedoms and unaccustomed to school routines, find these new things stimulating and fun.

Of course, you might not have access to a decent school, and Avraham and I have discussed other solutions to the burnout problem and have concluded that at present there are no ready answers. Taking a year off to build a house, a family farm, or perhaps travel, can relieve the problem. One homeschooling parent comments, "I don't know of any easy solution, comparing the advantages of homeschool and public school. Sometimes the parents and children just need to realize that they will go through difficult times and must patiently work through them." You may be surprised that in your patient search, an unexpected solution will present itself, thus transforming one of the most difficult problems of homeschool into a blessing. It can certainly open us up to things that we would not have considered before.

For me, facing this problem helped me resolve my unproven assertion that all school experiences would ultimately be negative. When morning sickness, burnout, family changes, and personal changes all converged upon me, I faced the reality that homeschool was not my ultimate priority in every situation. The other concerns had to take precedence before I could properly homeschool. I also learned that at certain times, I could place my own pressing needs before the needs of the homeschooled children, an idea I did not entertain before. However, during all of this, I still saw myself as a homeschool mother, and only sent those children to school that I felt should go. At one point, I had only a six, a four, and a two at home, while expecting our eighth child. This was a stressful attack on my homeschool ego, but through it I realized that even with my older children in school at the present, I was still a homeschooler. To my delight, the six-year-old began to learn and progress at an unprecedented pace, receiving the intense attention that only my first children had heretofore enjoyed. And I realized that we could always resume homeschooling in a larger way whenever we all felt that the time was right. Burnout, therefore, became a learning experience and another source of growth.

Surely I need some special training. In a day when specialists cut our hair, cure our illnesses, make our clothing, grow our food, and do everything that many folks did for themselves a short time ago, we find it hard to trust our ordinary selves with our own children. A credentialed teacher must be necessary to "teach them everything they need to know!"

Emerging from college as a credentialed teacher, I was shocked to find how little of my training applied in the actual classroom. And, beginning my own homeschool, very little of my hard-won classroom experience worked at home. In schools, most teachers fall into the mode of lecturing/testing; few conduct fruitful discussions, and fewer yet provoke independent thinking and learning. In homeschools, the parent acts as a guide, a motivator, a channeler of resources and energy. Most good mothers do this instinctively—it is the mothering instinct to do so.

Did you know that in many places private school are not required by law to hire credentialed teachers; and that they hire many uncertified teachers, not for their education, but for their success at working with children? A teaching certificate simply means that a university student has completed a certain course of study and has student-taught for a prescribed length of time. Any and every kind of teacher emerges from these programs, good ones, horrific ones. They basically come out what they were to begin with.

And while a university graduate might be able to marshal more facts and figures than his unschooled counterpart, most of us really don't remember that much. In the typical university program, we amass facts and pour them out for exams. In rare cases do we learn how to learn—how to read well, to write well, to think well, to utilize the math facts, to integrate the science facts. If we are fortunate we may graduate having read and thought about higher things than we might have otherwise, but some general-education programs permit us to skirt even that.

So university training does not necessarily qualify us to be a good homeschooler, and it may even hinder us if we take our teacher-training so literally that we cannot approach children in other ways.

Far more important are these two basic things: first, your commitment to find a better way to raise and teach your children than our society now offers; and second, a continuing desire to keep learning yourself. John Holt would have added a third: that we genuinely enjoy our children's company. As you read, explore new ideas, think, wonder, try new things, you keep growing, and that is what your children need most of all—a vital, self-educating model to follow. So many of us feel bad because we have never had a chance to try weaving, making aquariums, identifying specimens from the world around us, learning new languages, reading good literature. With a homeschool we not only can but must enjoy new things—together with our children. This transforms our own lives, makes us happier.

Once, curious to envision a composite of what the scriptures say about learning and schooling, I was struck by how the following revelation applies to everyone, busy mothers included:

And I give unto you a commandment that you shall teach one another the doctrine of the kingdom. Teach ye diligently and my grace shall attend you, that you may be instructed more perfectly in theory, in principle, in doctrine, in the law of the gospel, in all things that pertain unto the kingdom of God, that are expedient for you to understand; Of things both in heaven and in the earth, and under the earth; things which have been, things which are, things which must shortly come to pass; things which are at home, things which are abroad; the wars and perplexities of the nations, and the judgments which are on the land; and a knowledge also of countries and of kingdoms. (D&C 88:77-79)

One way we can interpret this is by saying that we can strive to know everything worthwhile that we can, and that we can measure and evaluate everything we learn by the scriptures, by the Spirit. And we can also assume that if we go about teaching and learning diligently, God will facilitate our efforts. To me, this offers much more direction and motivation than a teaching certificate ever did!

Don't I need some sort of study course or correspondence course for my children? I usually object to study courses because they entrap us into thinking that someone else knows best what we should be studying and how much we need, how long it should take, what point of view we must adopt. So many of these courses use the fill-in-the-gap method, which pulls us back into the right-answer test mentality that most of us abhorred in school. Some of that can be okay, as in math workbooks, but home study courses often lockstep us into too much of it—after all, we paid for the course so we had better use it.

Many Christian-oriented courses plug scripture or moral quotes into the texts, or worse, use moralistic tales for their literature selections. I object to this because I feel that the scriptures have their own integrity, and usuing them to indoctrinate during other study matter offends my sense of their dignity. Furthermore, great literature carries with it its own powerful morality; preaching is a much less effective method, and it offends the aesthetic sense. Finally, I feel that many study courses lack the depth and intellectual challenge that homeschool is meant to provide.

Still, despite these objections, I think there are some situations in which a correspondence course—if it's a good one—can have a place in a homeschool. When you are dealing with a large family of many ages, a course or study guide can ensure that somebody doesn't get neglected. Usually the seven- or eight-year-old gets pushed aside by the demands of the babies or the older children. By using a quality study course, you can be sure that the child's needs are being met and that you spend a modicum of time with him. Also, when a child is preteen through early teens, he often seeks structure. He enjoys classes, group activities, and a predictable state of things. At that age, a good correspondence course fills the inherent need—and takes the demands off your hands as well, for often at this age the child begins to resist Mother. An instructor at another location—or even just a friendly written voice—can take the burden for you.

How do you choose a correspondence or study course? There are so many available! My first criterion must be that it should not cost inordinately—and most of them do. You are not purchasing "education"—just a little help, and the cost should reflect that.

Secondly, the course should be flexible and interesting enough to adapt to the child's current bent of thought and intellectual needs. As I mentioned above, it should not be didactic nor push one philosophical point of view. Hopefully, it avoids a constant workbook, fill-in-the-blanks approach. And it should provide a pleasant and encouraging learning experience so that the children generally look forward to using it.

After looking at a few study courses, I found a couple that seem to meet at least part these criteria. One is the *Oak Meadows* courses (P. O. Box 712, Blacksburg, VA, 24060), which I like because they include activities with their studies, and because they provide good-quality, interesting texts to go along with the courses, at least in the upper elementary grades. They stem from the Waldorf approach to education, which I don't totally agree with but that gives a loving, relaxed approach to growing up. The early grades especially reflect this feeling, though these require a good deal of parental involvement. I also like very much the materials from *Learning at Home* (Dept. 8810, P. O. Box 270, Honaunau, Hawaii 96726). They seem to have an intellectual integrity and flexibility, a perfect homeschool approach. They also offer lots of different options from many sources. I feel their prices are fairly good, although if one were to buy everything that looked appropriate, he could tot up quite a bill! Also, their materials sometimes take a long time to arrive.

For the older ages, there are so many high-school curricula available, but the one that seems to suit me best is *American School* (850 E. 58th Street, Chicago, Illinois 60637). I like theirs because they use the thought-question approach, with open book, rather than a tense, examination orientation. Further, their questions are challenging and provoke thought. Their coursework load seems moderate enough, and people who value a "real" high school diploma can get one. Quite young people can easily handle the level here—even a twelve-year-old or some precocious elevens won't mind doing these courses. They can thus "graduate" very young indeed and perhaps start some university level work if they want to, having acceptable qualifications. Of course a teenager can take an equivalency examination, but most school districts require that you be at least eighteen. Also, many people feel that the equivalency exam carries with it a social stigma—a person is not good enough to graduate from high school.

Some younger people like to take college level courses and often do quite well at them. If one of the parents teaches at an institution, a youngster can take courses for free, especially in night school or during summer sessions. Correspondence courses from colleges, whether they be high school or university level, usually cost too much for the average homeschooling family, though they might be quite good quality.

Before you buy any study course, ask for a sample of their lessons and a curriculum overview. You can immediately get a feeling for whether they will suit you. And the *Learning at Home* folks in Hawaii allow you to return anything you don't like within fifteen days, unused, a nice way to be absolutely sure of your choice.

Is there such a thing as an ideal school?   If I were to imagine an ideal school, it would allow for the child to elect to play outdoors all day, if he wanted. School would provide a community resource, an optional adjunct to the home, rather than a compulsory babysitting service. Instead of force-feeding children with information and facts that they supposedly must know to be successful in society, a teacher would act as a guide and facilitator, just as the homeschooling parent does.

The advantages of having a school rather than doing all the work at home might be access to a larger variety of materials and tools, such as science lab equipment; or a nice variety of art supplies and methods; a superior library and someone to guide the children as they read through it; musical instruments, and the opportunity to learn them, and the chance to play them together; and a structure that drew on specialists in the community to help children learn about unusual subjects. Children would be able to enjoy each others' company, play sports together, and thus experience a nice outing away from home. And parents could be freed to work on their own when they arrange to do so, without the necessity of monitoring all of the children all of the time.

The success of such a school would hinge, of course, on the teacher. Some people have a natural gift for drawing the best out of children, of seeing their interests, sensing their potentials, bringing them to experiences that will help them most. A majority of teachers nowadays feel obliged to "teach," and, of course, some things must be taught. But the ideal teacher fades into the background as soon as possible.

I remember observing, during a family visit, two younger cousins as they watched their older cousins knit leg-warmers and scarves. "Do you know how to knit?" one aunt asked. Neither girl did. "Do you want to learn?" Of course they did. Needles and wool appeared, and with some difficulty the two found themselves casting on, preparatory to knitting. At that moment the aunt's baby woke up, and she went off to tend him. Then the best moment occurred: the two older cousins migrated to the younger ones, helping them loosen the tension, pull the yarn around—to knit.

Most of us do not easily let go of the idea that school attendance must be compulsory, that certain subjects must be taught, and that students must be graded on their work. From observing many homeschool families, I feel confident in the following: home can be just as instructive and positive as school, even if no formal lessons occur (remembering our three months in the wilds in Alaska, when the boys' reading abilities soared, and where they accumulated incredible knowledge about plants, weather, mining; and of social studies and literature, from the books they read).

Given a variety of learning materials and a safe learning environment, children will learn, broadly and deeply, many subjects. They may need to be assisted and encouraged in the ones they falter in; but the main business of being a child is learning, and they do it passionately, without the lure or pressure of grades. Finally, if a home or school and the people in them radiate love and excitement about learning and living, children will choose to work without compulsion, mirroring the adult's enthusiasm for these things.

John Holt's Music and Bookstore rents and sells a film, *We Have to Call it School*, about the Ny Lil Skule in Denmark, which resembles the model I am seeking for. If you can see this film, it might give you courage in teaching in this way. In brief, it shows a school run like a homeschool, possessing and illustrating the advantages of both.

Unfortunately, most of us can only dream about such a community and its school, at least for the time being. But this doesn't mean that we give up hope for it. We can still utilize existing schools somewhat, depending on the agreeableness of the teachers and principals there. Some districts in California offer a program called *Independent Learning*, in which parents can utilize school programs to whatever extent that they themselves choose. Children may attend school with this individualized approach, but homeschoolers can also use it.

In other areas, parents send their children to school half days. Some friends whose children practiced their music three hours or more per day did this. Interestingly, when their oldest girl turned twelve, she could no longer attend the elementary school but had to be bussed to a farther-away Middle School. After a courageous half-year there, she came home again, because she felt she was frittering her time away, and because the social and emotional environment was so stressing.

Again, some young people go to school for woodworking, swimming lessons, orchestra, English. If you live near a friendly school, your children could enjoy the outing and instruction but still spend the bulk of their days in the loving nurture of home.

Some schools offer textbooks, paper, crayons, art materials, and standardized tests. Once we received a call from the local principal offering these things. We went to the school to check it out, finding the staff there exceedingly friendly (because of a Distict mandate, we found out, which we considered a happy improvement). We later learned that by accepting any assistance we placed our children on the school's rolls, permiting it to collect the $20 or so per day allotted for students from the Federal Government. This may offend your conscience; you will have to decide for yourself if you find that your school takes this approach.

I feel it is very important to maintain a good relationship with your local schools. You should try to support its positive activities, such as School Fairs, plays, concerts, etc. One homeschool mother served on the PTA, though none of her children attended school! Speak positively whenever you can; it doesn't help to air your negative feelings to the community at large, even though you may feel quite critical of things you see going on. Be cheerful and confident when you speak to school officials.

I often call our homeschool an "educational experiment," noting how successful our children's performance has been. You can come across as intelligent, informed, and sympathetic to the school's needs and problems. Dress nicely when you deal with school people, perhaps leaving the baby at home. (Babies are welcome in the New Zealand schools, teachers sometimes bringing theirs along as they teach, but they are treated as unwanted creatures in American schools.)

I have not referred to the serious political implications of schools, such as socialism and humanism: indoctrinating children in the flawed beliefs of the society, whether boldly or subtly. Nor have I tackled the grave problems inherent in many textbooks. These are good matters to evaluate yourself. They, like schools themselves, will not go away for a long time, so we do need to deal with them. Perhaps, by thinking carefully through the important and fundamental issues of learning and schooling, we will prepare ourselves someday to help form more positive educational institutions.

In the meantime, our mental efforts will sharpen our commitment to our homeschools.

A final question people ask, *What about socialization?* I treat in the chapter on that subject, not as the final answer to the question, but by way of seeking to articulate some things we have experienced.

Myths about Children

We should find it ironic that most of us moderns don't really know what to do about children—how to communicate with them, how to feed their needs, how to love them. The scriptures warn us to teach them the gospel of repentance, to stop them from quarrelling, to ensure that they honor us; to train them up in the way that they should go, that when they are old they will not depart from it.

That sounds simple, but it demands more than we see at first glance, for it infers that we know the way we should go. Most of us in the modern world really don't know. Most of us are dissatisfied and unhappy and unsure of ourselves. Of course, we understand very well the negatives we should avoid, lying, stealing, swearing, unchastity, and so on, but as for the positives, the day-to-day practice of being happy in life, most of us mix the standards of the world into our perceptions of the good life. Consider, for example, how we vary so incredibly in our standards at home. Some people listen to the radio from their first waking moment until they go to bed at night, inviting into their homes an uncensored stream of sound and idea. On the other hand, some people never listen to anything but carefully-chosen classical music. Some people watch television in the same indiscriminate way, even on the Sabbath. And some others don't own televisions.

We once shared a rental house with a young man who ate TV dinners and sweet foods almost exclusively. Comparing his diet to our whole-wheat bread, vegetables, and so on, he thought it didn't make any moral difference what you ate, as long as you could afford it. Most of us close our minds to anyone who is dressed in clothing that we esteem as unstylish or old, although our spiritual sense tells us to do otherwise. The standards of the world dictate whether or not we are happy in the size and decorations of our homes, although around the globe, people in other cultures live very cheerfully and contentedly in homes arranged quite differently. Is there a moral difference between a family that sits itself down in front of the television each night until bedtime, and that which spends its evening time talking, making music, reading, knitting, or whatever?

By pointing out these contrasts, I am only saying that "the way we should go" in today's world is not as clear as it seems to be, the world view of industrialized society having so infiltrated our way of perceiving the world, and ourselves in it.

It certainly has muddled the way we deal with our children. In contrast to Liedloff's discription of the peaceful mothering of babies just described, I remember reading in a child-care book (and what a condition we have come to on our society, that we have to look into books to understand how to love and care for our offspring!) that you should put a baby into his crib for some hours each day, so that he be won't become spoiled. That is a big, tragic myth—that babies can be spoiled. If God intended babies to take care of themselves for some hours each day, he would have given them means to do so. But babies, helpless and dependent, crave to be held and carried about, and constititionally that's how they are built. For a full explication of these ideas, you should read Liedloff's book. Even if you, as we, don't believe in evolution, which figures in Liedloff's argument, her point of view can still change your life. Having mothered babies both ways (although I must confess that I picked up my babies whenever they cried, even though I tried to supply means for them to amuse themselves in their cribs). I am convinced that holding infants in arms while they are young creates exceedingly, intelligent, peaceful, independent, and happy children.

A closely-related myth: that children need to be kept busy by adults. We seem, to fear that if we don't keep them occupied, they will have nothing to do and therefore get into mischief (our next myth). So we buy various toys, turn on the television, supply lots of games; somehow we trust them to enjoy themselves out-of-doors, but inside we seem to be ever-concerned about them, thinking that children are basically naughty, that they desire to anger us, deep-down, and if we don't keep a tight control over their activities, they will over-run us. This develops an incredible tension between parents and children, between teachers and children. On the other hand, however, I believe that children are basically good. They want to please us; they love us. They may become naughty, however, if they miss that basic rightness of being held in-arms as babies and somehow try to squeeze out of us that loving closeness they still lack. Children who constantly demand their parents' attention could be suffering from this lack.

Liedloff recommends sleeping with the child until the need seems to be filled. She cites examples from families with overbearing children who let them sleep between their parents until the child himself opted to return to his own bed. After some tossing, turning nights of adjustment, the children slept happily with the parents for a time, and then on their own initiative returned to their own rooms, happier and more content.

Children also become naughty because they find this the surest method for getting attention. If they sit mute before the tube, no one bothers with them, adults being quite satisfied to pursue their own interests and pleasures without them. Many children don't get spoken to unless they provoke an adult into remonstrating them. And when we do speak to them, we sometimes feel that we have to talk a variation of baby-talk, a child-talk as it were, as if the children could not understand and participate in the adult world. If you talk mature English to a tiny infant, he will grow up understanding and speaking it; why not? It is the only model he has! Very small children can understand and speak using a large and mature vocabulary. Sometimes visitors will turn around to see who I'm speaking to, when I say to a little child, "Put the utensils on the counter," or "Process the contents of your backpack before playing."

Many homeschool parents find it their greatest adjustment, including children in their everyday world. It certainly brings more interruptions. And it involves seeing things from a child's point of view.

Your eight month old might be sitting in the floor, for example, screaming her head off, or so it seems to you. Our adult reaction is to make the child stop its irritating noise. But look at what is causing the problem: she is trying to remove the lid from a plastic jar, and it is maddeningly stuck. Instead of getting angry, we can sit down on the floor with her and show her how to put the lid on and off. A quick cuddle, and both of you are ready to continue your work. One day my littlest one, after having put on her shoes, was trying to get me to put on mine. I was busy mopping the kitchen floor, and didn't want the Sunday shoes she brought. So continuing my mopping, I kept trying to dance around, avoiding her efforts to buckle onto my ankles my good shoes, and she kept roaring and screaming after me, shoes in tow.

Finally I stopped and tried to understand her. Did she just want me to put on my shoes? The flash of intuition which is a gift to parents, if we just will bother to listen, came: she wanted to go for a walk. "Do you want to go outside?" I asked her between roars. Immediate silence and vehement nodding, yes, she wanted to go outside. "Well, go get your sweater, and I'll get mine, and we'll go for a walk." While she got her sweater, I swiped clean the few remaining spots, grabbed my sweater, and we enjoyed a beautiful outing.

Of course a child might be ill or tired, and his or her cries could be intended to get our attention much of the time, however, their noise does not mean that they want to anger us, but rather that they have exhausted their small means of handling what seems to them a difficult problem. Understand what it is and facilitate it, and peace will resume.

Probably the most damaging myth of all, to homeschoolers and really to anyone who lives and works with children, is that adults must teach children all the things they should know. If we really think about this, we see the obvious silliness of it, yet our schools promote the idea that teachers teach and test those essential items that children need, and that if they don't teach it, the children won't learn it. Even from our homeschool, we have seen abundant instances to the contrary. I have chosen to actually teach very little in the way of social studies or science; when you read the chapters on these subjects you will see how we approach them. Yet when the children have taken the standardized tests on them, they have scored right at the tops of the charts, usually getting all the answers right. Furthermore, they know so much about countires, histories, rocks, plants, animals, etc., that they quite startle us. They will discuss the relative heights of the world's mountains, including those under the sea; or they will identify some of the native plants around us, talking about what they're good for; or they will detail what animals or birds live around us.

Where do they get this knowledge? I check out books from the library wherever we are, emphasizing those that discuss local matters. Because we are living in the reality they are reading about, they are keen on learning whatever they can about it; a book on seashells, when we are living at the beach, produces labelled displays of the finest specimens of shells that they can find. Much of the time the children relate details that I do not know. And they retain this knowledge. Often when I cannot accomplish a certain move in origami or knitting, I let David read the chart and show me how to do it.

A teacher might ask if we can trust the children to learn all the things they need to know by themselves. That question presupposes that teachers know what children will need to know; that their teaching techniques will effectively teach the needed information, that the children will truly learn and retain the knowledge; and that they will be able to apply the learning in real situations. All of which are really heavy questions, aren't they? Most standardized tests assume that the children have not learned some things; they are built so that some children will miss some of the questions. When my children take the tests, they expect to be able to answer all of them correctly, getting frustrated and upset when they miss some.

When Peter Reynolds was taking his oral examinations for his doctoral dissertation dealing with home schools, one professor asked him how our children, who read three or four books a day sometimes, could really read them well and understand them without adult supervision. How, for example, could they understand foreshadowing, the technique by which an author builds his plot by dropping hints of major happenings earlier in the work? Peter answered that often we read the books together and discuss techniques; and of course this is correct. But also I trust the children to garner much of this themselves through constant and good reading.

Overhearing some of their discussions about books they are concurrently reading, I can tell that they are indeed getting it. Often when we read poetry aloud together, they point out repetive consonant sounds that please them (alliteration), or the similar use of repeating vowel sounds for certain emotional effects (assonance)—and so on and on. Do children really need adults to point everything out to them? Do they even need adults to give names and explanations of the things they notice—at first—or can they experience and enjoy them without their names?

Parents and teachers alike fall into the trap of believing that children learn step by step, steadily amassing a store of knowledge. In reality, people learn differently: sometimes they learn very rapidly, and then suddenly they may plateau, seeming to make no progress at all for a time. Just as suddenly, they quantum-leap to a level of expertise of understanding you never expect, the unconsious mind having been at work assimilatng and sorting facts. Insisting that the children produce top work every day is like asking an artist to hand over a masterpiece on schedule; the human mind deosn't work that way. Days of reading, play, conversation, music, and so on, may precede a really remarkable output in in math or poetry, I have noticed. We just need the understanding and patience (and intuition) to facilitate the child's rhythms of learning.

A rather more widespread myth is that children—indeed people in general—will not work unless they are coerced into it, fanned into flame by competitions, shamed by slighting comparisons or bribed with rewards, or payment. Modern society assures us that we want leisure, relief from work, although our leisure pursuits require work, some of it demanding: golf, woodworking, sewing, gardening, sports of all kinds. What seems to delineate work from pleasure is our enjoyment in doing it. And while it is true that most occupations include the drudging sort of work that no one likes, like mucking out the barns, digging the fence holes, office work many of us plough through, still, ideally, our work should be the joy of our lives, the spark of interest to our days.

Jean Liedloff describes a Yequana Indian who was raised in the city. He decided that he belonged with his tribe, and so returned, but he didn't want to do the work expected of a man. He didn't garden, didn't like to fish, and only once in a while went hunting. The members of the tribe tolerated this for a year or more, cheerfully giving him food, until the man decided for himself that he wanted to make a garden. The others helped him clear the spot and plant the crops, chuckling that here was a man who wanted to work, and didn't know it! People who are forced into idleness or imprisonment chafe for some productive activity.

The same applies to children: if they live in a positive, giving environment free of the technological pollutants that destroy working energy (i.e. television, videos, etc.) they will pour themselves into productive work, into learning. They may not do it in the ways prescribed by the teachers' college, but if a child learns about levers by prying up boulders with a stick, or about fulcrums by homemade seesaws, the principles of these physics make sense to him in his muscles before he ever meets them in books.

Similarly, our society solemnly declares that nobody can get a good job unless he gets the prescribed education in order to qualify for it. This might seem to disqualify homeschoolers, who can get equivalency certificates, it is true, but who certainly learn outside of the prescribed routine of diplomas. Yet homeschoolers make some of the best workers: adaptable, skilled in their hands, able to understand the present need, able to learn quickly. Most employers admit that the young person's training at school rarely qualifies him for the specific job he is going to do; in almost every case he still has to be trained. "We get these university students in here," moaned one electrical engineer, "who don't even know how to use a hacksaw. Of course, they eventually learn, but what a lot of wasted time! They have to be told everything!"

My husband recalls a job doing construction work. He was hired during an economic boom, but soon after, the market depressed, and worker after worker was laid off, diminishing the staff from about thirty to three, including himself just a young worker alongside experienced builders. He remained because he worked intelligently and well, having only left this job by his own choice, wishing to have the experience of living on a sheep ranch, where he worked as a gardener and cook.

John Holt tells a story of a young man, wanting to be an architect, who found work rehabilitating inner-city houses instead of attending a school of architecture, which might have cost him about $80,000. Instead, he stands to earn about that much and have ten to fifteen houses on which to base his reputation after the same amount of time so that a prospective firm can hire him on the basis of his work rather than a diploma that may say little about his actual qualifications.

Although I have a graduate degree, my money-earning skill, free-lance editing, I developed chiefly on my own. When I applied for part-time work with BYU Press, the test results were so good that they thought I might have been tricking them. I like writing and editing, and it comes naturally to me (unlike gardening or interior design, for example) and I would do it whether or not I could earn by it.

I believe that everyone is born with talents and disposition to certain work, and that homeschooling is a way to find one's work in life, the thing we would do anyway even if we couldn't earn by it. Usually we do it so well that we can earn a good living by it, and there are many people who make a good living doing the things they love. Indeed, it is a sorry state of affairs when most people in our society earn their bread doing work they detest. Margaret Mead, Thomas Edison, Noel Coward, and Woodrow Wilson are famous people who were educated outside of schools and yet achieved brilliance in their chosen fields; there are many more, perhaps not famous but noteworthy because of their excellence and happiness, at their work.

I discuss other myths in other places in this book, such as the idea that adults need to be credentialled teachers in order to effectively instruct children, their own or others'. Another is, the earlier children learn anything, the better it is for them.

In fact, the whole notion of homeschool explodes the biggest myth of all: that children need an institution to help them grow up, rather than the resources of their own loving home.

FOOD AND HEALTH

At least three aspects of food interest me as a homeschooler. First of all, when the children stay at home, they eat much more than they do when away at school, partly because at school the food is not always available, but also because they get more stressed and less able to eat. In New Zealand schools everyone enjoys a morning tea-time, all the children being encouraged to eat fresh fruit for their "play-lunch." Not very many of them actually do, though they do munch crackers, sandwiches, cookies, perhaps a box of raisins. At home the children are always reaching for fruit, juice, nuts or dried fruit; and often they will go into the kitchen to put together something: peanut-butter balls, cookies, cakes (from wholesome ingredients), juice popsicles. Many mothers notice that their school children tank up with after-school snacks, while preferring to eat small lunches at school, or sometimes no lunch at all.

Secondly, the food we send to school doesn't compare to the soup-and-salad lunches we have together at home (usually Avraham is available at lunch-time, and we often eat the main meal of the day at noon, talking and enjoying each others' company). After some weeks at school, the children's health, I found, diminished somewhat because of the small breakfast and inferior lunches (usually just a whole-wheat peanut-butter sandwich and a piece of fruit). They certainly need more than that. School lunches, on the other hand, when the children have chosen to take them, provide lots of protein, but few vegetables and too many sweets and starches.

Lastly, the children learn different things about food at home than they do at school: there, they see a stunning procession of candy, pastry, cookies, cakes—twinkies!—soft drinks, and chips. These foods allure them, as I believe they do many of us. But our children don't often get these kinds of foods to eat themselves because we teach them to eat mostly natural foods. At home, with only good foods around, the children content themselves with that. They enjoy it; they learn to prepare it.

When I taught high school, I noticed that food visibly affects learning. Those students who brought reasonably healthy lunches from home, or who ate in the cafeteria, starchy as that food was, held to their work better than those who subsisted on junk food. If my own children happen to fasten onto something sugary early in the day, I can count schoolwork negligible. The children spin about aimlessly, their attention span severed. Chemicals such as preservatives and flavoring and colorants work on us somewhat the same way. And it seems to take about two or three days to eliminate the offenders from the system.

I make it a point to discuss the nutrients in certain foods, along with the notion of balancing one's meals—to have fruits and vegetables to provide alkalinity along with the proteins and grains and dairy foods that we eat. "What should I have to balance this?" the children often ask.

Anyone who likes has permission to cook, though I usually veto sweets before meals. The children feel cooking is easy, that anyone can do it. All of the younger children love to help me prepare meals, grating cheese or carrots, beating egg whites, mincing parsley, mashing potatoes. The older children know how to bake bread, to make birthday cakes for each other (though to be truthful they create a horrendous mess when they do!). They know how to make yogurt and grow sprouts. When I am not home or not available to cook a meal, almost everyone, from the six year old to the fifteen year old, can put together a decent meal.

They don't always like to cook; much of the time, they let me do it, though they might volunteer to give a hand when I am in the kitchen. They especially like to whip cream, separate eggs, and taste the cake batter. Occasionally they undertake something on their own: Yoni likes to make cobblers and peanut-butter balls and "seed candy," which is made from ground-up nuts and seeds, honey and milk powder. Once David created a nice batch of meringues, sweetened with honey. They don't blink at scrambling eggs, making toast, preparing finger salad, or following a recipe for almost anything. Usually one thing deters them: they must responsibly clean up their own messes after cooking.

There must be something more to the Church leaders' urging us to produce much of our own food than just to help out our budgets. It might be a tangible way of leading us to be independent. Producing our own food gives us plenty, while purchasing it often stints us. When we raised goats for milk, we overflowed with it; we had plenty to share with friends who had allergies or milk intolerance—who then shared their offerings, such as haircutting and babysitting, with us. Raising chickens for eggs and meat gave us an abundance as well. Although Avraham is a much better gardener than I am, over the years I have been putting in successful gardens on the French-intensive method. It is surprising how much food can be produced in such a small space.

I still retain hopes, however, for a family garden that will yield the many bushels of tomatoes, beans, corn, etc, that our family preserves each year, as well as the veggies and fruits that comprise the mainstay of our diet. We saw superior greenhousing in New Zealand, and I would like to provide our winter needs with one. The children like to garden, and with the consistent and kind guidance from a good cultivator—Avraham—I feel sure we could do well, another step towards self-sufficiency.

As it stands, we are learning to produce our basic foods at home, another important lesson in the appropriate economy of consumption at home. We buy our grains in bulk—mostly wheat, but also a good deal of rye, barley, millet, oats, as well as smaller amounts of buckwheat and brown rice—and grind our own flour for breads and other baking. We sprout seeds we have bought in bulk, and we make yogurt. Our homemade contributions to Church dinners and Scout meetings may not look outstanding compared to the fluffy white beauties there (though sometimes people hover over our whole-wheat cookies, gobbling them up); but in addition to baking nutritious foods I like to think that our family is learning something about being responsible in home production.

As I have mentioned, Avraham, lately with the children's help, bottles a large proportion of fruit and staples each year. We also freeze corn off the cob, and green beans, but not peas—they are easier to buy frozen. In the freezing of veggies, the children all help, some husking corn, the adults blanching and cooling it, some children stripping the ears, and others packing it into bags. We also raise and slaughter and freeze meat chickens—big, clumsy, stupid birds that grow into the size of small turkeys and yield high-quality protein. When we process fifty chickens, the children learn first-hand where meat comes from. For Sammy, who terms himself the Chicken King, knowing each fowl by name and habit, this might be heartbreaking, but he takes it all in good stride (except one time when Avraham mistakenly killed Rosemary the Buff Orpington hen who turned out to be Anthony the rooster, the only gentle and tolerable male in the flock; the other roosters had to go to the pot when they began attacking the little children, but we all mourned to lose fat, good-natured Rosemary-alias-Anthony).

When Avraham masterminds the bulk canning, however, the rest of us just stay clear out of the kitchen, do the cooking and dishes outdoors, and let him work. I like for the children to see a man doing this kind of work! We all put in a hand sometimes, as with the applesauce, or with placing the halved and pitted apricots on drying screens.

We hope to be teaching them that your diet forms your health, that "you are what you eat." By using a plain foods diet, we try not to be health fanatics, and we usually don't spend on fancy health foods. We all notice how cranky and tired we feel after we indulge much in sugar or chocolate (which we can't seem to resist, when it's around). When Chava develops symptoms of some chronic problems she has had, she asks for lots of fresh fruit of her own accord to put her system back in order—quite admirable in a little child. Sammy, prone to grouchiness and fits of temper, helps himself to brewer's yeast when the pressure is on. I always smile when certain foods—like mashed potatoes flecked with chopped Swiss chard—seem gourmet treats to them.

Having researched and used medicinal herbs over the years, we try to handle most family ailments with these simple remedies. Sometimes when mullein or red-raspberry leaves are ready for picking, we troop out to gather them together. The children recognize common ones—plantain, docks, marshmallow (eating the "cheesie" flower buds), and know somewhat how they are used. Chava (and now Sarah) begs for a daily green drink, made by blending comfrey and wild greens into pineapple juice. I like for the children to know how to find simple remedies growing out in the fields and orchards.

We do visit the doctor, of course, for serious problems. Before Sarah was hospitalized briefly, as a small baby, we had dragged our feet about employing the medical profession, having handled virtually all of our childhood diseases ourselves. But the shock of Sarah's illness swung us back the other way a little, something we needed.

Watching us, the children have learned to give a decent back massage, relaxing head rub, effective foot massage. They understand the simple principles of reflexology, massaging out sore spots to help heal the body. The master massager has to be Yoni. His small hands seem to hold a gift of healing. Once the family visited a playground when he was only five years old. Chasing after the baby, I stepped on a bee. In the van, while Avraham drove, I sat together in the back, with the other children, while I complained of the swelling pain on the bottom of my foot. Yoni reached over and took the sore spot in his hand, just holding it. Somehow the pain melted away, and never came back. His touch soothes away headaches and back tensions.

The others massage well too. David has the power and skill to work out tightness in an adult's back, and can give a good foot massage, too—if you can corner him. Chava will walk all over your back for you, if you ask her, patiently soothing away tightness. Even baby Sarah, at only twenty months, would smooth and caress one's hair and head into relaxation. You read stories about primitive people using their hands to massage, groom, touch each other; I am convinced that it is a very healing part of being a family.

Children learn easily about good air, good water, good food. You don't have to become fanatics or rigid to teach them lifetime attitudes. I grin with secret delight when I see them choose plain vegetables and whole-wheat bread at a dinner out, though they also reach for cake and ice cream! We follow this dictum: it is not what you occasionally eat that harms you, but rather what you live on—day to day. So when they stuff themselves with candy during Easter weekend, we bite our tongues and ladle out the soup for a few days. Similarly, we try to moderate our meat intake, but occasionally Sammy or Chava will gobble up an inappropriate amount. We tolerate it, and then supply a series of vegetable meals to make up for it. Better to avoid the reaction that some children have, being brought up on a strict whole-foods diet. When they are left to themselves, they swing all the other way, swiftly tucking in the junk food to make up for their long-seeming deprivation.

Customs of food and medicine are very much dictated by one's culture, and breaking away from the norm can make us feel uncomfortable. Just think, we eat three or more times each day! How great a portion of our resources—and time—we sink into food! We should think about this and refine the attitudes that underlie our eating. Similarly, taking responsibility for our own health rather than running to the doctor at the first symptom of a cold or fever may seem to challenge a powerful cultural practice. Quite apart from the way our health improves as we undertake preventative, gentle methods, we have found a higher law of independence.

And the children intuitively understand these healing methods. They break off a stem of aloe vera for a burn; they ask for vitamin C for a sore throat; they bravely gulp camomile tea for a headache. Once Chava and I were walking in rather rough country, and a bee (barely) stung her. How she howled! Just after a rainstorm, the leaves were laden with droplets, and I picked a wet leaf and wrapped it around her sore finger. It soon stopped throbbing, until the moisture dried up, so we picked another—and another. Soon the pain went away. She was full of excitement about the magic leaf water that takes away the pain.

Never wishing to become fanatics, we try to stay moderate. We go to the doctor occasionally, and we follow the M.D.'s directions in those situations that require medical help.

Still, for us, a natural, gentle, approach to food and healing form a central part of our homeschool, one of those things that children learn from consistent, daily practice, rather than heavy-handed teaching. I feel like we're getting somewhere when Sammy heaps his plate with broccoli—or when Sarah makes a meal of sprouts and homemade salad dressing, ignoring all the other goodies on the table. Like most other children, mine still like their treats and goodies, but I am hoping that they are also learning good health habits along the way.

LEGAL MATTERS

During a talk on homeschool, a young man interrupted me. "Is this legal?" he inquired. I answered that in my home state, Utah, the laws were very favorable to homeschool; at present, if a child receives a certain amount of hours in the basic subjects, comparable to the school curriculum, he is considered being legally schooled, whether he attends an institution or not.

Having never concerned myself with the philosophical base of legality, I don't worry about the question of homeschooling being an inherent or constitutional right of the parents. To me, that is an obvious, foregone conclusion. Neither does the question of strictly adhering to curriculum subjects for each grade concern me much, for our holistic sort of study comprehends the basic subjects every day, as well as embracing many more. If a child doesn't master a certain skill, as expected of him at his grade level in school, what does it matter? He will learn it later. It is better to learn easily to count by twos when you are seven than to cry over it when you are six.

When my children attended public school for a short time in Utah, I felt provoked by a skill mastery program the district was implementing. Every child was required to perform correctly a list of skills, each time receiving a computer statement about whether he succeeded. After the skill was duly checked off at school (and at home on the parents' master list), the children didn't look at it again. If the children did not master all the skills, theoretically they would be held back a year.

These skills seemed to me to be chosen arbitrarily, some appearing basic and important, others to be out of kilter. Many of them seemed too advanced for the ages involved, such as alphabetizing down to the third letter for third grade, or doing addition and subtraction up to twenty in the first half of the first grade. Not that children could not learn these things, but pounding them into their heads, causing unnecessary stress to those who do not, at that age, conceptualize these abstractions easily, seemed to me to fruitlessly waste precious childhood time that could be pleasantly passed learning things that the children wanted to learn.

Discussing my feelings with Yoni's third-grade teacher, a very open, loving sort of woman, I commented, "With all these advanced skills, I don't see very many advanced scholars running around the school"; and she definitely agreed, uncomfortable herself with the curriculum demands. And Sammy's fifth-grade teacher said, "I see little use in checking off a list of requirements. If I want to know a child's skill on using a map key, I let him draw a map and create a key for it, drawing in the features he includes. I want my students to *think*, but I don't get much support in it. Sometimes the children go home crying because I ask them to do work that makes them use their brains instead of just passing off a multiple-choice test." I told him, "You sound just like a homeschooler!" and he took it as a compliment.

The Utah Home School Association actively monitors legal developments about homeschool. If they catch wind of changes in the law, such as a recent attempt to require annual testing, they inform all members, initiating a deluge of calls and letters and providing a powerful lobby. The Association encourages all homeschoolers to know the law exactly, pertaining to their legal rights.

Each state differs in its homeschooling laws. Some states, such as California, do not allow homeschooling; but in actual practice, many families continue to do it. Depending on the policy of the individual districts, they may or may not be hassled for teaching their children at home. Our friends in Wisconsin homeschool under an umbrella association, formally enrolling their children in an established private school, meeting with the school personnel every so often. In Washington State, for a long time, such meetings were supposed to happen weekly, but recently, the law changed to allow homeschooling itself.

If you are contemplating homeschool, Holt Associates provides information on the current legal status in your state. Their newsletter, *Growing Without Schooling*, contains legal updates, including information on court cases. I have found these people unfailingly friendly and helpful—and always up-to date—in legal matters. They can also recommend lawyers well-versed in legal precedents about homeschooling and willing to assist people who are being hassled by local authorities. When friends moved to another state, they called up Holt Associates to find out what the laws were there. Those folks knew exactly what they were (there was just then a new law), and put our friends in touch with homeschoolers in their area!

Possibly the best way to avoid legal troubles is to comply with the letter of the law, though perhaps you might be violating the day-to-day requirements. For example, you are teaching English if your children read each day, write letters and make entries in their journal, make tape recordings of their favorite stories, and even if they watch classic movies. They will not be receiving the exact equivalent their peers get in the classroom, but you are certainly within the law. And of course you will not be spending fifty consecutive minutes each day on math or science; but remember that you run school 365 days a year (even on Sundays we are learning)—many more than 5.42 hours per day, so you can provide a good argument.

This leads us into testing. When my older children were six and eight, the school district sent us a letter offering testing services at the school if we desired them. I didn't want to have my children tested. I felt they were not test-wise, and perhaps in my secret heart I feared that they would muff the tests and show us up as failures. So that year I went to the district and requested copies of the Stanford Achievement Test, which I administered at home over a week or so. The children scored so well—everything in the ninetieth percentiles and often in the 99th (except for math, which was in the 80s)—that I lost my fears about testing. We have tested bi-annually since then, and when the children attended school in New Zealand, their school tests placed them in the 99th percentile in all subjects.

If your state requires testing, and if you work with your children during the day, I think you should relax and let them take the tests. Although they should be tested at the same intervals and with the same tests as their peers, sometimes authorities give difficult tests at closer intervals as a harassing technique, and you should be right on top of that. You will be pleased at how well your children score, even in subjects you don't spend much time at. Their active reading supplies the needed general knowledge. An exception of course would be a child like Yoni who read late; he might need more science experiments and reading aloud.

Needless to say, if you travel, you can usually homeschool legally without any problems, because your American citizenship gives you the right to educate your children outside of the regulations of the foreign country where you live. However, you might consider part-time or temporary attendance at a foreign school, if it is a decent place, because this is a good way to learn languge and customs and to become involved in the culture.

Consider options before you give up in despair. We met one family in New Zealand that moved out into the bush and lived very minimally so that they would not have to face the hassles of dealing with school authorities (children could legally receive correspondence education if they lived a certain distance away from the schools). This same concept works in Alaska. Some authorities accept enrollment in an authorized correspondence course, such as Calvert, an adequate substitute for school attendance. These courses might seem lock-step and confining, but perhaps you can find a way to fit the work into a more creative schedule.

Some families begin with correspondence courses and let them lapse as they create their own curriculum, not notifying the local authorities, and thus letting the problem solve itself by attrition. Enrolling under an umbrella school can help, and sometimes schools form to provide just this service (contact your local homeschooling association and/or Holt Associates for information on this). Some families have actually moved to a friendly state, like Utah or New Mexico, so that they can homeschool in a free, open atmosphere without oppression from the law.

Most important is your attitude. Some school districts might work well with a family that approaches them professionally, confidently, and with a friendly attitude. If you interact with a chip on your shoulder, you could find yourself unnecessarily harassed. Many times a school district will ask a homeschooling parent to provide a curriculum. This can seem a monstrous task—there are so many things you do during the day that include learning; how can you write all of that down? Again, Holt Associates direct you to people who have written successful curricula and who might be able to share them with you. You might actually enjoy writing one of your own. A simple way to handle this problem is to save a file of the children's work, including short notes of what you do each day. (By the way, I never have done this consistently. I always feel that I barely cope with each of my children's needs and my own, much less writing everything down.)

In extreme situations, homeschoolers have been jailed for teaching their children at home, and some have been threatened with removal of their children to state custody unless they comply with demands. Before you panic, should you find yourself confronted with legal threats, investigate thoroughly the actual education laws in your state. Visit with other homeschoolers to see how they have operated within the law. Inquire at Holt Associates; they sell a book, *Home Education and Constitutional Liberties*, summarizing the legal history of homeschool and offering a legal argument for it. Quite often you may find that the local authorities are pressing you unfairly and that the actual state laws allow home-study alternatives.

Whether or not you invite visiting officials into your home is a personal decision. I have never faced this problem, but one homeschooler suggested that you greet them pleasantly and ask them to call for an appointment rather than letting them arrive unannounced and intimidate you in your own home.

And if you live in a state that allows homeschooling at present, be sure to keep up with legal changes. Some homeschoolers hold the opinion that although the authorities might permit homeschool now, the idea rankles them; and if they get the chance they will look for ways to pull the children back into the system. Perhaps this view sounds unfair and negative, but better safe than sorry. We have watched the UHEA professionally and powerfully prevent bad laws from passing. Their work has been intelligent and impressive, and I am confident that homeschoolers everywhere could organize to do the same

HOMESCHOOL THEORY

The term "educational theory" smacks of dry and not-too-useful educational courses, but some important ideas underlie the undertaking of a homeschool. Homeschool parents find themselves thinking through these ideas, asking themselves these questions, sorting through their emotional reactions to bucking the system. It's important to do this; otherwise, when the autumn leaves sweep the September streets and all the neighborhood children, decked out in their sweaters and sneakers, books in hand, set out for school, you may be seized with a nostalgic panic that something is terribly wrong: your children are gathered around the dining room table, some still in their pajamas, measuring juice into cups and spooning out the oatmeal.

Or worse, if a relative or nosy neighbor attacks you for letting your five-year-old play with blocks, Legos, and sand all day long instead of doing the real work of school, you may find yourself inarticulate and feeling vaguely guilty.

I like the anecdote about Bertrand Russell, who ran an alternative school at his home between the world wars. A conventional headmaster of a state school, looking at some of the pupils' work was aghast at what seemed to be irresponsible untidiness and a lack of control; but being a gentleman, he said nothing. Russell perceived that he thought the work dreadful, however, and commented, "You see, your aim is to produce good children. Mine is to produce good adults."

Dr. Rex Wadham spent much time seeking and articulating what might be called eternal or true principles of learning, of teaching. When I attended one of his undergraduate classes as part of my teacher training, I recall him teaching in an unorthodox sort of way. I carried away from his course mainly the idea of the Holy Spirit in the classroom.

Rex developed many striking concepts about teaching/learning; they form a foundation for much of my thinking. He taught that each person comes to this earth with certain gifts, talents, and—most interestingly—knowledge sealed upon him. This is harmonious with the important Mormon teaching about the nature of man. Knowing that each child has inside a mature spirit, blessed and endowed with capabilities, dispositions, personality, and a mission to perform during his life, changes our approach to bringing him up. Not a *tabula rasa*—blank slate—as some theorists would have it, but a complete individual, even at birth. Children therefore need us to feel and understand what they are, so that we can draw them out.

Rex showed the contrast: classroom education resembles pouring in, as a teacher might hold a pitcher above the opened mouth of a complacent student, pouring in knowledge. True teaching, however, draws out the capabilities and knowledge already present in the child. Of course, this requires that the teacher, the parent, attune himself sensitively to the child, and to the Holy Spirit, to sense what activities will develop and round out those gifts. When we exclaim at young children's unusual skill or understanding ("out of the mouth of babes," we say), we are seeing a manifestation of a mature knowledge in the child's mind and spirit. You have probably seen many instances of this, if you have children.

One evening I was driving home from an appointment, with Sarah in the car, then eighteen months old. She was cranky and wanted her dinner; she kept trying to crawl over me to nurse. The roads twisted and climbed crazily (there is nothing in the world like New Zealand roads), and I couldn't put her in my lap and still control the wheel and gears. So she sat back and began to howl. All of a sudden she stopped; I paid little attention, just glad to have some peace. But then I noticed that she was singing a little song we enjoy in our family, "The wheels on the bus go round and round." Where did she learn that you can sing to help you endure trials? At the time, I was struck that this was an example of knowledge or intuition in a very young child.

Little Avi, only three years old, loved weaponry. Sticks and leaves, nails and knives he transforms into war toys. No one else in the family cares so much for guns or daggers, except in sporadic bursts of interest. Nor have outside stimuli such as television affected him; he hasn't had them. He simply seems born with a disposition for warfare, which at his age he translates into spurt of aggression but without a sinister side to them.

If I need a babysitter, I don't have to look further than Yoni. Even when he was seven or eight years old, he instinctively knew how to hold, feed, distract, entertain, and communicate with babies. Seeing a newborn, he asks permission to cuddle it in his arms. When Sarah, close to two years old, was learning to sleep through the night, Yoni, upset by her cries, took her to be with him and gave her a bottle of water. She slept, arms around his neck, till morning.

As for Sarah, how surprised we were when, at only eight or nine months old, she spied a doll and scooted over to clasp it to her breast. Here, I felt sure, was an innate knowledge of mothering, of femininity; none of our boys has held baby dolls in that way. On the other hand, Chava has had this from the time she was a baby. And what a child for make-up, jewelry, ribbons, perfume! She doesn't take her example from me because I have little time or interest for fussing much. But, visiting with other little girls, or her cousins, she solemnly puts on make-up, paints her fingernails, and winds ribbons into her hair. She loves to decorate herself with necklaces and bracelets. It's a trait that I will have to train into tastefulness, but we enjoy her attempts to beautify herself.

Sammy read early, and reads voraciously, evidencing a remarkable memory. Of all the children, he is the one you can ask for definitive information; he often chronicles his research in notebooks, illustrating, labelling. But Sammy doesn't draw very accurately, as Yoni and David do. Both of these boys seem gifted with their hands; David can conceptualize and create, with pencil or with three-dimensional media, far better than anyone else in our family. At school in New Zealand, he completed his class handicraft project weeks before the rest of the students, and then began creating projects of his own that the other students copied. (At first, the teacher wasn't sure about letting him do it, but soon she saw he worked responsibly.)

David innately, intuitively understands the scriptures and spiritual concepts; he did from the time he was small. It was as if he knew these things before; you didn't need to teach him much. Yoni, on the other hand, understood the workings of the Holy Spirit from the time he was small, even before he was baptized. When Yoni prays, you sense a beautiful spiritual feeling; he often comments that the words are given to him, which is the ideal the scriptures teach. The other children are alive to spiritual things (Sammy, as you might expect, is becoming a master of the scriptures), but haven't evidenced the spiritual keenness of these two boys.

Parents everywhere recognize these marked tendencies for certain things in their children. Homeschool mothers have sometimes confided to me that they just know what certain of their children will do when they grow up, not so much from the children's wishes as from the Spirit. Not surprisingly, parents discuss these things little, but "keep them in their hearts." I firmly believe as a parent that God may open up our understandings about our children's missions in life, so that we can more precisely train them. Not that we limit their learning to these subjects, but that we provide examples, experiences, and materials for them.

A close corollary to the idea that we come to earth with talents and knowledge sealed upon us must be concept of a mission in life—not in the grand, dramatic splash of the world, necessarily, but something quite unique and individual to do. For example, from the time I was small I dabbled in pencils and typewriters. Whenever I decided to do something else, such as becoming a biologist or an artist, having enjoyed these activities for a time, I found myself channelled back into the paper, books, and typewriters. Some people just naturally love working with wood, with metal, with fibers. One woman we met in New Zealand couldn't keep away from spinning and knitting. Before long she had developed a lucrative business knitting unusual, bulky sweaters, eventually providing cottage-industry work for other home knitters.

We watch our children, we observe their predispositions for certain kinds of work, and we provide the resources to keep developing it, I don't mind when Yoni uses up most of a pad of paper practicing drawing a tree. Each drawing improves in some way; each is beautiful and unique. His portfolio is a delight to shuffle through. When Chava demands to crochet, I drop what I am doing and help her to draw through the loops of wool. She and Avi always want to help me cook, and I try to give them a grater and the cheese, a wire whip and the egg whites, peeler and the carrots, to work alongside me. (When I am under pressure, I do refuse.) The children model their work on our work or on the instruction books that we continually bring from the library; with only minimal guidance, they themselves refine the necessary skills.

A very important book for understanding how children learn is Walter B. Barbe's *Growing Up Learning*. Barbe demonstrates three different modalities of learning: auditory, visual, and kinesthetic. He calls them learning strengths. Most classrooms operate in the visual mode, using printed materials and written assignments. But people work in other modes: the kinesthetic learner uses body movement to learn and understand, and best responds to learning methods that involve him physically or speak to his physical sense. The auditory learner hears better than he visualizes, and often requires the chance to talk a lot and sound out the learning material. The visual learner has to be able to see the thing at hand.

Of course there are mixes of these. I found myself, on the interesting checklists included for infants through adults, to be an auditory-kinesthetic learner, which explains why my own school experiences left me cold. This way of looking at learning modalities also helps explain other things: how people use and require space, how they use their time, how they relate to each other. I found this book emancipating, just as valuable as the left-brain, right-brain theory of learning. If you are homeschooling, you will want to read it, to help understand how best to approach your children.

Ideally, we provide what Rex Wadham termed "a safe place" for learning. Most classrooms—and many homes—are far from being safe places, places where adults and children can be themselves without undue tensions or fears. In most schools, teasing and ridicule reign, so that the children's self-concepts plummet. I have seen it happen with each of my children that attended school. Sometimes they would explain what names they were called or how the bully shoved them against the wall or how the teacher made them stand for a half-hour with their hands on their heads because they had not tidied their desks in exactly two minutes. But even without explanation, we could *see* the effects: extreme sensitivity to any criticism, with bursting into tears or temper. Fortunately at home they have never reached the stage where they were afraid to try something for fear or ridicule; but if they had continued going to school for a long time, I suspect this would have happened too.

In a safe place we can ask questions without fear. The questions might seem silly or even stupid; if one is really outrageous, someone might laugh, but not in cruelty. We can also hazard answers to questions without the terror of coming up with the wrong one. We can crack jokes, spin puns, unravel stories. We can sing and dance (try that in a regular classroom!).

We used to visit the schoolground during recess when we lived in Provo. As children played, I used to idly add up how much money was walking around that playground in designer jeans, expensive shirts and dresses, name-brand shoes. Suddenly, my children's faded jeans and flannel shirts looked dowdy. At home, fashion doesn't matter; we do squawk if a child wears his dungarees till they're stiff, but we don't insist on fine appearances. I have noticed that homeschool children reared without television care much less about name-brand clothes and high fashion than their mainstream counterparts.

Unfashionable as I am, I like it; I like to see children in levis or shorts and t-shirts, comfortable. In New Zealand, where children seem like children longer than they do in the U.S., I was delighted to see them running up and down in such clothes, barefoot, at school.

In a safe place, a child can read and experiment and explore until he knows everything he wants to know about a certain subject. In one family, the son decided that his passion for rocks would help him grow up into a geologist. The family bought him sample cases, took him rock-hunting, and joined the local Geological Society. After a couple of years and some admirable expertise, the boy lost interest and went on to something else; the parents, philosophically, packed up the rocks in case another child wanted them someday.

In a safe place, a child can spend time walking, thinking, daydreaming, playing, without constant demands that he perform certain paperwork or assignments. As I explain in **Myths About Children**, humans do not learn cumulatively, piling block upon block of knowledge. Rather, they learn in the pattern of peak and plateau. Sometimes we need the quiet, seemingly unproductive time of plateau for our minds to regroup and prepare for the next peak.

In a big family, of course, our children cannot daydream endlessly; some little one always needs a drink, a walk, a book to be read, and the older children are in demand by the younger ones. Yet they still enjoy time for private reflection when compared to the frantic pace imposed at schools. There, teachers tend to fear the innate naughtiness of unherded masses of unruly youngsters. Discussing these concepts with school people, I find that despite their enthusiasm for child-initiated learning, they always balk at the prospect of trusting children to use their time productively, without compulsion.

A safe place is comfortable. It has soft furniture, a pillow to read on, and plenty of natural light. It flows with fresh air. You can eat and drink when you need to, as much as you need to. You know where the tools are and you know which you can use without permission.

A safe place operates by rules, of course, but sensible rules, enforced as much as possible by internal rather than external discipline. Seemingly paradoxical, our family operates by quite strict principles, and yet our children live freely and self-reliantly. I wonder if the discipline problems in school today arise from the lack of governing principles—anything goes in some families, so the children have no backbone standards to behave by. Of course we experience our share of nagging: "Sit up straight!" "Take your feet off the table!" "Have you brushed your teeth?" But I keep striving for spontaneous good behavior, so that when the baby cries, someone immediately goes to pick her up; when night comes, someone closes windows and curtains without being told;

when there seems to be nothing much to do, each child stirs himself to pick up a book, a project, a craft.

Related to a safe place is the inherent dignity of children. Have you ever wondered what childhood is for, what adolescence is for? They last, altogether, perhaps a fourth or a fifth of our lifetime; in childhood and youth we are different than we are during the rest of our entire lives. Certainly, childhood is for play, but children's play is more than just entertainment. It is the way that they piece the world together, the way they try on adult roles, the way they develop skills. Although good mothers have always done so, Maria Montessori was perhaps the first widely recognized educator to take play seriously, and to provide play experiences that would help children learn.

We can hardly resist thinking a baby darling when he sits with a book, pretending to read aloud in the peculiar, halting style that his older siblings, just beginning to read, use. We can hardly help thinking how cute a young cook or carpenter or painter is. Yet we should take all their efforts very seriously. When a tyke hands up a drawing or painting, we should compliment him on aspects we truly admire. One mother-artist insists we should avoid the refrigerator art display; if a painting is worth showing, we should frame it (in cheap frames from the five-and-ten store or a garage sale) and hang it up for the family to enjoy.

When children create practical items, such as ceramic bowls or cups, wooden doorstops, bird feeders, toothbrush holders, fabric placemats, potholders, we should gratefully use them, as serious about them as the children themselves are. Whenever we give presents, one of the children paints designs on clean newsprint to employ as wrapping paper (which we rarely buy); when birthdays or anniversaries come up, we send homemade cards. When Yoni hums an original tune over and over, we take out the music paper and notate the melody; perhaps someone writes words, a harmony part, or chords. We all sing it and remember it, as in Yoni's memorable discovery, at five years of age, of the Alberti bass, which he called, "Buy me scotch tape."

Serious work demands serious tools, and we let the children use many things at will, without permission. We cut with sharp scissors (the dull, rounded ones provided for children's use are maddening when you want to cut anything accurately). We chop with sharp knives (though I let the tiniest chefs use dulled kitchen knives, not razor-sharp ones). A very young child gets some reminders, "That's sharp," "That's hot," but my motto is, "Say less." Without baby talk, without too many oohs and ahs, we guide the children through their serious work of play. Interestingly enough, they soon find that they *can* knit, draw, sculpt, write, garden acceptably, and later perhaps very well. Especially in a society such as ours where so few people really *do* anything, children's skills come across as impressive indeed.

Rex Wadham called this idea "the whole plant, not just cut flowers." Fragmented and regimented, most school curricula offer cut flowers, preformed learning experiences often unrelated to anything else children do. There might be exceptions, as in New Zealand where children read about, wrote about, made experiments with, and played in the wind and the rain. Still, even these experiences were regulated and initiated by the adult; better that the children themselves, after rushing about in the March gales, look up books and articles about wind, find library sources and poems about it, make kites and anemometers, write stories and verse, draw and paint wind.

How ironic I found it when, in a beginning research class for graduate work, the teacher intoned, "It is not intellectually honest to begin research with a question that you already have the answer for. You need to ask a question then look at the material with an open mind, considering both sides of the matter." After many years of being told what to learn, how to do it, how long it should be, what form it should take, and then being told whether it is good or not—according to an often capricious judgment—now suddenly graduate students are told that there are no predetermined answers after all! It all goes back to the whole plant—seeing subjects in their proper contexts. As often as possible, we experience the foundation of our learning in the real world. We collect leaves and classify them; we don't just memorize pinnate, palmate, spathulate. When we wonder if the books' illustrations of snowflakes are really accurate after all, we take our microscope and catch a few, focus, and gasp in wonder. After that, making paper snowflakes means something close to our hearts. We study the water cycle; we learn about different kinds of storms. After we went through the devastation of a hurricane, we checked out every book in the library on cyclones, typhoons, and hurricanes, learning how these storms form and how they behave.

In the springtime when the animals give birth, we consider reproduction. We speak about birth control, abortion, miscarriage, and adoption. In the fall when all greenery changes color, sometimes brilliantly, sometimes just fading, we find out what makes the colors change and what happens to the plants and animals during dormancy. Which animals truly hibernate? Where? Which animals are predators?

Why? When we consider the whole plant, unpleasantness alongside pleasantness, we begin to understand the world.

Rex Wadham illustrated how the Hero Journey, an important pattern in the scriptures and in literature, powerfully provides a learning tool. Rex thought that public school attendance provided some of that, a journey away from and back home each day. As our children enter adolescence, perhaps part-time attendance at a school or university for especially desired courses can become Hero Journeys.

Yet the physical leaving might not be essential. Joseph Smith did not travel far for his experience in the Sacred Grove, an event that changed him and the world forever. Sometimes even certain courses of study can constitute a Hero Journey. At the time I studied American Literature for my master's degree, I didn't mind the nihilism, despair, and disjointedness of much modern writing. Recently, Avraham purchased a paperback set of Dicken's works, and I confined my reading to them and other works of the same period. To my surprise, having brought home a library book or two of the modern stuff, I found myself unable to read it. Even Dr. Zhivago repelled me for its immorality. An an extreme example, you may recall Buckminister Fuller's complete year of silence as he sorted out his new, burgeoning ideas.

Children naturally embark on Hero Journeys of their own—camping out, staying over with friends, working with a neighbor, studying something new—or you may construct Hero Journeys for them. As the young people mature, the Journeys may become more daring. We trust our young heroes because we have trained them at home, and when they return, new and expanded, we enjoy their new selves. I like this pattern of the Hero Journey; it becomes a progressive letting-go as the children grow up.

Rex taught that enthusiasm (from the Greek root, "inspired by God") was a necessary part of learning something, not the football-game hip-hip-hooray kind of enthusiasm but rather what we might describe as animation, or a heightened sense. Anything that I have truly learned, as opposed to memorizing for a test, has originated with this kind of excitement. We feel that we want to know, we work at finding out, we remember. A teacher's enthusiasm can animate his students toward learning, perhaps in the same way that bearing your testimony strengthens others. You may remember the early Mormon church leader, Brigham Young's instructions to teach nothing—not even the multiplication tables—without the Holy Spirit. In the heavy world of academia, the Holy

Spirit seems to have little place; yet scientists, artists, linguists, scholars of all kinds, frequently describe their discoveries in terms that echo Joseph Smith's description: you "begin to have strokes of ideas."

If you are filled with a holy animation about learning something, anything, the children will feel it and enjoy learning it with you, even if it's something as mundane as typing or chopping wood; or something as work-intensive as learning a new language or mastering equations.

Although I mention this throughout the book, one of the most important concepts in homeschooling must be learning from the real world, especially through the natural world, but also by experiencing what goes on in the world of work. You will smile at Reed Benson's observation—made about socialization, but also applicable here—that if we are hoping for our children to learn to function in the real world, sending them to school is not a very good way. How real is sitting all day long in a confined classroom with thirty companions of your own age? Adults doing the work of the world certainly don't live that way. So much interesting work goes on in the world; all you have to do is enter into it. Hang around a construction or road-building site. Observe horse- or dog-training. Learn from the local shoe repairman. Sometimes one of your children will be able to help in the stable, carpenter's shop, florist's, electrician's. The real world around the home, especially if you live in the country, contains so much: plants and animals, farming and building.

If the clever parent secures books that explore the underpinnings of these real-world experiences, the children obtain a thorough education, superior to those ensconced in schools who receive only the academic side; the homeschooled child understands how the facts are used. The preoccupation with academia as the end of all education must be misplaced; in the extreme, such a student can become a pedantic bore or an academic wonder who often cannot perform any real, useful work; and in the eternal sense, he can be left far behind in the quest for God's kingdom.

We want to grow into individuals who can think and reason, love and forgive, work skilfully and persistently. The high-academic track in the secondary schools so often leaves all these skills behind. It is a bitter irony: the young people who take this track are the elite, while those who take the shop classes are considered red-necked inferiors. One boy who was skilled with his hands as well as his mind wanted to take carpentry and auto mechanics, but he was terribly sensitive to the fact that the so-called intelligent, well-reared kids didn't take these classes. For a while he suffered through trigonometry and college-prep English, which he didn't really

enjoy. Finally he settled for a middle course, which left him still unsatis-
fied. Such a boy, in a homeschool, can train his hands and his head as well.

For us, the theoretical concept that convinced us to homeschool
was the notion of family stewardship. Fragmented and confused, most of us
moderns turn to institutions to assure us of quality care in our lives, notably
schools and the medical profession. But God does not hold the schools
accountable for our children's upbringing; the scriptures pinpoint us, the
parents.

Intuitively, many parents feel the discrepancy of turning over their
impressionable young ones to a system which, however hopeful, still grinds
out a standard of mediocrity. Forbidden to teach spirituality or morality, the
teachers are stuck with the teachings of textbooks, which preach con-
sumerism, humanism, socialism, evolution, and similar ways. As I
describe in **Socialization**, the structure of the school tends toward
behavior of middling quality. Noting the many good qualities of New
Zealand schools, Avraham wryly commented, "It produces good kids, but
not prophet material," alluding to Moses' wish that all the men of Israel
could be prophets.

Like other parents, we began homeschooling to be good stewards
of our family responsibilities, as endless, exhausting, and demanding as that
may be.

Nearly as important as stewardship is our inner conviction that our
children will be growing up, as I have said, into a world far different than
the one we live in today. Speaking with acquaintances as we travel, I have
been impressed that people of many different religions share our feeling that
we live in the last days.

The scriptures paint a picture of the status quo continuing on
without seeming disruption as the moral state as the world steadily declines;
then suddenly, everything falls apart. How important to be the kind of
person who can quietly take care of himself or herself and assist others as
well! How vital to possess life skills, survival skills, work skills! A
generation of television babies who squall when they cannot have their
sugar-frosted flakes will be in trouble when those times come. Family
members who know how to work together and sacrifice for one another will
be at an advantage.

Other ideas may constitute homeschool educational theory, such as
the family as a unit of production, not consumption; voluntary simplicity;
the spiritual foundation for all learning, academic and practical; the

parent/teacher as facilitator; child-initiated learning. Sorting through the ideas that motivate us strengthens our commitment to our children and to our alternative way in life.

CONCLUSION

At present, homeschool is a happy choice, a good alternative for raising children, an appropriate assumption of parents' natural rights. I do not think that it is a moral imperative, though. I believe that it is as wrong for us to say, as one homeschooler did, that school is theoretically and functionally incorrect, that he would rather do anything than allow one of his children to attend, as it is to insist that only professional teachers possess the characteristics to teach children what they need to know.

I have often felt that the time may come when public schools as they exist today will not be available—whether this results from financial strictures (of which the writing is already on the wall), moral breakdowns (in some cities schools are actually dangerous places to be), or problems of disease (some hypothesize that serious, rampant contaminations will soon compel us to keep our children at home). In the meantime, families may face temporary needs to educate their children at home, such as our friends who are spending a year overseas and will opt for homeschool rather than put their children into a foreign system.

But I feel confident that in the long run schools will not be the chosen way to educate children. Recently I ran across an article in *BYU Studies* (volume 10, number 1) entitled "Education: Moving toward and under the Law of Consecration." These ideas reflect our religious view that the thousand years of peace—the millenium, a notion we share with other religions—will embrace a better educational order. People of other faiths may still enjoy thinking over the following comments, even though their religious view may differ from mine. This was a series of questions and answers with President Alvin R. Dyer of the First Presidency of the Mormon Church, given in Autumn 1969. Twenty doctoral candidates in religious education put questions to him in a telelecture. Although the entire article is worth reading carefully, I summarize items important to my point here.

President Dyer reminded us that twenty-four temples were planned in the city of New Jerusalem, but no separate school buildings. He inferred that the schools will operate in the temple itself. He said that there will be a vast broadcasting system, communicating from an order of the priesthood

306

to all the world. He asserted that the home will be the only medium of teaching children—through the family, in the patriarchal order—that is, under the direction of the father. Professional teachers are now just standing temporarily in the place of the fathers, who will and should eventually take their proper places in the education of their families. In the ideal system, professional educators will function as resources for the fathers in the homes, since these teachers have developed the skills and media for teaching well.

President Dyer emphasized that the Lord has given us no organization other than the Priesthood to work through, and that all other systems will grow subordinate to it. He emphasized that the fathers comprise the Priesthood in the home, and he said that being informed in spiritual matters, being without prejudice, and having the Spirit of the Lord are the most important attributes that any teacher can have. Everything we teach and learn can be evaluated by these principles. He further pointed out that the principle of repentance applies to learning—not always repentance from sin, but repentance from having the need to change, the need for regeneration. He felt that this should be looked at as a principle of conversion. And the methods, the procedures of learning, are a way of attracting people's (and, we can add, children's) attention. But true learning is a spiritual, personal thing.

I found President Dyer's remarks comforting and forthright, assuring me that child-raising in the home—evidently in the supportive environment of extended family and a wholesome neighborhood—was a true principle. The more we can learn of good ways to teach our children at home, the further we may be moving toward this ideal situation, the millennial way of educating families.

Surprisingly, though, these ideas are in no way new. I was just recently given a copy of an old manuscript titled *Home Education*, by Isaac Taylor, published in 1838. Although this book is somewhat difficult to master because of its old-fashioned style, it is delightful to read. I was so surprised because he advocates many of the principles I have been seeking for: the quiet, moral influence of the home and of a loving family; the development of spiritual sensitivity, and of emotional stability as well; the idea of practical and manual training as central to a child's sense of worth and happiness; the love and intuitive teaching of the parents, both mother and father; the vital importance of childhood play, outdoors, ideally in a rural environment; careful selection of play and household materials, to promote good taste; the same care in selecting reading materials; the encouragement and enhancement of a child's natural, God-given talents; and the movement of youth into farm and neighborhood responsibilities of work as a way of removing children from too much domination by the mother's influence.

In particular I was pleased to read Taylor's insistence on delayed rather than accelerated learning. He explained that children are often readier to learn academic skills and concepts at a later age; and that it is better to let children fully experience the world at their own level than try to force them to greater and greater demonstrable skills. Schools feel compelled to do this, he noted, so that they can prove that they are doing a good job. But at home we can delay teaching things until the child is ripe and mature for them.

Taylor also stressed reading aloud to younger children to develop their minds and vocabularies; and he pointed out the importance and delight of learning science directly from nature. It all sounds very familiar, doesn't it? Yet, Taylor's volume was published a century and a half ago (we have simply removed ourselves far from sound principles); and I have found myself struggling hard to rediscover so many of them independently. Rarely have I read them as clearly expressed in any modern writing on education.

Indeed, President Dyer also pointed out that home education under the direction of fathers goes far back, to the time of Abraham and before; and we are just lately finding our way back. It is fascinating and stimulating to me to realize that there is an ideal approach to raising children—the Lord's way—and that we can find it out ourselves through our experience.

Today is certainly a difficult time to raise children, and homeschooling is no panacea for all the ills of our society. Since most of us homeschool in city or suburban neighborhoods, isolated into nuclear families, homeschooling can be draining and sometimes frustrating, even creating new problems.

For now, I see the challenge of parents as being able to find good ways to educate their children without "carrying the world into their homes in backpacks," as Reed Benson once said. Someday soon it may be clear that homeschooling is not only a superior alternative but a necessity; and I am confident that everything we have learned toward doing it well will pay off amply then. As one mother, who had homeschooled for some years and then put her children in school expressed it, "For some of us, when the public schools are no longer available, it will be a glad time; we'll have a celebration! But others, as yet inexperienced and unsure of educating their own children at home, will find themselves challenged to the very core, confronted with the need to educate their children without that public support system."

I hope that this book will provide some direction to both groups, so that we can handle both the negative as well as the hopeful, millennial challenges in the years ahead.

Index